DIPLOMACY
WITH
CHINESE CHARACTERISTICS

Rachel A. Winston, Ph.D.

Copyright © 2021 by Lizard Publishing

All rights reserved. No part of this book may be reproduced, stored, or transmitted by any means. In accordance with U.S. Copyright law, the scanning, uploading, and electronic sharing of any part of this book without the permission of the publisher constitutes unlawful piracy and theft of the author's intellectual property. Prior written permission must be obtained. Inquiries concerning the reproduction of any material from this book must be submitted to Lizard Publishing.

Lizard Publishing ®

7700 Irvine Center Drive, Suite 800

Irvine, CA 92618-3047

www.lizard-publishing.com

Our mental process is fueled by three tenets:

• Ignite the hunger to learn and the passion for making a difference

• Illuminate the expanse of knowledge by sharing cutting edge thinking

• Innovate to create a world that may only exist in our dreams

Maps and Illustrations by graphic designer, Abiyy Suryowibisono

Book design by Michelle Tahan and Obinna Chinemerem Ozuo

Typeface: Garamond

Book Website: southchinaseabook.com

First Edition: July 2021

Rachel Winston is available for speaking events.

ISBN: 978-1946432278 (paperback), 978-1946432285 (hardback), 978-1946432261 (ebook)

LCCN: 2021913622

This book was published in the U.S.A. Lizard Publishing is a premium quality provider of educational reference, career guidance, and motivational publications/merchandise for global learners, educators, and stakeholders in education.

This book is dedicated to William and Esther Mirvis, who endured life circumstances during WWI and WWII but never had the chance to see what the fruits of their labor were to achieve.

Acknowledgments

"If I see so far, it is because I stand on the shoulders of giants."
– Isaac Newton

There is never enough room to acknowledge every person who contributed to an individual's perspective, assisted in the development of a person's knowledge base, or taught indelible lessons that last a lifetime. In this book, I gratefully acknowledge my family, friends, colleagues, and professors.

I would also like to thank my fellow students I have met along the way from whom I have learned from their perspective and wisdom.

Isaac Newton once said, "If I see so far, it is because I stand on the shoulders of giants." A few of those giants in my life whose shoulders have lifted me higher and helped teach me invaluable lessons include: Suzanne Crawford, Matt Robledo, Steve Harrison, Fred Smoller, Lyn and Thomas Penna, Candice Katayama, Jik and Chelsea Lee, Trudy Naman, Cheryl Tobin, Cliff Sobel, Kym North, JT Geehr, Michael Castro, Sarah Emory, Dana Sampson, Wendy Harris, Carol Lewis, Michael Okaisabor, AbiyySuryowibisono, and Jasmine Flores.

Meet the Author

Rachel A. Winston, Ph.D.

As a retired university professor, Full-Time Faculty Member of the Year, elected statewide leader, and winner of the McFarland Literary Achievement Award, Dr. Winston writes and publishes on key educational, societal, and international issues. She taught at UCLA, Brandman University, Chapman University, Embry Riddle Aeronautical University, Cal State Fullerton and holds graduate degrees from Harvard University, the University of Chicago, the University of Texas at Austin, George Washington University, Claremont Graduate University, Pepperdine University, and Cal State Fullerton.

Inspired by trips with U.N. officials in the 1960s to the Golan Heights, Crimea, Caucuses, and Ukraine during the Cold War, and East Germany when still behind the Iron Curtain, Dr. Winston later worked on Capitol Hill and with the White House. As a mathematician, chemist, and computer scientist, her life led her to more than fifty countries. Attending graduate school in Hong Kong, presenting at speaking events in China, and conducting research in Southeast Asia, Dr. Winston's research for her theses for Harvard University and the University of Chicago offered numerous insights as she built relationships with people throughout Asia.

Dr. Winston turned her research into the book *Raging Waters in the South China Sea* and continued to write *China's Power Grab and Expanding Claims*, followed by *Belts and Roads Under Beijing's Thumb*. Her graduate work in World War II Studies and visits to concentration camps in Germany, Poland, and the Czech Republic led her to research genocide and write the books in the *Awakened Now* series: *Awakened to Tomorrow's Future*, *Nazi Germany to Xinjiang Province*, and *Persecution of Uyghur Muslims*.

Foreword

Diplomacy with Chinese characteristics is taking shape globally with, as yet, the world not knowing exactly what that is. Evidence is mounting that does not support China's claim that it is a beacon for the world. Examples to date are horrific with China's early abrogation of its signed and sealed promise of honoring the United Nations Convention on the Law of the Sea, known as UNCLOS. China does not just work around the law, but rejects it altogether, replacing its precepts with a supposedly historic map with dotted lines outlining China's presumed longstanding and superior claim to the South China Sea that extends well into the sovereign land and sea rights accorded by UNCLOS.

Presently, the tragedy of Hong Kong is playing out before us - another gross violation of an agreement worked out with the UK many years ago wherein for 50 years, ending in 2047 to be exact, Hong Kong would retain its free status as an administrative district of China. No longer. Freedom lost. Newspapers shut down. Journalists shut out. China has subjugated, restricted, and arrested anyone seeking freedom.

Flagrant violations of the enumerated civil liberties embedded in The United Nations Declaration of Human Rights are everywhere seen to be trampled on without regard to the world's consensus. China itself has a Constitution that, at face value, presumes to protect its people from the oppression regularly inflicted on them. Yet, there is no rationale that can be made for the intentional genocide, forced labor, and abuse of the peoples of the Xinjiang Uyghur Autonomous Region in Northwest China. The fate of the Falun Gong is another excellent example of state terrorism inflicted on the harmless practitioners of meditation and movement.

Even in the littlest of things agreements are meaningless. For example, at the March 2021 meeting between the US and China's foreign policy leaders, an agreement to a two-minute opening introduction was brazenly trashed by China's well-planned intention to open with a 15-minute rant more than seven times longer than the agreed-upon time.

In *Diplomacy with Chinese Characteristics*, Winston spells out in detail the references made above, but these are but the tip of the iceberg with many more examples of diplomacy in action promises made and not kept, looming threats to global peace, and the inroads China has made in its stranglehold on the financial stability of countries around the world. In some cases, the noose has closed, standing as examples of what is likely to happen if debts are not paid. Make no mistake, many will not be paid, and those countries will pay dearly in territory and natural resources as other countries will attest.

Diplomacy in practice takes many forms, and rightly so, but rarely is it held in so little regard and so often used as a tool of control and conquest without regard to a moral compass that will allow both sides to live in peace and to expect no harm.

The reader will be fully enlightened reading this book on China's words and actions, including its aims, strategies, and practices. Irrespective of which book you read first in the Raging Waters series, the colorfully illuminated pages, and writing will provide a clear picture of the China the world faces today.

Dr. David Waugh, United Nations (Retired)

Table of Contents

1. China's Remarkable Growth — 1

1. Piecing Together the Puzzle: Uncertainty, Intention, and Pressure — 2
2. Onward from the Century of Humiliation: China's Bold Moves — 6
3. Mao's Massive Failures: The Great Leap Backward — 10
4. Deng Xiaoping: Opening China to the World — 16
5. Shoring up Productivity: Harnessing the Skills of China's Population — 22
6. Foreign Direct Investment: Remarkable Growth in Income, Trade, and FOI — 30
7. Xi Jinping's Larger Than Life Personality: Chairman and Dictator for Life — 38

2. The Belt and Road Initiative Is Born — 46

1. Celebration, Collaboration, and Coercion: The EU Celebrates as Xi Offers Benevolent Leadership — 48
2. China's Belts and Roads: Wrapping Beijing's Arms Around the Planet — 56
3. A Match Made in Heaven: Offering No-Questions-Asked Loans to Developing Countries — 62
4. China's Money Lending Benevolence — 68
5. Not Technically A Debt-Trap: Sri Lanka's Former Hambantota Port — 76
6. China's Name Controversy: Why Did China Change Its Name from OBOR To BRI? — 84

3. Xi Jinping Thought and China's Diplomacy — 90

1. Win-Win Diplomacy: China's Soft Power Sprinkling the Planet — 92
2. Vaccine Diplomacy: The Pandemic and Vaccine Rollout — 98
3. Facemask Diplomacy: China's PPE Generosity, Failures, and Economic Enrichment — 104
4. Wolf Warrior Diplomacy: China's Aggressive Verbal Attacks, Institutionalized During the Pandemic — 112
5. Hostage Diplomacy and Extradition Treaties: Showing Who's Boss by Taking Foreigners Hostage — 118
6. Economic Diplomacy: China's Spider Web in Africa Interwoven with Soft Power — 122
7. Death Metal Diplomacy: Taiwan's Sovereignty, Energy, and Not-So-Chinese Characteristics — 130

4. Near and Far – China's Claims Extend Its Reach — 136

1. Benevolent Development or Nefarious Goals: Will China Rise Peacefully or Change the Rules-Based Order? — 138
2. A Global Trading Network: Shipping Transport and Trade Breakdowns — 144
3. Financial Transactions: Renminbi or Chinese Digital Money as a Global Currency? — 150
4. China's Largest Banks and State-Owned Enterprises: Understanding China's Socialist Businesses and Beijing's Control — 156
5. Fueling the Hungry Giant: China's Stake in Global Liquid Natural Gas, Oil Fields — 164
6. Dark Fleets: China's Fishing and Shipping in Ecuador, the Arctic, and Elsewhere on the Planet — 172
7. Three Poles Environment and Climate Change: China's Ministry of Science and Technology (MOST) Project — 180

5. International Pushback — 186

1. Free and Open Indo-Pacific: Attempt to Prevent China from Taking Over a Non-Adjacent Waterway — 188
2. ASEAN, Code of Conduct, and the South China Sea: Unlawful Militarization and Relentless Aggression — 198

3.	Five Eyes Alliance: Australia, Canada, New Zealand, U.K., & U.S.	206
4.	The Quad: United Countries to Oppose China's Coercion and Aggression	214
5.	Beijing Warns about Boycotting Its 2022 Winter Olympics: 180 Human Rights Groups Voice Opposition	220
6.	Questions and Quarantine – Power and Benevolence	226

6. Conclusion 232

1.	Uncertain Future for China and the World: Achieving Xi Jinping's Chinese Dream and Global Ambitions	236

7. Index 242

Acronyms and Terms

Acronyms and Terms	
3 Buckets of Oil	China's 'Big Three' oil corporations or "Three Buckets of Oil" - PetroChina, Sinopec, and CNOOC
5G	5th generation mobile network
60/40 Rule	Under Philippine law, Philippine government must own at least 60% of capital used in contracts involving natural resources. Furthermore, 60% of the profit must remain with the Philippine government.
99-Year Lease	This was the length of time Great Britain leased Hong Kong after the Opium Wars and the time China leased Hambantota Port in Sri Lanka when Sri Lanka struggled to pay its debt.
AC	Arctic Council
ACAP	Arctic Contaminants Action Program
ACFTA	African Continental Free Trade Area
ADB	Asian Development Bank
ADF	Australian Defense Force
ADIZ	Air Defense Identification Zone
AECO	Association of Arctic Expedition Cruise Operators
AEI	American Enterprise Institute
AFP	Armed Forces of the Philippines
AIIB	Asian Infrastructure and Investment Bank
AIV	Advisory Council on International Affairs
AMAP	Arctic Monitoring and Assessment Program
AMM	ASEAN Foreign Ministers' Meeting
Anarchy	The idea that the world lacks any supreme authority or sovereign. In an anarchic state, there is no hierarchically superior, coercive power that can resolve disputes, enforce law, or order the international system.
APEC	Asia-Pacific Economic Cooperation
ARF	ASEAN Regional Forum
ARIA	Asia Reassurance Initiative Act

Acronyms and Terms

ASEAN	Association of Southeast Asian Nations - (One Vision, One Identity, One Community) - Regional, intergovernmental association of ten Southeast Asia countries. The 10 member nations include: Brunei, Cambodia, Indonesia, Laos, Malaysia, Myanmar (Burma), the Philippines, Singapore, Thailand, and Vietnam.
ASEAN Plus Three	This cooperative group includes the 10 ASEAN states plus China, Japan, and the Republic of Korea
ASEAN Plus Six	These sixteen countries (the 10 ASEAN states plus Australia, China, India, Japan, South Korea, and New Zealand) form the Regional Comprehensive Economic Partnership.
ASMA	Antarctic Specially Managed Area
ASPA	Antarctic Specially Protected Area
ATCM	Antarctic Treaty Consultative Meeting
AU	African Union
BBNJ	Biodiversity Beyond National Jurisdiction
BCIM	Bangladesh-China-India-Myanmar Economic Corridor
BEAC	Barents Euro-Arctic Council
BRI	Belt and Road Initiative
CADF	China-Africa Development Fund
CAFF	Conservation of Arctic Flora and Fauna
CBP	U.S. Customs and Border Protection
CCAMLR	Convention on the Conservation of Antarctic Marine Living Resources
CCAS	Convention for the Conservation of Antarctic Seals
CCFFA	Central Commission on Foreign Affairs
CCP	Chinese Communist Party
CCWRFA	Central Conference on Work Relating to Foreign Affairs
CDB	China Development Bank
CDIS	Coordinated Direct Investment Survey
Century of Humiliation	The approximately one hundred years from 1842, with the Treaty of Nanjing, to October 1, 1949 when the People's Republic of China was formally established.
CEP	Committee on Environmental Protection
CFR	Council on Foreign Relations
CGA	Coast Guard Administration
CGIT	China Global Investment Tracker
CHEXIM	Export-Import Bank of China
CHIIA	China Investment in Australia
CICA	Conference on Interaction and Confidence Building Measures in Asia
CICIR	China Institutes of Contemporary International Relations

Acronyms and Terms	
CIIS	China Institute of International Studies
CIS	Commonwealth of Independent States
CLCS	Commission on the Limits of the Continental Shelf
CLETC	China Light Industrial Corporation for Foreign Economic and Technical Cooperation
CMC	Central Military Commission
CMREC	China-Mongolia-Russia Economic Corridor
CNOOC	China National Offshore Oil Corporation (Chinese State-Owned Enterprise - SOE)
CNPC	China National Petroleum Corporation (Chinese State-Owned Enterprise - SOE)
CoC	Code of Conduct
COMNAP	Council of Managers of National Antarctic Programs
COMPLANT	China National Complete Plant Import and Export Corporation Group
COVID-19	The coronavirus COVID-19 pandemic that broke out in the fall of 2019 in Wuhan, China
CPEC	China-Pakistan Economic Corridor
CPI	Consumer Price Index
CSFAC	China State Farm Agribusiness Corporation
CSIC	China Shipbuilding Industry Corporation (Chinese State-Owned Enterprise - SOE)
DoC	Declaration of the Conduct of Parties in the South China Sea
DPJ	Democratic Party of Japan
DPP	Democratic Progressive Party
DRC	Democratic Republic of Congo
DSM-IV	Diagnostic and Statistical Manual of Mental Disorders
ECOSOC	Economic and Social Council
EDCA	Enhanced Defense Cooperation Agreement - An agreement signed in 2014 between the U.S. and the Philippines with the goal of supporting U.S. Philippine relations and military cooperation. The EDCA was declared constitutional in 2016.
EEAS	European External Action Service
EEU	Eurasian Economic Union
EEZ	Exclusive Economic Zone – The United Nations Convention on the Law of the Sea (UNCLOS) defines the region as the band extending 200 nautical miles off the shores of a coastal state in which that state has the jurisdiction over the exploration of natural resources and exploitation of marine resources in its adjacent continental shelf.
EIA	Environmental Impact Assessment
EPB	European Polar Brand

Acronyms and Terms

ETIM	East Turkestan Islamic Movement
EU	European Union
EXIM	Export-Import Bank of China
Facemask Diplomacy	This initiative was China's effort to sell facemasks to countries worldwide during COVID-19.
FAO	Food and Agriculture Organization
FDI	Foreign Direct Investment
First Island Chain	A string of islands from lower Philippines up to the top of Japan that are a near-in region. China hopes to push the U.S. presence outside of this area.
Five Eyes Alliance	An intelligence sharing alliance between Australia, Canada, New Zealand, United Kingdom, and the United States founded in 1941.
FOCAC	Forum on China-Africa Cooperation
FOIP	Free and Open Indo-Pacific Strategy
FONOPs	Freedom of Navigation Operations
FPA	Foreign Policy Analysis
FTA	Free Trade Agreements
GDP	Gross Domestic Product
GNP	Gross National Product
GPEA	Greenpeace East Asia
Gray Zone Operations	Intense political, economic, informational, and military competition that is just short of war. China uses 'Gray Zone' tactics to "win without fighting" to further its maritime claims and alter the status quo without going to war.
Great Power	The ability of a sovereign state to exert its influence on a global scale.
GRINGOs	Government-Run or Government-Initiated NGOs
Hedging	The management of risk relationships between two opposing parties to protect security and sovereignty by diversifying commitments and simultaneously balancing and engaging. The term 'hedging' is increasingly found in the U.S. strategic discourse, particularly regarding China. The White House 2006 National Security Strategy document stated that the U.S. strategy "seeks to encourage China to make the right strategic choices for its people, while we hedge against other possibilities."
Hegemon	A political state having dominant influence or authority over others. States can have global or regional hegemony.
HYSY	Hiayangshiyou "Ocean Oil" - CNOOC deepwater oil platforms
IAATO	International Association of Antarctic Tour Operators
IASC	International Arctic Science Committee
ICAO	International Civil Aviation Organization
ICC	International Criminal Court

Acronyms and Terms	
ICE	U.S. Immigration and Customs Enforcement
ICJ	International Court of Justice
ICPR	International Covenant on Civil and Political Rights
ICRW	International Convention on the Regulation of Whaling
IDF	Indigenous Defense Fighter (Taiwanese Fighter Jet)
IFIs	International Financial Institutions
IISD	International Institute for Sustainable Development
ILO	International Labor Organization
IMF	International Monetary Fund
IMO	International Maritime Organization
IPCC	Intergovernmental Panel on Climate Change
IR	International Relations
IRCT	International Rehabilitation Council for Torture Victims
ISA	International Seabed Authority
ISAF	International Security Assistance Force
ITC	International Trade Center
IUU	Illegal, unreported, and unregulated fishing practices
IWC	International Whaling Commission
JADIZ	Japanese Air Defense Identification Zone
JASDF	Japan Air Self Defense Force
JMSU	Joint Marine Seismic Undertaking – a collaboration between China, the Philippines, and Vietnam to survey for hydrocarbon resources
KADIZ	(South) Korea Air Defense Identification Zone
KIG	Kalayaan Island Group
KMT	Kuomintang
Kowtow	Kneel and touch the ground with the forehead in worship or submission as part of Chinese custom
LAC	Line of Actual Control
LDP	Liberal Democratic Party (Japan)
LNG	Liquefied Natural Gas
Maglev	Magnetic Levitation - A train system that operates using magnets that allow the train to levitate off the track, reducing friction.
Malacanang	The Philippine presidential palace is a high governmental meeting location and residence of the Philippine president. It is incorporated into written text and speeches in the same way as the White House is in the U.S.
MERICS	Mercator Institute for China Studies
MFA (MoFA)	Ministry of Foreign Affairs
MFEZ	Multi Facility Economic Zone (Zambia)

Acronyms and Terms

MIC2025	Made in China 2025
MoC	China's Ministry of Commerce
MOFCOM	Ministry of Commerce
MOFTEC	Ministry of Foreign Trade and Economic Cooperation
MOU	Memorandum of Understanding
MPA	Marine Protected Area
MSR	Maritime Silk Road
NATO	North Atlantic Treaty Organization
NBA	National Basketball Association
ND	Northern Dimension
NDB	New Development Bank
NDRC	National Development and Reform Commission
NGO	Non-Governmental Organization
Nine-Dash Line	China bases its determination of rights to the South China Sea based upon a nine-dash line drawn on a map in 1947. At times, this demarcated map had ten and eleven dashes in a roughly U shape. The boundaries of what they term their 'historic claim' are vague, but roughly encompass about ninety percent of the South China Sea. The ICJ determination in Philippines v. China was that, based upon UNCLOS, China has 'no basis' for their claim.
NM	Nautical Miles
NOC	National Oil Companies
NSC	National Security Council
OBOR	One Belt, One Road
ODA	Official Development Assistance
ODI	Overseas Direct Investment
OECD	Organization for Economic Cooperation and Development
ONGC	Indian Oil and Natural Gas Corporation (Indian State-Owned Enterprise - SOE)
ONI	Office of Naval Intelligence
OPEC	Organization of Petroleum Exporting Countries
OSPAR	Convention for the Protection of the Marine Environnmment of the North-East Atlantic
PAME	Protection of the Arctic Marine Environment
PAP	Singapore's People's Action Party
Paracel Islands	A disputed archipelago with 130 coral islands and reefs in the South China Sea that is occupied by China and claimed by Taiwan and Vietnam inhabiting a population of over 1,000. They are also called Xisha Islands and Hoang Sa Archipelago.
PCA	Permanent Court of Arbitration

Acronyms and Terms	
PetroVietnam	Vietnam Oil and Gas Corporation (Vietnamese State-Owned Enterprise - SOE)
PH	The Philippines
PLA	People's Liberation Army (China)
PLAAF	People's Liberation Army Air Force (China)
PLAN	People's Liberation Army – Navy (China)
PLANAF	People's Liberation Army Navy Air Force (China)
PPE	Personal Protective Equipment
PPP	Purchasing Power Parity
PRC	People's Republic of China
PSSA	Particularly Sensitive Sea Area
R2P	Responsibility to Protect
RCEP	Regional Comprehensive Economic Partnership
RIMPAC	Rim of the Pacific
RMB	Renminbi – The official name for China's money introduced in 1949 is considered "the people's currency". A yuan is one unit of RMB.
ROC	The Republic of China (Taiwan)
SAFE	State Administration of Foreign Exchange
SAIS	School of Advanced International Studies
Salami Tactics (Salami Slicing)	A process of cutting away at the opposition by utilizing threats and alliances and politically dominating a landscape by slicing the opponent's power piece by piece.
SAR	Special Administrative Region
SASAC	State-owned Assets Supervision Administration Commission
SCAR	Scientific Committee on Antarctic Research
SCO	Shanghai Cooperation Organization
SCS	South China Sea
Second Island Chain	An extended region into the Pacific Ocean out to Guam from Asia.
Sinopec	China Petroleum & Chemical Corporation (Chinese State-Owned Enterprise - SOE)
SME	Small and Medium-sized Enterprises
SOE	State-Owned Enterprise
SONA	State of the Nation Address
Sorties	An air sortie is a military mission where aircraft are sent out on a combat mission.
SREB	Silk Road Economic Belt
SSA	Sub-Saharan Africa
THAAD	Theater High-Altitude Area Defense

Acronyms and Terms

TIP	Turkestan Islamic Party
TPP	Trans-Pacific Partnership
Twitter Fingers	An individual who uses social media rapidly and rabidly, retweeting incessantly.
U.S.	United States
UDHR	Universal Declaration of Human Rights
UN	United Nations
UNCLOS	United Nations Convention on the Law of the Sea – This is an international treaty that was signed in 1982 and came into force in 1994 as an agreement that defines the rights and responsibilities of the world's oceans and seas. As of 2019, 168 parties have joined.
UNCTAD	United Nations Conference on Trade and Development
UNDP	United Nations Development Program
UNEA	United Nations Environment Assembly
UNEP	United Nations Environment Program
UNESCO	United Nations Educational, Scientific, and Cultural Organization
UNFCCC	United Nations Framework Convention on Climate Change
UNIDO	United Nations Industrial Development Organization
USAID	United States Agency for International Development
USD	United States Dollar
USSR	Union of Soviet Socialist Republics (14 countries; Founded on December 30, 1922; Dissolved on December 26, 1991)
VAT	Value-Added Tax
VPN	Virtual Private Network
WB	World Bank
WHO	World Health Organization
WIPO	World Intellectual Property Organization
Wolf Warrior Diplomacy	The newly introduced, aggressive method of diplomacy used by China in 2020 and named after Chinese blockbuster action films.
WPS	West Philippine Sea
WTO	World Trade Organization
WWF	World Wide Fund for Nature, previously known as World Wildlife Fund when founded in 1961.
XUAR	Xinjiang Uyghur Autonomous Region
Yuan	A unit of renminbi (RMB)
ZOPFAN	Zone of Peace, Freedom and Neutrality – Declaration signed in 1971 by the foreign ministers of the ASEAN member states.
ZTE	Zhong Xing Telecommunications – a Chinese communications and technology corporation.

Part 1

China's Remarkable Growth

Painting with Broad Brushstrokes

Stepping back from the fray of international politics with its inherent beliefs and prejudices, the fundamental core of America rests in its values. The vast majority of Americans were raised with the belief in freedom, liberty, and human dignity. Some were immigrants who came to this country for a better life. Others have long legacies in the United States, also coming here, fighting for, and working hard to create a better life. Still, others have suffered because the 'better life' they sought was fraught with limits, inequity, and racism. Yet, in the end, those who call America home are all Americans, each seeking a life and a world where peace, hope, and engagement can thrive with equal opportunity, security, and prosperity for themselves and their posterity.

There is no doubt that we are a divided country and, I suggest, a divided world as well. Freedom to voice an opinion or express a particular faith is not a given, which has many people around the world concerned – not just in America. This suppression is gravely worrisome as individuals modulate their words around barriers of speech, political correctness, and a new lexicon of 'appropriate' comments, pronouns, and assumptions.

Yet, through it all, we are stronger together than we are apart. We are more alike than we are different. We care about the same fundamental beliefs, even if our hopes, opportunities, and challenges are viewed from a different vantage points. On a global scale, our greatest strength as a nation is that, though we have enslaved people like a hundred or so other countries, we have not executed millions like Mao, Stalin, and Hitler. These tragedies remind us of the horrific consequences of totalitarian countries and their oppressive and dictatorial leaders.

It is at this juncture, we begin the discussion about the Belt and Road Initiative and why we should be concerned with the new silk road, the polar silk road, debt-trap diplomacy, Made in China 2025, and China's plans for 2030, 2050, and beyond.

Chapter 1
Piecing Together the Puzzle
Uncertainty, Intention, and Pressure

Introduction

The planet is a giant set of puzzle pieces. Nobody has them all. Governmental leaders, university researchers, and think tank fellows, many exceptionally brilliant, investigate, collaborate, and fit together pieces until a journal article, white paper, or governmental decision can be produced or action taken. There is no "Royal Road", as Euclid stated, to know all. However, each individual can learn and become more aware.

Furthermore, though individuals can make reasonable predictions based on known capabilities, words can be hollow or intentionally misrepresented. Individuals, researchers, and government officials must widen their perspectives. In the complex world that lies ahead for ourselves and our posterity, we need to gather more puzzle pieces since one can never know a state's future intentions as John Mearsheimer eloquently explains in his book *The Tragedy of Great Power Politics*.[1]

Individual and State Survival

Personal and state survival remain a paramount quest, which is why individuals and states hungered for survival tools during the COVID-19 pandemic and greater preparedness for looming political, economic, or military challenges. For the sake of an individual's family, community, and country, knowledge is life itself. No entity would willingly be vanquished; no state would simply relinquish their sovereignty unless forced into submission.

Humankind's intrinsic self-determination propels states toward survival at almost any cost. There are great incentives to solidify alliances and reduce uncertainty. Thus, as rational actors – individuals or governmental entities – possessing some level of fear, a great deal of uncertainty, and no 9-1-1 to come to the rescue on the international level, states must maximize on their capacities to control outcomes, as treaty allies Japan, South Korea, and the Philippines are well aware.

This is why great power entities, Russia and China, for example, seek to secure their future, gain widespread control, and protect their sovereignty in the face of perceived competition. This fear and uncertainty motivates states to use their relationships, resources, and human capital to enhance economic and military power. History, though, reminds us that power does not assure survival. Further, great power is feared by smaller states more than it is admired, forcing states to hedge, ally, and protect.

Even when puzzle pieces are placed in a general area and a few are connected, the image is not completely clear. The final decisions about where to put the remaining hundred pieces and the ultimate result is still unknown. Plans change and new information emerges. The probabilistic components culled from game theory's strategic modeling are scrapped for another day. Sadly, strategic maneuvers with high levels of success require an element of surprise, which will never be in the puzzle box. That one missing piece is the tragedy of a possible attack and the lack of omniscience emanating from a blind spot.

With a world full of loose puzzle pieces, it is critical to make better decisions by

---

1 John Mearsheimer, *The Tragedy of Great Power Politics* (W.W. Norton & Company, 2001).

reducing uncertainty. In a world where misinformation and disinformation are readily transmitted and a single push of a button has the potential to kill millions of people, transparency is essential. With clearer understanding of state capabilities, better decisions can be made.

Knowledge is the name of the game, which is why the 2021 GameStop shakeup challenged society and the Security and Exchange Commission to question hedge fund information access, stock manipulation, and those who trade in the market. Fairness is certainly part of the equation in international politics. Power is another. Leaders with insider knowledge and under-the-table trades have the ability to manipulate the outcome for the body politic, the people, the seemingly inconsequential members of the larger community, like you and me, who merely use the information available to fit together the end pieces so we can see the rest a bit better. This lack of access to puzzle pieces is the bigger problem for the average citizen..

Conclusion

On the global scale the stakes are high. More puzzle pieces mean more moving parts. However, we should not abandon our quest to learn and understand despite the bigness of the picture. By putting more pieces together we, like those we have elected to be our leaders, can reduce society's uncertainty and tension. Knowledge and clarity are two of the reasons why this book was written.

What's at Stake?

First, since no individual or state has all the puzzle pieces, there are always blind spots and misperceptions.

Second, due to fear and uncertainty, states will seek greater control. The stakes are raised when one entity perceives that another is upping its claim.

Third, as humankind strives for survival, individuals will seek ways to persevere, though it may not be for the good of the state. This quest for relevance, security, and self-preservation may have consequences that blur the puzzle, increasing leaders' need to further control their citizenry.

China's Remarkable Growth | Part 1

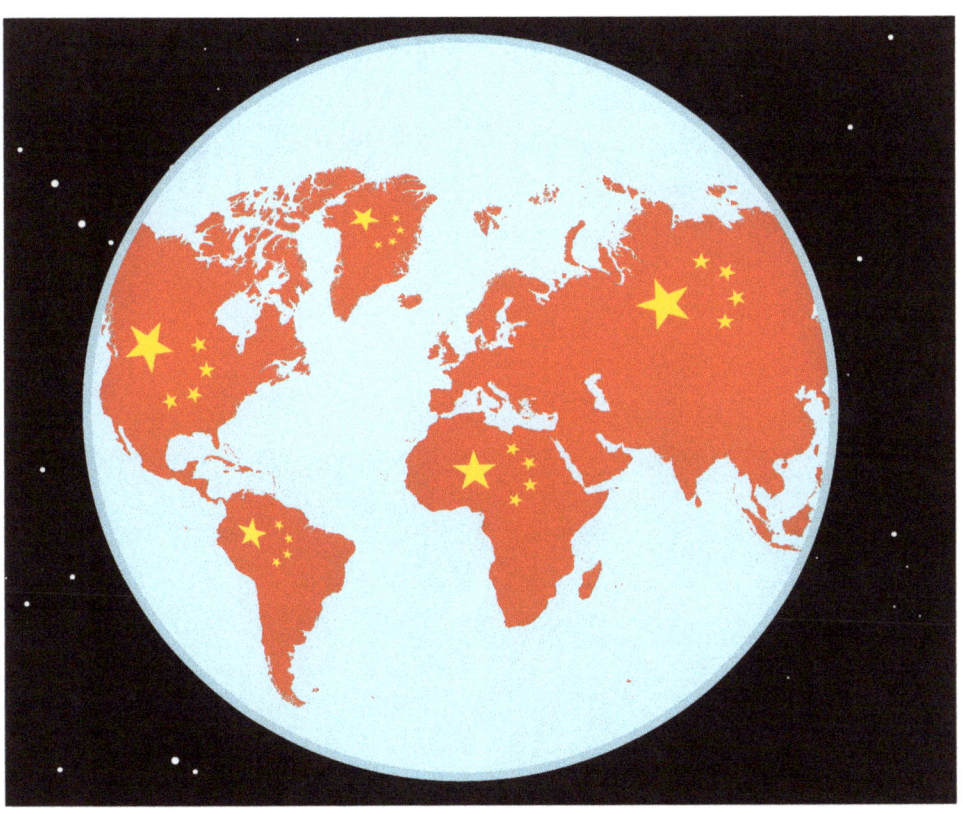

Chapter 2
Onward from the Century of Humiliation
China's Bold Moves

Introduction

After its 'Century of Humiliation', China emerged as a formidable economic and military powerhouse. The legacy of imperial powers fighting the weakly mobilized Chinese military and citizenry was over. China vowed to never feel powerless again. Fueled by nationalist pride, China sought regional hegemony with an eye toward global hegemony. With a history that is 3,000 – 5,000 years old, depending upon revisionists perspectives, China does not think in decades or even centuries, but in millennia.

Thus, the horizon for China is long and every small step is an inch closer to its ultimate goal. Nevertheless, the pandemic created the perfect backdrop for Beijing to manufacture more, loan more, and extend its reach into the South China Sea, East China Sea, Indo-Pacific, Arctic Sea, Antarctica, South American Pacific Waters, and beyond.

Historic Rights

China believes that much of Asia is 'rightfully theirs'. This belief, along with the COVID-19 pandemic, emboldened Beijing to make claims to territory belonging to more than a dozen countries. China instigated fighting in the Himalayas, placing its military squarely inside India's borders. In the South China Sea, Beijing threatened island by island by intimidating or buying off countries for their complicity. China's maps continue to be redrawn as Beijing asserts its dominance, rams boats, threatens commerce, prevents oil drilling, and brashly creates administrative districts in areas claimed by other countries.

As China rolls back the clock centuries past to determine what they believe should rightfully be theirs, these claims do not jibe with 21st-century society nor with 20th-century history. Beijing bases its claim on the fact that once, centuries ago, they fished in a certain area. Not only would that kind of claim work for other countries but, in 2016, the International Court of Justice ruled against Beijing in the case *Philippines v. China*, stating that China did not have these rights under international law.

That fact has not thwarted China in its active pursuit of the South China Sea as they press ahead with their newly created rules that violate rule of law and impose their dominance upon claimant states. Regional states have sovereignty based upon the United Nations Convention on the Law of the Sea (UNCLOS). Although China is a signatory, Beijing does not obey these laws or other related international norms and ethics. This situation is ripe for conflict no matter how much in loan guarantees President Xi uses to buy loyalty and votes from states as a carrot or threatens sovereignty as a stick.

In addition to aggressive acts to gain economic dominance, China's remarkable growth lays on the backs of its people. Their hard work, determination, and output are extraordinary, whether nationalistically driven or brutally forced. Most Chinese citizens work assiduously to better their homeland, though tens of millions throughout the country are essentially enslaved or imprisoned with no rights or freedoms. With no way out of their high-walled, barbed wire laden encampments, these manufacturing workers are threatened into submission and forced into slavery while being indoctrinated and re-educated into believing they are doing this for the good of the country. Imprisoned in hundreds of concentration camps in Xinjiang Province, Beijing's 'work sets you free' doctrine, harkening from nearly a century ago, has helped fuel an empire and created a global marketplace of cheap goods, purchased by people worldwide.

China has shifted the balance of global economic power to assert regional hegemony. While the Opium Wars of the 1800s wounded the proud and mighty 'Middle Kingdom', those painful scars are now a source of energy, a determination to claim what is 'rightfully' theirs, and a vision to regain its central role in a world where state-by-state is pulled into its sphere of influence.

China no longer pays indemnities, but they do commit to never again relinquish ports. In fact, today the tables are turned, and other states must surrender their ports with similar terms used on them more than a century ago. China's economic revival is nothing less than impressive, though also oppressive and repressive at the same time. While creating a massive banking structure with loans administered globally through its signature Belt and Road Initiative, China has aggressively asserted itself in multinational institutions.

China's 'Century of Humiliation' ended. Its maps have been re-drawn 'with Chinese characteristics', islands renamed, and states forced to comply with Beijing's wishes in much the same way the West demanded that China pay earlier. China's remarkable growth has increased with the pandemic, while at the same time stoking the flames and threatening countries in a way that demands attention now before it is too late.

Conclusion

Concern abounds. Both business and political leaders are aware of China's abject cruelty, tremendously long hours, and harsh conditions. Yet hundreds of individuals, companies, and political entities in the U.S. and abroad buy their products. Meanwhile, multinational corporations knowingly violate their publicly-stated moral principles in an illustration of cognitive dissonance that defies the imagination. It is here in the midst of moral disorder that this book begins to lay the groundwork of China's quest to shape a world in its own likeness through the Belt and Road Initiative.

China has taken bold steps. In 2015, China launched new policy guidelines, including Made in China 2025, which heralded China's future as the dominant manufacturing center for high technology, including telecommunications, electronic vehicles, robotics, and drones. The effort has proven to be successful in reaching its goal by hiring technology leaders with intimate knowledge of trade secrets, forcing the transfer of intellectual property, and producing phones, computers, and devices with China's labor. By incorporating surveillance, facial recognition, DNA collection, back door programs, artificial intelligence, and ubiquitous social media collection mechanisms, Beijing has orchestrated a coordinated pursuit of cyberespionage. China's quest is to reduce its dependence on foreign countries while increasing other country's dependency on its manufacturing centers in an attempt to dominate and control markets. China has also been successful in this effort by withholding rare earth minerals, semiconductors, and other inputs necessary for supply chains. Through subsidies, company acquisitions, and social control, China is determined to end its Century of Humiliation with a new era of unparalleled success.

What's at Stake?

First, since China's method of attaining supremacy is to divide and conquer. Beijing uses carefully-tailored rhetoric to pacify those who sign onto its Belt and Road Initiative. However, if the Indo-Pacific unites or ASEAN even partially gels, Beijing's 'diplomats' may stop labeling smaller regional states weak.

Second, there is no doubt that China wields economic dominance, exemplified by its grip on trade 'partners' and used as a sharp weapon against Australia.

Third, China's political dominance and coercion effectively silenced Hong Kong and terrified Taiwan.

Fourth, China's military dominance against Delhi as its People's Liberation Army (PLA) encroached on India's Himalayan territory with firepower.

Chapter 3
Mao's Massive Failures
The Great Leap Backward

Introduction

While it may be hard to imagine now, China was once a third-world state where vast stretches of the countryside were undeveloped. The majority of the occupants lived in catastrophic poverty. Most families lived in villages where they developed and farmed small plots of land for their own consumption and to share, sell, or trade with others. The work was mainly done by hand, but they often had plows with whatever animals they had to pull them. The country was defined by its extreme scarcity and dearth, with people hoping for a better life. Deng Xiaoping remarked, "These things cannot be cut away from the entire history of our Party and our country. To grasp this is to grasp everything. This is not just an intellectual issue – it is a political issue."[1]

The Great Leap Forward

The Great Leap Forward (1958-1962) resulted in China's Great Famine where thirty million Chinese starved to death. Mao Zedong eliminated private agricultural production, forced peasants onto communes, and ensured that the ruling elite was fully stocked.[2] On these communes, grain was produced and sold to other countries while leaving only the bare minimum for the workers. Meanwhile, Mao, wanting to prove that his efforts were successful, exported food, while turning away offers for international relief.

Steel production was necessary for industrialization. To meet the need, families were asked to melt down everything they owned containing metal. Tools and equipment were confiscated for this massive effort. These steel production furnaces, large and small, were coordinated by the Communist Party in cities and farms. Targets were set to out-produce major economies; though results fell far short of expectations. Most of the material produced was worthless. Even so, there was a great thrust to use the strongest civilians to produce steel.

With the Communist Party overseeing all production and ensuring citizen compliance, everyone was put to work. Quotas and incentives were in place to stimulate productivity. However, with few skills and no fertilizers or equipment, the people nevertheless valiantly toiled, though yield output rates still dropped. Since men were taken away to work in steel and construction, women, children, infirmed, and the elderly remained to work in the fields. Furthermore, threats to farms mounted as people became sick, crops were infested with locusts, and birds and animals became a menace. Malnutrition and starvation were endemic. Millions died. As people began to parish in droves, family members sought alternative avenues to get food. Some who attempted to escape were beaten, tortured, hung, or buried alive.

---

1 François Bougon, *Inside the Mind of Xi Jinping* (Hurst, 2018).

2 Vaclav Smil, "China's Great Famine: 40 Years Later," *BMJ 319*, no. 7225, 1619-1621, https://www.ncbi.nlm.nih.gov/pmc/articles/PMC1127087/

The Great Leap Forward
Smelting Furnaces in the 1950s

The Great Proletarian Cultural Revolution (1966 – 1976)

On January 5, 1964, Mao's *Little Red Book* was published. Mao wanted citizens to know why they needed to work hard, face challenges, and relinquish control of their lives for the betterment of China's posterity. Packed full of quotes, this small book, "Thoughts of Chairman Mao" spoke of his country's struggle and provided wisdom for a stronger China to emerge. The book soon became required reading for all subjects of Beijing, young and old. More than a billion copies of Mao's Little Red Book have been distributed.[3]

Mao Zedong launched the Cultural Revolution in 1966 with the goal to strengthen communism in China, purge the state of tradition and capitalism, and institute Mao's ideology. A loyal and growing clan of young followers emerged called the Red Guards who vowed to support Chairman Mao. In turn, Mao Zedong heralded their coming in his

---

3   BBC, "Who, What, Why: What is the Little Red Book?," *BBC News*, November 26, 2015, https://www.bbc.com/news/magazine-34932800

16-point set of guidelines, endorsed by the CCP Central Committee on August 8, 1966.

Mao wanted to eliminate educated leaders, business owners, and landlords, beckoning the proletariat to rise up and remove capitalism wherever they saw its roots growing. Mao saw this as a struggle for the masses of workers and peasants to crush anyone in authority and repudiate education, literature, and art that did not conform to Marxist socialism. Mao's transformational plan met resistance, but only for a short time. Mao stated,[4]

This resistance comes chiefly from those in authority who have wormed their way into the party and are taking the capitalist road. It also comes from the old force of habit in society. At present, this resistance is fairly strong and stubborn. However, the Great Proletarian Cultural Revolution is, after all, an irresistible general trend. There is abundant evidence that such resistance will crumble fast once the masses become fully aroused.

---

4   Alpha History, "Mao's 16 Points on the Cultural Revolution (1966)," *Alpha History*, n.d., https://alphahistory.com/chineserevolution/mao-zedongs-16-points-on-the-cultural-revolution-1966/

The Red Guards were encouraged to rise up and rebel. Tens of thousands rallied in support of Mao's violent class struggle aimed at removing power from politicians, intellectuals, leaders, and farm owners. Their rallying cry was to "Bombard the headquarters",[5] remove the bourgeois, and eliminate the business owners.

On June 1, 1966, the *People's Daily* called for the citizenry to "Sweep away all the monsters and demons,"[6] thus the Red Guards began their violent campaign across the country. The Cultural Revolution condemned religion, banned faith, and closed temples which they either shuttered, turned into factories, or destroyed. The faithful were castigated as "enemies of the people." Catholics, Protestants, Muslims, and people of other faiths were imprisoned. To demonstrate their disdain, they forced believers to wear tall hats inscribed with their 'crimes', watch as they set statues and paintings on fire, and be rounded up and sent to hard labor encampments.[7]

Mao's Cultural Revolution (1966-1976)
Destroying the Four Olds

---

5   Howard W. French, "'Bombard the Headquarters'," *The Wall Street Journal*, May 27, 2016, https://www.wsj.com/articles/bombard-the-headquarters-1464373894

6   Thomas F. Farr, "The Assault on Religion in China and What to do About It," *Testimony Before the House Committee on Foreign Affairs, Subcommittee on Africa, Global Health, Global Human Rights, and International Organizations,* September 27, 2018, https://docs.house.gov/meetings/FA/FA16/20180927/108730/HHRG-115-FA16-Wstate-FarrT-20180927.pdf

7   Sergio Ticozzi, "The Persecution of Catholics During the Cultural Revolution," *AsiaNews.it*, May 17, 2016, http://www.asianews.it/news-en/The-persecution-of-Catholics-during-the-Cultural-Revolution-37513.html

The next campaign, highlighted in an August 18, 1966 speech, was to eradicate the 'Four Olds' – old traditions, old customs, old culture, and old ideas. The Red Guards amassed in Shanghai and the revolution was in full swing with the proletariats overtaking cities as the CCP's eight Central Committees approved the dictates of the Cultural Revolution in August 1967.

Conclusion

As the Red Guards grew in numbers and power, they successfully eliminated their professors, destroyed the businesses, seized farmland, destroyed artwork, burned books, and started anew. Without the teachers or books they created a revolution that decimated the past with devastating consequences. The irony of the phrase "Cultural Revolution" is left for all to ponder.

What's at Stake?

First, the CCP's Ministry of Education continues to burn books with any content that do not conform to their societal norms, including Bibles and other religious and Western texts.[8] Publishers of 'illegal' texts are imprisoned for printing and distributing books that criticize the Chinese Communist Party (CCP).[9] These actions are illustrated by the imprisonment of the Hong Kong book sellers.[10]

Second, besides the fact that millions died, many suffered through the maligned belief that there was value in murdering or imprisoning fellow citizens. This moral bankruptcy is at the core of the problems in which generations were raised.

Third, religion was banned, which took away the practice of faith and spirituality of millions. Churches were demolished as representing Old Customs, Old Habits, Old Culture, and Old Ideas. Even today, religion is stifled. Likening himself after Mao, Xi Jinping has called for his comrades to be "unyielding Marxist atheists", imprisoning millions of faith and thrusting them into forced labor camps for global production, distribution, and sales.

---

8   James Palmer, "Why is China Burning Books?," *Foreign Policy*, December 11, 2019, https://foreignpolicy.com/2019/12/11/china-burning-book-censorship-online-outrage/

9   Helen Davidson, "Chinese Publisher who Spoke Up for Dissident Academic is Jailed for Three Years," *The Guardian*, February 9, 2021, https://www.theguardian.com/world/2021/feb/10/chinese-publisher-who-spoke-up-for-dissident-academic-is-jailed-for-three-years

10 Reuters Staff, "Hong Kong Bookseller Jailed in China Releases Smuggled-Out Poems," *Reuters*, May 5, 2020, https://www.reuters.com/article/us-china-sweden-bookseller/hong-kong-bookseller-jailed-in-china-releases-smuggled-out-poems-idUSKBN22H1OT

Chapter 4
Deng Xiaoping
Opening China to the World

Introduction

Deng Xiaoping became the de facto leader of China in 1978, two years after Mao Zedong's death. His life to that point had taken him across the world where he witnessed various systems of thought and governance. In 1919, he participated in a work-study program in France. In 1926, he studied in Moscow with the son of Chiang Kai-shek, Chiang Ching-kuo, who later became the leader of Taiwan, overlapping a decade of leadership between the two countries. Deng also served in China's early 20th-century revolutionary march toward communism, World War II and, afterward, in China's Civil War.

During Deng's pragmatic leadership, the People's Republic of China's (PRC) policies transitioned from those Mao championed during his rule to an open trading market society, harnessing the power of the country's large population. China's economy progressively rose as he traveled the world examining intersections between social, political, and military programs. Meanwhile, he cultivated relationships with business executives and trading partnerships with other countries. His presence was so widely known that he was selected as *Time* magazine's 'Person of the Year' in both 1978[1] and 1985.[2]

During this period, of China's history Deng Xiaoping was credited with the country's vision of 'socialism with Chinese characteristics', which was identified by a market reform movement of foreign investment and domestic productivity. His approach combined the Marxist-Leninist ideologies he learned while studying and working in Marseilles and Moscow and the productivity required to embrace and incorporate the PRC's unique mass of peasantry who lived on farms. Deng established diplomatic relations with the United States in 1979. With an eye toward development, the country became one of the fastest growing economies in the world. Although his demise occurred after the 1989 Tiananmen Square massacre, his influence continued to be present in Beijing.

Looking Back, Stepping Forward

Over the past four decades, China's transformation from a principally agriculture-dominated economy to a global market distributor has changed the job distribution of its citizens, perception of the country, and its leadership.[3] China's unprecedented growth lifted many to a comparatively high standard of living as cities grew larger. Six of China's cities are in the top 25 largest,[4] more than any other country. Foreign direct investment (FDI) from hundreds of multinational corporations helped to infuse cash, resources, and human capital into the country. While this extraordinary growth uplifted the citizenry within China, other countires have paid the price of China's rise and economic power. These costs are likely to increase as explained in subsequent chapters.

---

1   Time Magazine, "Man of the Year: Visionary of a New China," *Time Magazine*, January 1, 1979, http://content.time.com/time/subscriber/article/0,33009,916563,00.html

2   Time Magazine, "Deng Xiaoping, Man of the Year," *Time Magazine*, January 6, 1986, http://content.time.com/time/covers/0,16641,19860106,00.html

3   Yi Wen and Scott Wolla, "China's Rapid Economic Rise: A New Application of an Old Recipe," *Social Education 81*, no. 2 (2017) 93-97, https://wwwJuly.socialstudies.org/system/files/publications/articles/81021793_0.pdf

4   World Population Review, "World City Populations 2021," *World Population Review*, n.d., https://worldpopulationreview.com/world-cities

Opening the Middle Kingdom to Foreign Investment and Trade

In the late 1970s, China had about a billion people, a long history of challenges, and a few hundred years of war and torment. The story that proceeds afterward is nothing less than miraculous. A freer, fairer, and more open China was no longer isolated from the world. Furthermore, China was beginning to be modernized in an ambitious quest toward economic advancement. Deng Xiaoping is considered the 'principal architect' who improved agriculture, industry, science, technology, and defense.

Meanwhile, across the strait, Chiang Ching-kuo ruled Taiwan. Chiang did not oppose the Chinese Communist Party. Chiang Ching-kuo had been classmates with Deng Xiaoping in the Soviet Union and began forming cross-strait economic relations with mainland China in the late 1970s. As China entered the world stage, led by Deng Xiaoping, Taiwan began investing in China. Economically, Taiwan has maintained its financial relations ever since, though more recently, these have become more tense.[5]

The bold moves that Chinese Communist Party (CCP) leaders took came on the heels of the PRC's economic and military rise which began more than forty years ago after the failure of Mao Zedong's "Great Leap Forward" (1958-1962) and "Great Proletarian Cultural Revolution" (1966-1976). After years of social and economic chaos, Deng Xiaoping led China from 1978 to 1989 toward a more liberal, market-driven economic approach with global potential.

---

[5] Eleanor Albert, "China-Taiwan Relations," *Council on Foreign Relations*, January 22, 2020, https://www.cfr.org/backgrounder/china-taiwan-relations

Deng Xiaoping was cautious, though, popularizing the notion "Cross the river by feeling the stones."[6] This note of caution reminded all that to reach seemingly clear goals within eyesight, currents may be swift, rocks may be slippery, winds may blow, and each step could stumble even the most skilled and confident. Furthermore, traversing an uncertain river may not be easy and could be dangerous.

Prudent and forceful, China crossed the river and now stands on the other side – strong, advanced, and savvy. The United States now finds itself face-to-face with a great power. Yet, China's population is more than four times larger and, when a butterfly flaps its wings anywhere in China, the strength of its power is felt around the world. America must now be alert when it treads on the perilous and slippery stones.

Deng Xiaoping realized that innovation would not emerge without risk-taking. Given Mao's legacy of top-down dictatorship, complete indoctrination, suppression of ideas, and the communist idea of sharing, Deng allowed companies to develop systems where profitability could arise without the government controlling the reins. In this environment privatization began; optimism surfaced. In a 1978 speech, Deng said, "Emancipate the minds, seek the truth from facts, unite and look forward."[7] A new orientation came out

> "It doesn't matter if the cat is black or white,
> So long as it catches mice."
> - Deng Xiaoping

---

6   Ezra F. Vogel, *Deng Xiaoping and the Transformation of China*. Vol. 10 (Cambridge, MA: Belknap Press of Harvard University Press, 2011).

7   Kong Qingjiang, "Opinion: Historic CPC Meeting Ushered in China's New Era," *CGTN*, Updated December 21, 2018, https://news.cgtn.com/news/3d3d674e776b7a4d31457a6333566d54/index.html

of this awakening with Deng Xiaoping's perspective of not assigning credit or method to outcomes.

"It doesn't matter if the cat is black or white, so long as it catches mice."

In 1919, just after World War I, Deng Xiaoping left China to participate in a French work program. Before leaving, Deng's father asked what he expected to learn in France. He replied, "To learn knowledge and truth from the West in order to save China."[8] He later studied in the Soviet Union realizing that fair and just leadership does not need democracy. Rather, China's system would benefit from a long-term strategic planning approach uninhibited by the vicious struggles of four-to-eight-year cycles of voting that dramatically shift foreign and domestic policies.

Deng's goal was economic progress beyond China's borders. He created the framework of greater freedom to empower businesses and produce intellectual property that individuals could use to create profit. Citizens, companies, and cities benefitted as Chinese entrepreneurs reached out past its borders toward the wider international sphere. While the uneducated and unskilled were not likely to attain middle-class status as quickly as those who had college degrees and technical skills, the economy of the entire country rose.

Conclusion

In the 21st century, China began a new mass population mobilization, achieving economic advances within a short period of time that took other nations decades to accomplish.[9] While China is most certainly not a poor country today, the tactics used in taking advantage of its vast human capital are both well-known and changing as this is written. With Xi Jinping's great push to shape China into a 21st century thriving marketplace after Deng Xiaoping's partnership-building economic transformation, China transformed itself from poor and weak to, one of the two most powerful nations in the world.

What's at Stake?

First, if China's leadership has the wherewithal to "develop systems where profitability could arise without the government taking the returns," at one point in its recent history, even after oppressive policies like those of the "Great Leap Forward" and the "Cultural Revolution", then it possesses the possibility of another great transformation.

Second, there are millions of genuinely good people in China with a heart of gold and both a conscience and sense of morality. These people could open the door to a new future with a 'peaceful rise'.

Third, China opened itself to the world with a model of being the lowest priced

---

8 Whitney Stewart, *Deng Xiaoping: Leader in a Changing China* (Twenty-First Century Books, 2001) 23.

9 Dali L. Yang, *Calamity and Reform in China*, (Stanford: Stanford University Press, 1996).

leader of cheap goods manufacturing. The only way to maintain that model is through its continued use of forced labor. Though abhorrent, these practices are either consciously ignored, equally complicit, or unknowingly accepted. Corporate enterprises and the global population look away and exchange low prices for the immorality of abject torture and slavery.

Chapter 5
Shoring up Productivity
Harnessing the Skills of China's Population

Introduction

In 1949, when the People's Republic of China (PRC) was founded, China was a poor, underdeveloped country.[1] Famine, floods, and disease were widespread. Periods during Mao's reign actually decreased economic output,[2] though its rise began to take shape when Deng Xiaoping led the country. Confidence and nationalism drove China toward achieving its "Made in China 2025" goals.[3]

Population and Employment

China is the world's most populous country with the world's largest workforce. With its total reform and opening-up policies in the late 1970's, China's national economy witnessed a sound, sustainable, and rapid growth. Nevertheless, in the 2020s, employment issues, industrial structure, and technological innovation remain essential, arduous, and pressing tasks for the Chinese Communist Party (CCP). The Chinese government asserts that employment is the first priority for its people's livelihood and is the top strategy for ensuring the stability of its society.[4]

Sustained Growth

The World Bank stated that China has had "the fastest sustained expansion by a major economy in history."[5] A 2019 Congressional Research Service report entitled, "China's Economic Rise: History, Trends, Challenges, and Implications for the United States", explains, "Since opening up to foreign trade and investment and implementing free-market reforms in 1979, China has been among the world's fastest-growing economies, with real annual gross domestic product (GDP) growth averaging 9.5% through 2018."[6] A 2021, *Wall Street Journal* article reported that China was the only major economy to report economic growth for 2020. "China's growth makes it an outlier among large economies," furthering that, "the World Bank expects the U.S. economy to have contracted by 3.6% and the eurozone's to have shrunk by 7.4% in 2020, contributing to a global economic pullback of 4.3%."[7]

---

1   Embassy of the People's Republic of China in the Syrian Arab Republic, "China's Socio-Economic Achievements During the Past 60 Years," *Embassy of the People's Republic of China in the Syrian Arab Republic,* October 27, 2009, http://sy.chineseembassy.org/eng/xwfb/t622842.htm

2   U.S. Library of Congress, "The Cultural Revolution, 1966-76," *U.S. Library of Congress,* n.d., http://countrystudies.us/china/90.htm

3   Jost Wubbeke, Mirjam Meissner, Max J Zenglein, Jacqueline Ives, & Bjorn Conrad, "Made in China 2025: The Making of a High-Tech Superpower and Consequences for Industrial Countries," *Metrics Papers on China,* December, 2016, https://assets.documentcloud.org/documents/3864881/Made-in-China-Paper.pdf

4   Yan DI, "China's Employment Policies and Strategies," *Ministry of Labour and Social Security, P.R. China,* n.d., https://www.oecd.org/employment/emp/37865430.pdf

5   EveryCRSReport, "China's Economic Rise: History, Trends, Challenges, and Implications for the United States," *EveryCRSReport,* June 25, 2019, https://www.everycrsreport.com/reports/RL33534.html

6   Ibid.

7   Jonathan Cheng, "China is the Only Major Economy to Report Economic Growth for 2020," *The Wall Street Journal, U*pdated January 18, 2021, https://www.wsj.com/articles/china-is-the-only-major-economy-to-report-economic-growth-for-2020-11610936187

What is Productivity?

Productivity is the amount of output gained from an input. If labor (human work) or capital (machinery or money) are used as inputs, then the question remains, how much output does that input produce? In economics, these numbers are divided and a ratio is produced. The productivity of a person can be measured by how many widgets are produced by a person per day, month, or year. On day one, for example, a person is hired to fill boxes to be shipped; they fill five boxes. When they are experienced, they can fill a hundred. Thus, how productive a person is in a job makes a big difference to a company or a country.

People can be more or less efficient with their time depending upon numerous variables (ability, strength, health, training, years on the job, etc.). The measurement of economic growth has much to do with the productivity of its people. This is why, in any society, education and experience are valuable. Trained people (human capital) have skills that help companies become more profitable and countries more economically successful. A manager might want to analyze ways to improve productivity and increase human capital.

An economist or statistician might want to examine whether a more efficient method of work, better training program, or type of leadership would improve productivity. They might create a simplified model, graph the data, or make charts to review the effectiveness of a plan. On the macro scale, one way of comparing productivity by country is to take the Gross Domestic Product (GDP) and divide this by the number of hours worked.

Productivity's Impact on Growth

In his book, "The Age of Diminishing Expectations", Paul Krugman explains, "Productivity isn't everything, but in the long run it is almost everything. A country's ability to improve its standard of living over time depends almost entirely on its ability to raise its output per worker."[8] This was particularly important for China in the 1950s to 2000s since it had a large population and thus significant underutilized human capital. From primarily agricultural workers, a new generation needed to be raised and prepared for 21st century technology skills. The modern world demanded educated, trained, and technologically-savvy people.

Thus, through the country's post-Mao leadership, productivity in China continued to rise. According to Zhu, "capital accumulation was the main source of economic growth in the 1952-1978 period while productivity growth has been the main source of growth since then."[9] Zhu considered human capital, physical capital, growth rate of labor participation, and per capita GDP to determine total factor productivity (TFP).

Persistent economic growth can only come from an increase in TFP.[10] Thus, in China, decades of rapid economic growth would not have been possible without significant growth in aggregate total factor productivity.[11] While foreign direct investment has played a significant role, productivity plays an even larger role.

Sociocultural and Economic Factors

Factors in human capital, labor, and social migration have played key roles. Chinese citizens are better educated. Millions have migrated from farms to urban centers for work. China has the largest labor force in the world. Agriculture continues to be critically important. With a population of nearly 1.4 billion people, food production is essential.

Additionally, this transformation could not have occurred without changes in the way China viewed its economic system and its people. China's fundamental economic, social, and political frameworks shifted with the institution of market reforms in 1978, movement away from state-owned enterprises, which failed to produce results and had significant negative fiscal consequences, and the creation of what Weingast terms, "Chinese style" federalism.[12]

Chinese citizens began to awaken to the possibility of greater freedoms. Deng Xiaoping's efforts "led to a range of experiments, emphasizing aspects that could be changed in the short run and that did not leave long-term investments vulnerable."[13] Citizens'

---

8 Paul Krugman, *The Age of Diminishing Expectations* (The MIT Press, 1994).

9 Xiaodong Zhu, "Understanding China's Growth: Past, Present, Future," *The Journal of Economic Perspectives 26*, no.4(2012): 103-124.

10 Robert M. Solow, "A Contribution to the Theory of Economic Growth," *The Quarterly Journal of Economics 70*, no. 1(1956): 65–94, https://doi.org/10.2307/1884513

11 Xiaodong Zhu, "Understanding China's Growth: Past, Present, Future," *The Journal of Economic Perspectives 26*, no.4(2012): 103-124.

12 Barry R. Weingast, "The Economic Role of Political Institutions: Market-Preserving Federalism and Economic Development," *Journal of Law, Economics, & Organization,* (1995): 1-31.

13 Ibid.

notions of business took root and were watered throughout the industries of agriculture, manufacturing, transportation, energy, communication, and finance.

As in its market approach, China took steps to improve productivity by providing incentives to growers who had delivered the state-required quota. Beijing allowed the farm workers on collective and state-owned farms to set their own prices and sell what they produced in the marketplace.[14] Those who worked harder were rewarded and productivity increased. More people took jobs in manufacturing, and still others took work in more highly skilled operations. The middle class expanded and opportunities for entrepreneurship increased. The poverty rate also decreased as more people were put to work. GDP grew and the labor market enlarged.

All sectors rose as people had greater mobility. Transportation networks improved with cars, trains, planes, and shipping mushrooming in numbers and quality. Workers continued to have new opportunities to take jobs requiring greater skills. The manufacturing sector gradually moved from labor-intensive industries to more capital-intensive finance and high-tech industries. "Accompanying the change in industrial structure was an increase in the scale of production, the required capital and skill, the market scope and the risks."[15]

Productivity did not come suddenly, but in steps. The vast supply of labor in China fanned the flames that were sparked by companies who recognized opportunity in the less expensive supply chain opportunities burgeoning throughout China - idle, but ready. This shift coincided with U.S. workforces demanding higher wages, more benefits, fewer hours, and better working conditions. Furthermore, in the U.S., governmental regulations, environmental restrictions, and federal reporting requirements were comparatively onerous. China offered tremendous cost savings and limited regulations.

This shakeup also occurred when Thomas Friedman proposed that our "flat world" could provide goods and services we needed at a fraction of the cost. Thus, in some industries, where labor costs were already $50 per hour, Chinese labor could be purchased for less than $50 a week. Multinational companies took the risk to retrain, retool, and reinvest to capitalize on China's cheap labor.

Massive shipping centers in China's port cities were built to transport the staggering quantity of goods. Manpower needed to be trained to manage the sophisticated logistical systems since mechanized flows moved thousands of containers each day on trucks, railcars, planes, and ships in a continuous cycle to all corners of the globe. Training in leadership and supply chain processes were also needed to boost the education level and increase productivity.

High tech processes and supply chains must navigate communication channels between global headquarters in San Francisco or New York and mega-centers in Beijing, Shenzhen, Tianjin, and other ports, receiving information about raw materials in Sao Paolo or Jakarta and delivery hubs in Los Angeles and Miami. Efficiencies in the supply chain improved product delivery to compete with even lower cost labor, mechanized production, and

---

14 Barry R. Weingast, "The Economic Role of Political Institutions: Market-Preserving Federalism and Economic Development," *Journal of Law, Economics, & Organization*, (1995): 1-31.

15 Justin Yifu Lin, "Demystifying the Chinese Economy," *Australian Economic Review* 46, no. 3 (2013): 259-268.

enhanced coordination. Without free market economics and a limitation on government intervention, none of this could possibly happen within the same timeframes.

Outsourcing and Market Disruptions

Outsourcing significantly benefitted companies in lowering overall costs. To be sure, there were language barriers, growing pains, and misinterpretations - intentional or unintentional. Despite the challenges, high labor costs in Western countries continued to increase opportunities for workers in China as more companies used less expensive Asian labor across industries. Telemarketing, order takers, writers, printers, graphic designers, virtual babysitters, tutors, and other online services were relatively easy to coordinate, set up, and terminate if unsuccessful.

However, each disruption in market forces required higher levels of education, while reducing unemployment, increasing per capita income, and improving productivity. Meanwhile, many manufacturing positions in the U.S. were eliminated. The dynamics changed along with the conception of a globalized labor force. This shift also changed product demand. The Chinese products we readily pick up in convenience and discount stores are significantly less expensive than those produced in the United States. At this point, it would be hard to turn back the clock.

Although the world is not quite as flat as it seems and environmental destruction during this industrial revolution will have long lasting effects, the world demanded China's less expensive products, and China was all-too-happy to be the world's supplier. Additionally,

Beijing reaped benefits as Chinese society "galvanized broad social constituencies that would support such a change."[16]

China hired experts, borrowed training courses, and ramped up productivity at a faster pace. The typical learning curve needed by early adopters, requiring trial and error investment and time-consuming evolutionary cycles, were overcome by using foreign intellectual capital. Experts were invited through China's 'Thousand Talents Program'.[17] Businesses were invited to enter the country provided the Chinese had a significant stake in operations. Thus, they could increase productivity at a much faster pace. Deng Xiaoping tapped into the knowledge banks, by importing trainers, attracting industries, and exporting goods. Soon, China was not merely manufacturing clothing, shoes, and toys, but highly sophisticated and technical machines, equipment, and communication systems.

GDP Growth

China was previously a relatively egalitarian socialist society with significantly greater equality among the working class. This has now diminished and new efforts are being made to improve education, health, and opportunity for those who have seemingly been left behind. With this effort, productivity will continue to grow and more people will have the chance to leave poverty behind and enter the middle class. Other opportunities for increased productivity include breaking up monopolies and privatizing state-owned business and financial sectors. This shake up would also allow more people to participate in these sectors that are often closed or cost prohibitive to enter.

There is no doubt that China's growth has been exceptional. "No country in human history has ever grown so fast for so long as Chinas did in the past three decades."[18] Growth rates, high levels of exports, vast foreign exchange reserves, robust economic systems, even during the 2008 international recession, are only part of the story. China has become the second largest economy in the world with a global GDP of 15 percent, second only to the United States with 24.5 percent. However, China's GDP growth rate expanded by 6.7 percent in the second quarter of 2016 versus the United States growth of 1.23 percent.[19] When GDP is based upon purchasing power parity (PPP), China is the global leader with a GDP of 23,194,411 in millions of USD versus the United States with 19,417,144.[20] China is the global leader in exports with $2,098,000 (in millions of dollars) with the United

---

16 Edward S. Steinfeld, *Playing Our Game: Why China's Rise Doesn't Threaten the West* (Oxford University Press, 2010) 28.

17 United States Senate, "Threats to the U.S. Research Enterprise: China's Talent Recruitment Plans," *United States Senate*, November 18, 2019, https://www.hsgac.senate.gov/imo/media/doc/2019-11-18%20PSI%20Staff%20Report%20-%20China's%20Talent%20Recruitment%20Plans.pdf

18 Justin Yifu Lin, "Demystifying the Chinese Economy," *Australian Economic Review 46*, no. 3 (2013): 259-268.

19 International Monetary Fund, "World Economic Outlook, April 2017: Gaining Momentum?," *International Monetary Fund*, April, 2017, https://www.imf.org/en/Publications/WEO/Issues/2017/04/04/world-economic-outlook-april-2017

20 Ibid.

States significantly behind with $1,471,000[21] and second to the United States ($2,205,000 in millions) in imports with $1,587,000.[22]

Conclusion

Acceleration is still possible in both foreign direct investment (FDI) and total factor productivity (TFP). Chinese citizens have tasted the fruit of the increasingly open economy. Many inspired citizens are hungry for opportunities and are willing to work to bring their ambitions to fruition. The state can and should both trust and empower its citizenry while developing stronger mechanisms for support and creativity building. There was no precedent for China's growth. Other countries attracted capital investment, foreign aid, and financial development mechanisms, so FDI cannot account for the greatest rise in history. China's growth was in its people and their work ethic, which serves as the envy of citizens and leaders of many other nations. There is no doubt that China's economic rise rests in the Chinese belief that they will no longer be a country of citizens fraught with destitute poverty and will soon realize economic domination.

What's at Stake?

First, with nearly 1.4 billion citizens, competition has become a driver for the motivated and ambitious. Job security is tenuous at best, and top positions often require extremely long workdays.

Second, sharp distinctions between China's rich and poor are more prominent today. However, there is also a growing middle class. This outcome is partly fueled by a growing number of businesses.

Third, by opening itself to the global economy, Beijing also perceives a growing threat – underground movements, banned religious beliefs, and citizen uprisings - which has led to extreme social control.

Fourth, leaders maintain a communist style totalitarian authority structure by blocking information sources. A growing number of communication channels exist – cell phones, internet, and social media - which have become both an opportunity for greater connectedness for those with access and a liability that enables thought control. Government paranoia abounds regarding freedom of thought, beliefs, and pursuits, which has resulted in blocking Google, Facebook, and VPNs.

Fifth, China has pulled in the reins of its corporations and re-instituted the state-owned, state-controlled corporation. These may look like a traditional and corporate entity, but China's government is in control.

---

21 Central Intelligence Agency, "Country Comparison: Exports," *World Factbook*, 2016, https://www.cia.gov/library/publications/the-world-factbook/rankorder/2078rank.html

22 Ibid.

Chapter 6
Foreign Direct Investment
Remarkable Growth in Income, Trade, and FOI

Introduction

China's remarkable economic growth in the past three decades far surpassed underdeveloped countries that had similar economic circumstances.[1] Economic reforms paved the way, starting with liberalized foreign trade, growth in capital assets, educating a broader population base, and the ability for citizens to create private businesses and form rural collective enterprises. To put these accomplishments into perspective, in 1978, China had a yearly per capita income of $154,[2] less than one-third of an average Sub-Sahara African country.[3] In 2021, the expected per capita income will be $8,840, an increase of 56 times.[4]

Furthermore, in 2021 China overtook the U.S. in Foreign Direct Investment.[5] Again, this phenomenal success is hard to imagine. In over only a few decades, China has grown, expanded, militarized, and used the global labor, economic, and political systems to harness its substantial growth.

China's Emergence from Its Dark Past

In 1989, during and after the Tiananmen Square protests, literally and figuratively, China's future looked dark. A few stores existed. Those that had an established presence closed early. Schools, jobs, and stations in life were prescribed – for life. Visitors "could not help noticing a singular feature of Chinese cities: their darkness. Urban centers at the time had very limited public lighting, logically enough, for there was precious little activity worth illuminating."[6] It was, therefore, nearly inconceivable that from this stifling, state-determined, political and economic hierarchy of Chinese socialism, a market-driven economy, thriving sense of entrepreneurship, and social self-efficacy could emerge.

The gleaming Chinese metropolises of today have progressively marched out of the dismal shadow of their past and into a modern age with a robust economy, bustling network of commerce, and scintillating skyscrapers. On the surface, the dramatically and colorfully lit buildings magnificently demonstrate the outward transformation of a country that has shed its perilous past. Equally apparent is the pride, hope, and spirit of its people. From the sluggish robotic motion of a people whose life was predetermined arose virtually unlimited possibility and rapidly rising productivity. The walking pace and determination to reach their next destination is clearly more rapid.

In 1978, China had "150 million people under the poverty line in rural areas, representing 26 percent of the rural population. By the end of 1999, this figure had

---

1. Jinghai Zheng, Arne Bigsten, and Angang Hu, "Can China's Growth Be Sustained? A Productivity Perspective," *World Development 37*, no.4 (2009): 874-888.
2. China Statistics Press, "China Statistics Abstract 2010," *China Compendium of Statistics* 1949-2008, 2010.
3. Justin Yifu Lin, "Demystifying the Chinese Economy," *Australian Economic Review 46*, no. 3 (2013): 259-268.
4. Trading Economics, "China GDP Per Capita," *Trading Economics*, n.d., https://tradingeconomics.com/china/gdp-per-capita
5. Paul Hannon and Eun-Young Jeong, "China Overtakes U.S. as World's Leading Destination for Foreign Direct Investment," *The Wall Street Journal*, Updated January 24, 2021, https://www.wsj.com/articles/china-overtakes-u-s-as-worlds-leading-destination-for-foreign-direct-investment-11611511200?mod=djemalertNEWS
6. Edward S. Steinfeld, Playing Our Game: *Why China's Rise Doesn't Threaten the West* (Oxford University Press, 2010) 3.

dropped to 34 million, and the poverty-stricken population had dropped to 3.9 percent in the total rural population."[7] In merely twenty years, these changes have been nothing short of remarkable. Agriculture, the main source of income for most Chinese flourished. "Farmers' per capita income increased from 133.57 yuan in 1978 to 2210.34 yuan in 1999 at an average growth rate of 7.69 percent."[8] Migration from rural areas to the cities escalated dramatically as did the rise in homeownership. There is also no doubt that the egalitarian provisions and protections of China's past socialist system are shrinking vestiges of what they once were. Many cannot afford to pay rising urban housing prices, quality health care, and educational enhancements.

Involvement in China's polity is occasionally encouraged if it enhances or supports the establishment. However, "Civic actors who step too far forward under the current situation run the risk of crossing some unknown red line. Not surprisingly, aspects of rule of law and civic association are intensely threatening to the state."[9] It is interesting to note that, "members of the Chinese middle class also tend to regard democracy as the best form of government. Thus, the middle class has the potential to initiate democratization in China if the Chinese government fails to keep satisfying the middle class' quest for economic well-being and protection of property rights."[10] Furthermore, with more than 500,000 Chinese students exposed to Western culture while studying abroad in 2015,[11] and with their Western-developed values, and information access, there is little doubt that these "sea turtles," or *haigui* in Chinese,[12] will return home seeking greater plurality, liberalism, and access.

Fueling China's Engine

Foreign direct investment (FDI) fueled China's economic engine, built infrastructure, created jobs, and opened international markets.[13] Meanwhile, China's average productivity increase was 13.5% over two decades.[14] For clarity, the productivity of a state is a factor used in economic circles commonly defined as the ratio between the volume of outputs and the volume of inputs.[15] This translates into a country's ability to improve its standard of living by harnessing the output of each of its workers. China's socialist system provides ample ways to exploit its available low-skilled and imprisoned workforce to remain on-task

---

7   Ying Du, "China's Agricultural Restructuring and System Reform under its Accession to WTO," *China's Agriculture in the International Trading System*, (2001): 52.

8   Ibid.

9   Edward S. Steinfeld, *Playing Our Game: Why China's Rise Doesn't Threaten the West* (Oxford University Press, 2010) 24.

10 Wen-Chin Wu, Yu-Tzung Chang, and Hsin-Hsin Pan, *"Does China's Middle Class Prefer* (Liberal) Democracy?." Democratization 24, no.2(2017): 347-366.

11 Chinese Ministry of Education, 2016.

12 Wei Sun, "The Productivity of Return Migrants: The Case of China's 'Sea Turtles'," IZA *Journal of Migration 2*, no.1(2013): 5.

13 Chung Chen, Lawrence Chang, and Yimin Zhang, "The Role of Foreign Direct Investment in China's Post-1978 Economic Development," *World Development 23*, no. 4 (1995): 691-703.

14 Yanrui Wu, "Has Productivity Contributed to China's Growth?," *Pacific Economic Review 8*, no. 1(2003): 15-30.

15 Paul Krugman, *The Age of Diminished Expectations*, Third Edition (The MIT Press, 1997), https://mitpress.mit.edu/books/age-diminished-expectations-third-edition

while producing significantly more output. These manufacturing production efficiencies with minimal labor costs are, in turn, utilized by many famous corporate brands to obtain low per product prices for the global marketplace.

Some argue that China's initial economic successes began primarily as a function of foreign direct investment (FDI), poured into China at a time when it needed to transition into a technologically more advanced modern state,[16] while others claim that China's rapid and sustained growth is a function of productivity.[17] While foreign direct investment has, undoubtedly, had a significant impact on China's remarkable economic growth, productivity increases account for a greater share of China's economic success.

Foreign direct investment infused capital and helped to build significant and critical Chinese infrastructure. Through joint ventures, cooperative enterprises, and foreign-owned enterprises, "by the end of 2003, China had accumulated more than $500 billion in FDI."[18] Now, with its massive war chest of assets, China continues to invest in its manufacturing for the post-pandemic world. A few of China's advances include banking, lending, and partnerships; technological advances in equipment, robotics, and militarization; and innovation in connectivity, surveillance, and artificial intelligence. Figure 1 depicts this dramatic growth.

Figure 1: Foreign Direct Investment in China: 1984 - 2003[19]

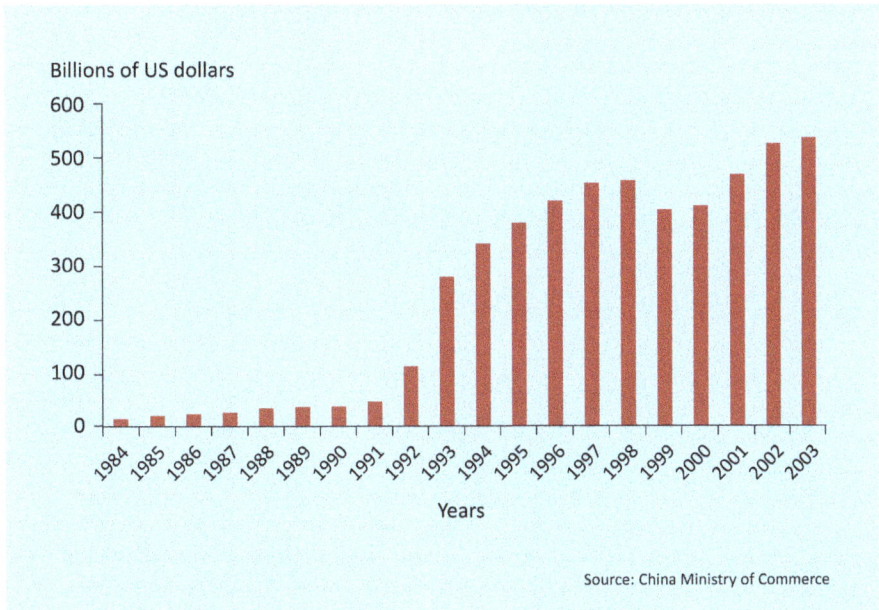

Source: China Ministry of Commerce

---

16   Mark Purdy, "China's Economy, in Six Charts," *Harvard Business Review.* November 29, 2013, https://hbr.org/2013/11/chinas-economy-in-six-charts

17   Xiaodong Zhu, "Understanding China's Growth: Past, Present, Future," *The Journal of Economic Perspectives 26*, no. 4 (2013): 103-124.

18   Guoqiang Long, "China's Policies on FDI: Review and Evaluation," (2005): 315-336.

19   Ibid.

This increase and the resulting exports are so significant that China has emerged in 2021 as the number one economy in the world based upon purchasing power parity. Over the years, China has wrestled with their policies in order to gain a competitive advantage. China's "Law on foreign direct investment in China" states that interested investors must meet certain standards and conform to a balance of payments before receiving approval, though the reigns of restrictions have been more recently lessened in order to attract additional money. Still, many companies have been hesitant to invest, held back due to marketplace uncertainties.

While some see China's meteoric rise as a threat, Beijing is still heavily dependent upon the West, particularly the United States for raw materials, trade, and corporate investment. "China's economic rise is not a miracle, but rather a result of opening trade barriers to businesses from advanced countries which want to take advantage of China's inexpensive manufacturing sector."[20]

Long explains, "Since 1993, China has attracted the largest amount of FDI of all developing countries while increasing its levels of both exports and technological advancement."[21] Purdy makes the claim in Figure 2, that capital has been the major driver in China's growth, not labor or productivity.

Figure 2: Labor, Capital, and Total Factor Productivity[22]

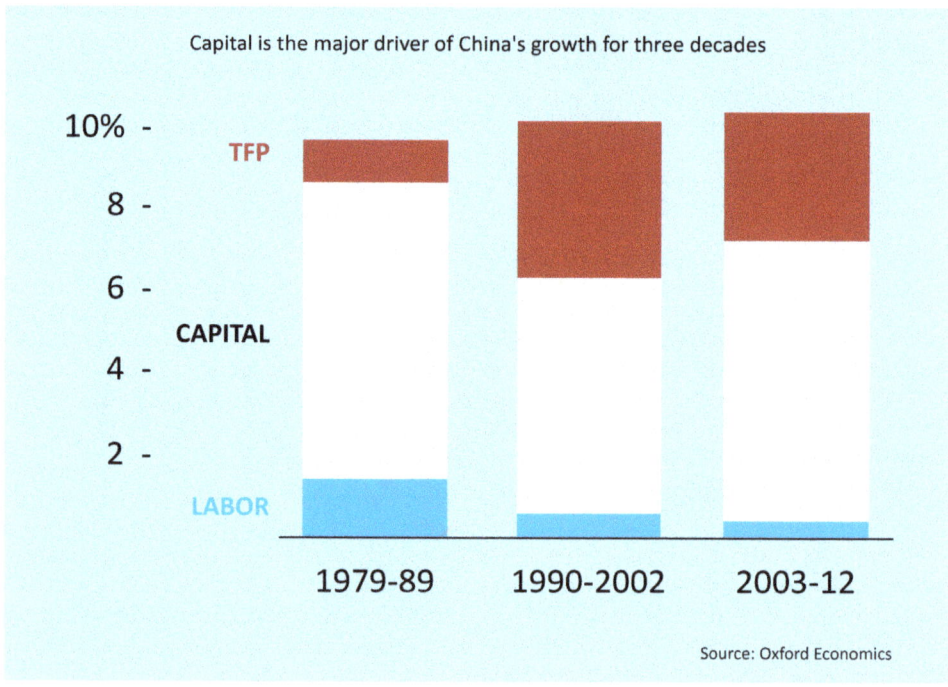

---

20 Michael Kennedy, China's Economic Growth (GRIN Publishing, 2014).

21 Guoqiang Long, "China's Policies on FDI: Review and Evaluation," (2005): 315-336.

22 Mark Purdy, "China's Economy, in Six Charts," *Harvard Business Review*. November 29, 2013, https://hbr.org/2013/11/chinas-economy-in-six-charts

Similarly, Chen explains that foreign direct investment (FDI) is positively associated with China's economic growth as well as its fixed asset investment.[23] With improved facilities and infrastructure, China can continue to attract more companies to invest. FDI's channel of technological progress has, in part, resulted in technology transfer, marginal capital productivity improvement, and further attraction of FDI through incentive policies.[24] The rise in China's manufacturing sector has forced other countries to compete and put pressure on their own industries to innovate and become more competitive.

Importance of Foreign Direct Investment

Foreign direct investment (FDI) has provided needed infrastructure, equipment, transportation, and manufacturing required for China to build its industries. FDI has been a critical component in China's economic growth. "The Chinese experience demonstrates that industrial policy and state spending on physical and social infrastructure can produce rich rewards; conversely, slavish reliance on foreign direct investment and trade are likely to limit the pace of growth."[25]

On the flip side, Chen, Chang, and Zhang explain that FDI created new phenomena including: (a) the accelerating uneven development between the coastal and inland provinces, (b) worsening income distribution, and (c) declining ideological commitment.[26] These occurrences provide a different take on the impact of FDI on China's society and culture on the macro level.

Zhu explains that increased entrepreneurship and incentives are the primary reasons for China's growth in productivity. China incentivized its supply of labor to come to urban centers and "subsequently scrambled to get its house cleaned up."[27] I contend that China still has some housekeeping to do. China must choose to make tough decisions regarding free speech and access that it has not yet been willing to make. Slave labor and intensified surveillance are also political lightning rods.

Another important point is that even though Purdy provided evidence for FDI's significant role in economic growth, he acknowledges that China's future growth will depend on increasing productivity. He explains that "if China wants to lower the investment ratio to below 40% of GDP by the end of the next decade, while keeping the rate of economic growth above 8 percent (essential for maintaining full employment), it must improve the growth rate of productivity."[28]

---

23 Chung Chen, Lawrence Chang, and Yimin Zhang, "The Role of Foreign Direct Investment in China's Post-1978 Economic Development," *World Development 23*, no. 4 (1995): 691-703.

24 Jean-Claude Berthelemy and Sylvie Demurger, "Foreign Direct Investment and Economic Growth: Theory and Application to China," *Review of Development Economics* 4, no.2 (2000): 140-155.

25 Chris Bramall, "Sources of Chinese Economic Growth, 1978-1996," OUP *Catalogue*, 2000.

26 Chung Chen, Lawrence Chang, and Yimin Zhang, "The Role of Foreign Direct Investment in China's Post-1978 Economic Development," World Development 23, no. 4 (1995): 691-703.

27 Edward S. Steinfeld, Playing Our Game: Why China's Rise Doesn't Threaten the West (Oxford University Press, 2010) 28.

28 Mark Purdy, "China's Economy, in Six Charts," *Harvard Business Review*. November 29, 2013, https://hbr.org/2013/11/chinas-economy-in-six-charts

Figure 3: Productivity Required for China's Future Growth[29]

China's Belt and Road Initiative
*Trains, Roads, Planes, Ports, and Tunnels
Productivity Needed to Drive Growth.
To keep a 10%+ growth rate, productivity needs to jump to 5.6%.*

3.3 %	2.5 %	2.1 %	5.6 %
2003-2012 GDP ANNUAL GROWTH RATE 10.5%	2013-2022 BASELINE FORECAST 7.4%	2013-2022 SCENARIO 1: 8.0%	2013-2022 SCENARIO 2: 10.5%

Source: Oxford Economics, Accenture Analysis

Productivity continues to be the most important factor, but this output will depend upon an increasingly aware and cosmopolitan recognition of socioeconomic and political undercurrents. China must overcome major challenges of internal social forces and external geopolitical tensions as it proceeds.

Conclusion

At this juncture, China can continue to make needed adjustments in their economic, social, and political spheres, develop greater efficiencies, improve the environment, and remove corruption. China must increasingly innovate and cultivate empowering relationships around the world while allowing its citizens to access information and provide opportunities for entrepreneurship and creativity. There are no guarantees that China's remarkable growth will continue at its historical pace. However, if it does, it will not be due solely to increased foreign direct investment, but in the development of human capital and productivity that will allow their citizens to thrive. Thus, as China proceeds down its uncertain road in an increasingly globalized economy, it should heed the advice of Deng Xiaoping and be forward thinking, wise in attitude, grounded when taking incremental steps, and "cross the river by feeling the stones."

---

[29] Mark Purdy, "China's Economy, in Six Charts," *Harvard Business Review.* November 29, 2013, https://hbr.org/2013/11/chinas-economy-in-six-charts

What's at Stake?

First, China continues to stifle free thinking and free speech and thus limits the type of innovative development and opportunity required to keep pace with a global marketplace.

Second, China's information networks limit communication. Global resources for information gathering, organization, and analysis are not available to most Chinese citizens. Google is banned, unrestricted social networking is limited, and information to make data comparisons is stifled.

Third, the environment is worsening with air and water pollution not only causing global concerns, but significant health care problems that can impact productivity and, eventually, some of its foreign direct investment.

Fourth, corruption is a factor that inhibits innovation. Rampant intellectual property theft through cloning, copying, or "adapting" has bred a lack of trust worldwide and an understanding that any innovation created or brand manufactured will probably be taken or reconfigured. This loss also lessens the willingness for entrepreneurs to create. Without controls and stronger government protections for licensing, copyright, trademarks, and patents, foreign companies will hesitate to invest and both creativity and productivity will stagnate or diminish.

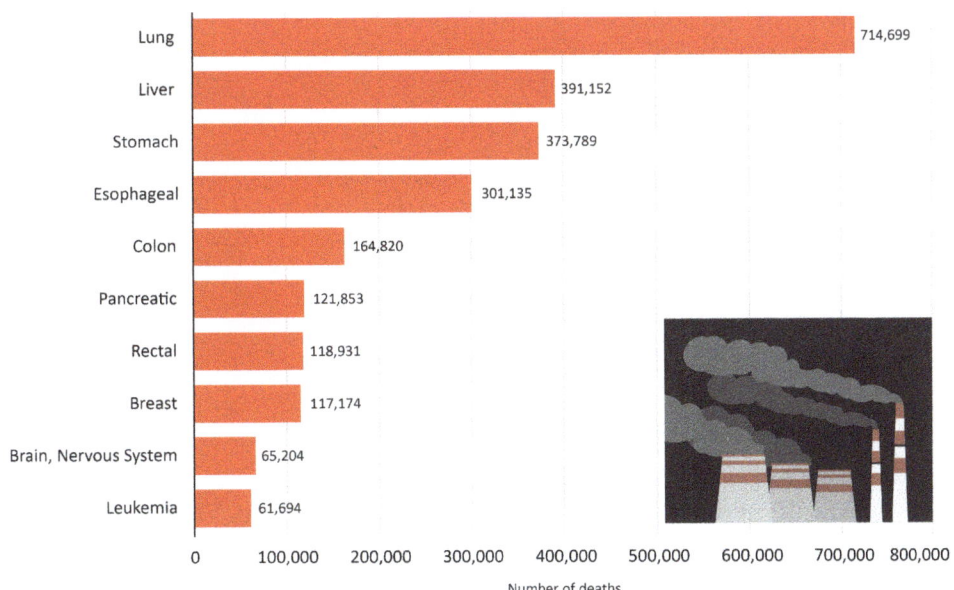

China's 2020 Data
Number of Deaths by Common Cancer Types

Cancer Type	Number of Deaths
Lung	714,699
Liver	391,152
Stomach	373,789
Esophageal	301,135
Colon	164,820
Pancreatic	121,853
Rectal	118,931
Breast	117,174
Brain, Nervous System	65,204
Leukemia	61,694

Chapter 7
Xi Jinping's Larger Than Life Personality
Chairman and Dictator for Life

Introduction

Xi Jinping stands firm in the Chinese Communist Party (CCP) kingpin position. When he took control of the CCP in 2012, he brought a bold vision of the Chinese Dream. With a population of 1.4 billion, President Xi has ensured his position of authority for life with concentrated power and an enigmatic control. Unafraid and unabashed about using force to quell dissent and silence opposition, even the most financially successful forces of human success, like Jack Ma, have been muzzled. The pandemic has not slowed President Xi's ambitions, as he pressed with his economic projects and demonstration of military might. In 2021, his take-charge presence and insistence on loyalty created a fierce persona on the global stage as one of the world's most influential and powerful leaders.

Xi Jinping's Beginnings

Xi Jinping was born on June 15, 1953, in Shaanxi Province, China. Xi Jinping is the son of Xi Zhongxun, who once served as China's Deputy Prime Minister. Xi Jinping's early childhood was spent in relative luxury, living in the residential compound among Beijing's ruling elite. During the Cultural Revolution, however, his father was purged from his position, out of favor with Mao's Red Guards, while his mother was tortured and sister killed. In 1969, Xi Jinping was sent to the rural countryside of Shaanxi Province, where he worked as a manual laborer for six years on an agricultural commune and joined the Chinese Communist Party (CCP).[1] After studying chemical engineering at Tsinghua University, he rose from one leadership position to another within the CCP until he was selected to be a member of the CCP Politburo Standing Committee in 2007.

He built a strong relationship with the peasants of Shaanxi Province. This warm and friendly bond ultimately aided in his ascent through the ranks of the CCP. President Xi currently serves as the President and Paramount Leader of the People's Republic of China (PRC) and the General Secretary of the CCP, a position he has held since 2012.[2] He served as Vice President of the People's Republic of China from 2008 to 2013. Xi Jinping was elected as the President of China for life and Chairman of the PRC's Central Military Commission on March 17, 2018.[3]

Since assuming power in 2012, Xi has launched an unprecedented set of ideological controls and enhanced domestic institutions needed to enforce them.[4] Xi Jinping set up a committee to monitor government officials and other related workers, including teachers, civil servants, academics, and journalists. This constant surveillance resulted in the suppression of freedom of speech, which, in effect, returned China to ideologies

---

1 Editors at Encyclopaedia Britannica, "Xi Jinping," *Encyclopaedia Britannica*, Updated February 9, 2021, https://www.britannica.com/biography/Xi-Jinping

2 GlobalSecurity, "Xi Jinping," *GlobalSecurity*, n.d., https://www.globalsecurity.org/military/world/china/xi-jinping.htm

3 Paul Mozur and Edward Wong, "U.S. Weighs Sweeping Travel Ban on Chinese Communist Party Members," *The New York Times*, Updated December 3, 2020, https://www.nytimes.com/2020/07/15/us/politics/china-travel-ban.html

4 GlobalSecurity, "Xi Jinping Personality Cult," *GlobalSecurity*, n.d., https://www.globalsecurity.org/military/world/china/xi-jinping-cult.htm.

reminiscent of those during the Mao Era.⁵

In 2013, Xi Jinping announced a policy prohibiting the formation of neighborhood associations and alumni meeting groups. Additionally, gathering after work is a violation in many areas. He expressed concern that such gatherings may provide an avenue for sects or political factions to grow within the CCP.⁶ With a heavy hand and iron fist, after term limits were removed, he took complete control of the PRC. He frequently referred to as "dictator for life", a totalitarian leader unseen since Mao Zedong.⁷

---

5   Human Rights Watch, "China's Global Threat to Human Rights," *Human Rights Watch*, n.d., https://www.hrw.org/world-report/2020/country-chapters/global

6   Xinhua, "Xi Focus: Xi Stresses "People First" on First Day of Annual Legislative Session," *Xinhua*, May 22, 2020, http://www.xinhuanet.com/english/2020-05/22/c_139080067.htm

7   Tom Phillips, "'Dictator for Life': Xi Jinping's Power Grab Condemned as Step Towards Tyranny," *The Guardian*, February 26, 2018, https://www.theguardian.com/world/2018/feb/26/xi-jinping-china-presidential-limit-scrap-dictator-for-life

Larger Than Life

With China's rising global presence looming large across all continents and the ability to wield control over the Chinese citizenry, there is no doubt that President Xi has a unique ability to take full charge. Exemplified through his push to build military installations throughout the South China Sea (SCS) and the Belt and Road Initiative (BRI), with investments on nearly every continent, Xi Jinping projects a persona that appears larger than life.

In 2017, the Chinese Communist Party offered President Xi the "core leader" status, putting him on par with previous strongmen Mao Zedong and Deng Xiaoping, though they hinted that his power would not be absolute.[8] He maneuvered his position and authority to remove the two-term limit on his presidency, which effectively allows him to retain control of China for the duration of his life with the economic and military authority to negotiate and construct projects that dot the planet.[9]

In March 2018, the National People's Congress (the PRC's parliament) passed changes to China's constitution. Fundamental among these changes included the removal of term limits for both the president and vice president, allowing President Xi Jinping to stay in office indefinitely. The vote was a rubber stamp of 2,964 members; 2,958 voted in favor; two delegates voted against the change; three abstained.[10]

Some suggest that dictatorship nearly destroyed China once,[11] while others proffer that his authoritarian control offers a grim future.[12] Meanwhile, China continues to grow economically and militarily, while its social control prohibits opposition, demanding "total submission" and threatening mass arrests.[13] Hong Kong is the latest casualty in the complete domination, subjugation, and forced indoctrination to Xi Jinping and the People's Republic of China's CCP.

With overarching social control and restrictions placed on Chinese citizens, President Xi is described as larger than life. China's propaganda highlights images that portray him as friendly, charismatic, and easy-going. He has been pictured playing with children, joking with local farmers, and kicking soccer balls in small communities.[14] These visual depictions

---

8 Nick Stember, "The Road to Rejuvenation: The Animated Xi Jinping," in *Pollution*, ed. Gloria Davies, Jeremy Goldkorn, and Luigi Tomba (Australian National University Press, 2015), 5-9.

9 BBC News, "China's Xi Allowed to Remain 'President for Life' as Term Limits Removed," *BBC News*, March 11, 2018, https://www.bbc.com/news/world-asia-china-43361276

10 Tetsushi Takahashi, "Connecting the Dots of the Hong Kong Law and Veneration of Xi," *NIKKEI Asia*, June 1, 2020, https://asia.nikkei.com/Spotlight/Beijing-Diary/Connecting-the-dots-of-the-Hong-Kong-law-and-veneration-of-Xi

11 Sergey Radchenko, "Dictatorship Nearly Destroyed China Once. Will it Do So Again?," *The Washington Post*, March 5, 2018, https://www.washingtonpost.com/news/made-by-history/wp/2018/03/05/dictatorship-nearly-destroyed-china-once-will-it-do-so-again/

12 Kevin Carrico, "A Deepening Dictatorship Promises a Grim Future for China," *East Asia Forum*, April 2, 2018, https://www.eastasiaforum.org/2018/04/02/a-deepening-dictatorship-promises-a-grim-future-for-china/

13 Shibani Mahtani and Theodora Yu, "'Total Submission': With Mass Arrests, China Neutralizes Hong Kong Democracy Movement," *The Washington Post*, January 6, 2021, https://www.washingtonpost.com/world/asia_pacific/hong-kong-arrests-national-security-law/2021/01/06/c3ccc248-4fbe-11eb-a1f5-fdaf28cfca90_story.html

14 CGTN, "Xi Jinping: Children Should Sharpen Mind and Toughen Body," *CGTN*, April 22, 2020, https://news.cgtn.com/news/2020-04-22/Xi-Jinping-Children-should-be-civilized-and-physically-strong-PTfLPxFRqU/index.html

offset the ruthlessness of his policies that have imprisoned more than a million, and instituted widespread genocide which global citizens consider ethnic cleansing.[15] The CCP rounds up anyone considered to be disloyal, even students preparing to enter college.[16]

Xi's rise in power is significant, both for China on a domestic level and for the world internationally. Domestically, Xi appears as the man who single-handedly holds all the power. Chinese people revere him and look to their paramount leader for strength. He projects power. He remarked in an October 1, 2019 speech, "There is no force that can shake the foundation of this great nation," furthering, "No force can stop the Chinese people and the Chinese nation forging ahead. ...Long live the great Communist Party of China. And long live the great Chinese People!"[17]

However, Susanne Weigelin-Schwiedrzik, China expert and sinology professor in the University of Vienna's Department of East Asian Studies, postulates that this picture is only accurate on its surface. She explained that while Xi removed officials during his anti-corruption campaign, he must manage obstacles in working with other CCP officials. Building his credibility, stature, and 'invincible' exterior, one major hurdle is to suppress existing factions. His anti-corruption campaign could backfire if his efforts shine a suspicious light as he attempts to eliminate his political opponents within the CCP.[18]

Universities and colleges across China have established research centers for Xi Jinping Thought. However, some say that these moves are driven more by research funding competition than genuine regard for Xi's social and political viewpoints. By including a broad set of policies and ideas, called "Xi Jinping Thought on Socialism with Chinese Characteristics for a New Era" within the Chinese Communist Party's constitution, the president took a giant leap toward consolidating his leadership beyond 2022.[19]

As described in an article headlined, "How Xi Jinping Became God," children and teachers are indoctrinated from a young age in Jiangxi province.[20] Propaganda methods help accomplish this goal, such as the children's song, "Grandpa Xi Is Our Big Friend," and stories of "Grandpa Xi." Additionally, since the PRC's education system fears "Western infiltration" into schools, the Party determinedly seeks to eradicate religion and eliminate the intrusion of Western messages through social media.

---

15 Frances Eve, "China is Committing Ethnic Cleansing in Xinjiang – It's Time for the World to Stand Up," *The Guardian*, November 2, 2018, https://www.theguardian.com/world/2018/nov/03/china-is-committing-ethnic-cleansing-in-xinjiang-its-time-for-the-world-to-stand-up

16 The Economist, "In China, Political Screening of University Entrants Causes an Uproar," *The Economist*, November 17, 2018, https://www.economist.com/china/2018/11/17/in-china-political-screening-of-university-entrants-causes-an-uproar

17 Evelyn Cheng, "China's Xi: 'No Force can Stop the Chinese People and the Chinese Nation'," *CNBC*, September 30, 2019, https://www.cnbc.com/2019/10/01/china-70th-anniversary-xi-says-no-force-can-stop-the-chinese-people.html

18 Eleanor Albert, Beina Xu, and Lindsay Maizland, "The Chinese Communist Party," *Council on Foreign Relations*, Updated June 9, 2020, https://www.cfr.org/backgrounder/chinese-communist-party

19 GlobalSecurity, "Xi Jinping Personality Cult," *GlobalSecurity*, n.d., https://www.globalsecurity.org/military/world/china/xi-jinping-cult.htm

20 Bitter Winter, "How Xi Jinping Became God," *Bitter Winter*, January 12, 2020, https://bitterwinter.org/how-xi-jinping-became-god/

Contents of literary classics like Daniel Defoe's (1660-1731) novel *Robinson Crusoe*, Russian writer Anton Chekhov's (1860-1904) short story *Vanka*, and Hans Christian Andersen's (1805-1875) *The Little Match Girl*, along with language and history books, have been altered.[21] The target population for framing this socially-controlled mindset is not just toddlers and elementary school children. College classes are not immune from the CCP's red-lined censorship. Since 2018, students and teachers at the Jiangxi Agricultural University must take an online course called "Young People Study Xi."[22] The active pursuit to convert holdouts to this ideology and political frame of reference across education levels is intentional.

"The Chinese President, like Chairman Mao before him, is trying to propose himself as an object of worship worthier than God," explains *Bitter Winter*, an Italian-based online website focused on religious liberty and human rights in China.[23]

A former professor at China's elite Central Party School issued an unprecedented rebuke of the Chinese leader, Xi Jinping, accusing him of "killing a country" and claiming that many more want out of the ruling Chinese Communist Party.[24] Speaking out however is dangerous, as Xu Zhangrun realized when he was 'detained' in one of the CCP's raids to realign and reeducate any faculty member who dared to criticize the paramount leader.[25] The discipline and detainment foisted on Xu was not the only casualty in the domino of faculty being 'punished'. Cai Xia, a retired Chinese professor who taught democratic politics at the Central Party School of the CCP, called Xi Jinping a "mafia boss" and the Chinese Communist Party a "political zombie". His CCP membership and retirement benefits were stripped , as authorities explained that his remarks "had serious political problems and damaged the country's reputation."[26]

President Xi Jinping has an affinity for punishing his enemies, whether openly or indirectly. China is an atheist state and, as such, is against any form of religion except for strict adherence to Communist thought and principles. President Xi has taken the fight against religion personally and considers any deviation from 'Xi Thought' or belief in religion as direct offenses against the state.

Thus, it is unsurprising that the CCP focused its efforts to eradicate the country's Muslim population and place the Uyghurs in concentration camps. Though China began its "War on Terror" against the Uyghur Muslims before President Xi Jinping took the reigns

---

21 Shen Xinran, "In China, Even 'Robinson Crusoe' is Censored," *Stella Del Matino APS.*, January 6, 2019, https://en.msa-it.org/freedom-news20190601/

22 GlobalSecurity, "Xi Jinping Personality Cult," *GlobalSecurity*, n.d., https://www.globalsecurity.org/military/world/china/xi-jinping-cult.htm

23 Ibid.

24 Lily Kuo, "China's Xi Jinping Facing Widespread Opposition in his Own Party, Insider Claims," *The Guardian*, August 18, 2020, https://www.google.com/amp/s/amp.theguardian.com/world/2020/aug/18/china-xi-jinping-facing-widespread-opposition-in-his-own-party-claims-insider

25 Chris Buckley, "Seized by the Police, an Outspoken Chinese Professor Sees Fears Come True," *The New York Times*, July 6, 2020, https://www.nytimes.com/2020/07/06/world/asia/china-detains-xu-zhangrun-critic.html

26 Yew Lun Tian, "Chinese Academic Disciplined after Criticising Xia nd Communist Party," *Reuters*, August 17, 2020, https://www.reuters.com/article/us-china-politics-professor/chinese-academic-disciplined-after-criticising-xi-and-communist-party-idUSKCN25D1DG

of the PRC,[27] Xi accelerated this effort to create Chinese social cohesion, 're-education', and transformation into atheism by defining all Uyghur Muslims as potential terrorists and coercing them into submission.[28]

Xi sought to stem ethnic violence, freedom fighting, and religious expression in China by taking a hardline stance with "absolutely no mercy" against Uyghur Muslims during a series of secret speeches in 2014.[29] Xi began by explaining in detail that the Uyghur Muslim ideology is incompatible with the Chinese belief system. The outcome

---

27 Chien-Peng Chung, "China's 'War on Terror': September 11 and Uighur Separatism," *Foreign Affairs*, July/August, 2002, https://www.foreignaffairs.com/articles/asia/2002-07-01/chinas-war-terror-september-11-and-uighur-separatism

28 Matthew Wilson, "Chinese Uyghurs: International Terrorists or a Terrorised Minority?," *Australian Institute of International Affairs,* December 23, 2019, https://www.internationalaffairs.org.au/australianoutlook/chinese-uyghurs-international-terrorists-or-terrorised-minority/

29 Austin Ramzy and Chris Buckley, "'Absolutely No Mercy': Leaked Files Expose How China Organized Mass Detentions of Muslims," *The New York Times*, November 16, 2019, https://www.nytimes.com/interactive/2019/11/16/world/asia/china-xinjiang-documents.html

was a religious conversion process that has culminated in the mass detention of Uyghurs, decried by human rights groups along with some international leaders across the globe as a smokescreen for China's efforts to suppress Islamic identity within the country.[30]

Conclusion

Surprisingly, the same belief system that banished Xi as a young boy, took down his father politically, and saw his mother tortured and sister killed persuaded him to become emotionally attached to a nostalgic determinism of Mao and the Cultural Revolution. President Xi does not fully comprehend international society's perception of what it means to be human or have freedom of thought.

With a complete dismissal of human dignity, Xi points with admiration to Mao's iron-fisted leadership as he inflicted what amounted to mass murder on tens of millions. He seems to only grasp his own personal plight as a young revolutionary, waving the Little Red Book with rabid fandom. Mao was extraordinarily larger than life. Xi similarly envisions his future, cast with the same spotlight and replete with his own 'Red Book'. 'Xi Thought' offers propaganda, inspirational messages of struggle, emergence, and other replications from China's torrid past that most Chinese would either like to forget or spin in some dystopian positive light.

With his family background, legacy, and course of action, President Xi Jinping is now on track to become the leader of his dreams. Xi projects his power onto the global stage, alongside Mao's long, dark shadow, as the longest-standing stronghold leader in Chinese Communist Party history. Using eloquent, historical references and colorful phraseology, Xi Jinping aims to eliminate dissent, breathe life into the Chinese Dream, and place China at the center stage of the international community's social, economic, and political spheres of influence by China's 100th year of Communist party leadership in 2049. With his larger than life personality, he is well on his way.

What's at Stake?

First, while eliminating adversaries, Xi Jinping warns all Party members that their futures are also in peril if they deviate from the CCP's prescribed course. No member is beyond the scrutinous eyes of the PRC's surveillance network.

Second, religion or the belief in any deity may not come before the supreme leader, Xi. All beliefs in a power higher than Xi are reprehensible.

Third, although 2049 may seem far away, this period is just a tiny moment in China's history. Much can happen in the next couple of decades. The probability is high that the prognosticators will hedge their bets in predicting the looming conflict and destruction that are likely to transpire.

---

30 Rachel Sandler, "Leaked Documents Show Xi Jinping's Secret Speeches About China's Uighur Crackdown," *Forbes*, November 17, 2019, https://www.forbes.com/sites/rachelsandler/2019/11/17/leaked-documents-show-xi-jinpings-secret-speeches-about-chinas-uighur-crackdown/?sh=ec86ad56bf5a

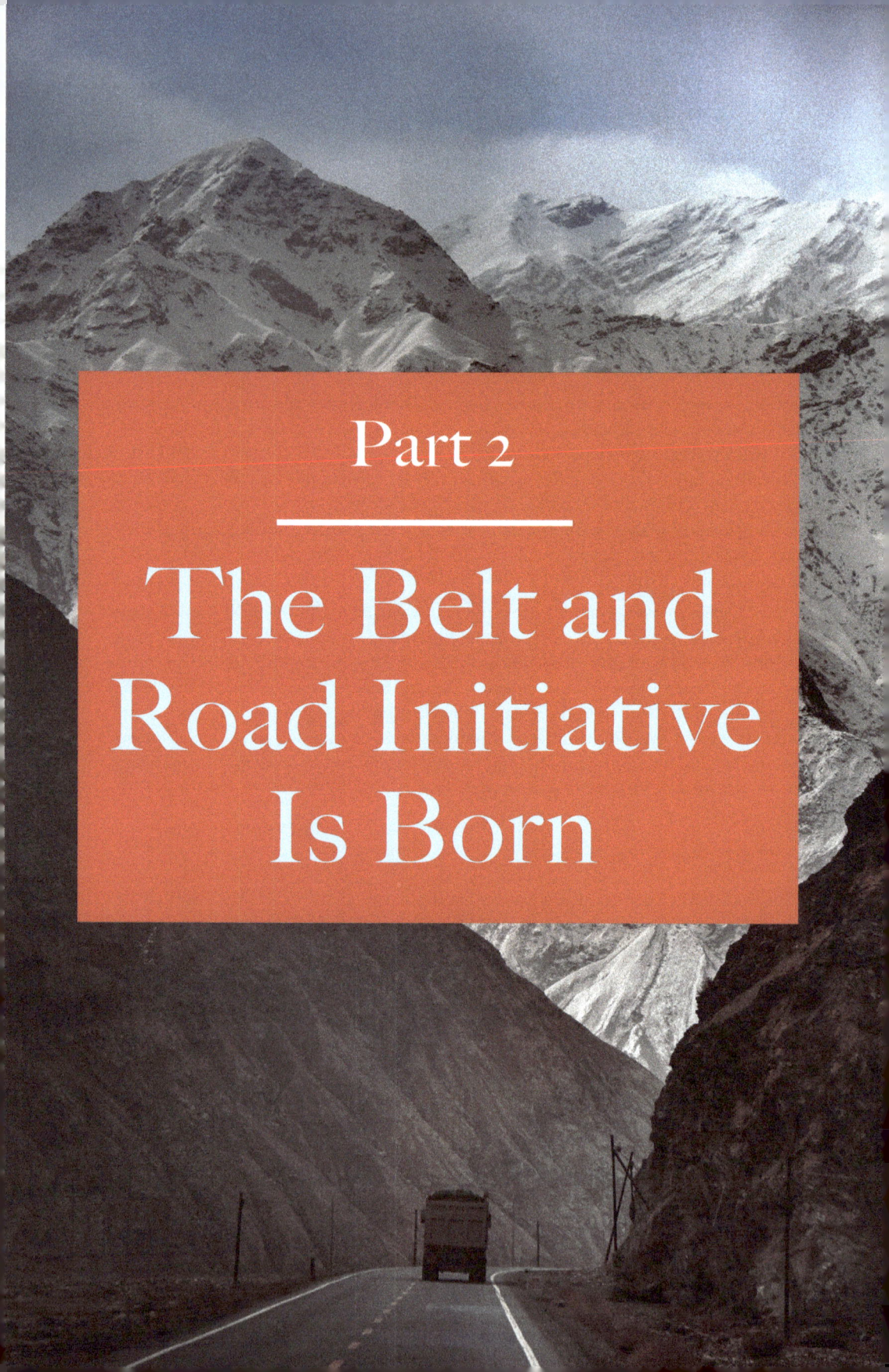

Part 2

The Belt and Road Initiative Is Born

Advancing China's Goals on Belts and Roads

Seeds of the Belt and Road Initiative were planted long before Xi Jinping entered office; the first tread was laid down in Tanzania during Mao's era. In the last decade, China's effort has steadily increased. When Xi Jinping was elected to office, one of his strategic priorities was to expand projects on all continents. President Xi has accomplished this goal as he increased funding on the Silk Road Economic Belt, Maritime Silk Road, Arctic Silk Road, String of Pearls, and Belt and Road Corridors.

With 140 countries signed on as of May 2021, the majority of the world has partnered with China, accepting its money and conditions to build out essential infrastructure for their country and citizenry. The money Beijing offers is too irresistible to pass up, though small-print conditions detail giving up sovereignty, resources, or another asset China wants in return.

Advancing China's goals, Beijing's banks poured money into countries for infrastructure, digital technologies, schools, and media. While the pandemic slowed other countries down, China's manufacturing sector pushed forward the throttle, thrusting the country to accelerate production. China's financial support in loans to countries also grew. China's diplomatic leaders began in 2021, meeting with its African counterparts on a five-nation tour that picked up two new Belt and Road partners.

The Belt and Road Initiative has completed numerous projects and China has proven that its people can deliver at a price that is lower than other counties in a timeframe that is significantly shorter. Money is given to the country's leadership with no questions asked. China's only requirements are that it brings its own manpower. However, since Chinese state-owned enterprises work outside of traditional state laws, they do not obey most traditional rules, do not consult with local residents, and frequently violate environmental norms: towns are demolished, rivers are polluted, and ecological habitats are irrevocably damaged.

Now fully developed with more than a trillion dollars in pledged loans, the Belt and Road Initiative has grown as planned, though near and far there are growing pains.

Chapter 1
Celebration, Collaboration, and Coercion
The EU Celebrates as Xi Offers Benevolent Leadership

Introduction

The 2021 – 2030 decade began with champagne as the European Union affirmed, in principle, China's benevolent free trade agreement. Though the deal, discussed for years, has yet to be ratified by the European Parliament, states are eager to manufacture products for the enormous Chinese market. "European companies would no longer be required to operate joint ventures with Chinese partners, for instance, or be forced to share technology."[1] Despite the United States' requests to reconsider, Germany's Chancellor Merkel was eager to increase Germany's economy and facilitate production to her country's flagship companies.[2] In the past, sticking points included technology sharing, intellectual property theft, Chinese control of operations, human rights, and forced labor camps. As Beijing championed this victory and the EU celebrated the chance to branch out into new markets of its own, many remained skeptical.

In the beginning...

President Xi Jinping became the paramount leader in November 2012, though his presidency began when Hu Jintao left office in March 2013. From the beginning, Xi was committed to economic growth and the global expansion. Xi Jinping took the People's Republic of China on a bold, transformative route with few holds barred. His power consolidation, including the removal, banishment, or imprisonment of his adversaries under the guise of 'corruption' has made his leadership fundamentally important to understand. Furthermore, he appears to have a 'paramount' ability to dictate the direction of the state.

Pouring concrete onto his intractable leadership, Xi Jinping abolished presidential term limits, making it possible to remain in power indefinitely. In May 2018, 2,958 out of 2,964 China's National People's Congress members voted in a mostly symbolic action to approve a plan with state-controlled media claiming that he "won the hearts of the people."[3]

According to Francois Bougon, in his book, "Inside the Mind of *Xi Jinping*",[4]

> There is a certain flexibility to China's leader: To financiers, he adopts the argot of debts and derivatives. To Davos revelers, he drifts easily into the trendy buzzwords of the global business class. To soldiers, he speaks in military idiom (on many occasions happily attired in army greens), and to party members, the jargon of Marxist theory.

---

1   Emily Rauhala, "E.U. and China Agree to Investment Pact Despite Concern about Forced Labor, Objections from U.S." *Washington Post*, December 30, 2020, https://www.washingtonpost.com/world/europe-china-investment-deal-eu/2020/12/30/089742a0-4ab9-11eb-9025-57b4c8818a4a_story.html

2   Ishaan Tharoor and Ruby Mellen, "The Awkward Timing of Europe's Deal with China," *Washington Post*, January 4, 2021, https://www.washingtonpost.com/world/2021/01/05/europe-china-deal-biden-awkward/

3   Emily Rauhala, "Xi Cleared to Rule Indefinitely as China Officially Scraps Term Limits," *Washington Post*, March 11, 2018, https://www.washingtonpost.com/world/china-approves-plan-to-abolish-presidential-term-limits-clearing-way-for-xi-to-stay-on/2018/03/11/973c7ab2-24f0-11e8-a589-763893265565_story.html

4   Francois Bougon, Inside the Mind of Xi Jinping (Westland Limited, 2018).

For the common people of China, he consciously models an ideal of patriotic service and loving family life.[5]

The Chinese people are lathered in "Xi Jinping Thought". This set of dictums are enshrined in the Constitution and contain ideas crafted into a belief system that all Chinese are expected to know. There is even a Certificate of Achievement that can be earned for mastering "Xi Jinping's Thought on Socialism with Chinese Characteristics for a New Era". The EdX course is taught by Angang Hu, Dean of the Institute of Contemporary China Studies at Tsinghua University.[6] In China's ever-increasing commitment to ideological purity among the CCP, along with business and educational leaders, the goal is the absolute commitment to the cause.

Yet, outside of China, Xi is seen as a humanitarian on the one hand and a ruthless punisher on the other. All leaders are warned – anyone who obeys Xi's directives and follows what China commands will be spared; anyone who dares to put up a fight will be viciously attacked. Just consider the venom China injected into Australia with a vengeance or the villages China is building on Bhutan and Indian territories.

There are other concerns too. In November 2013, China declared an Air Defense Identification Zone (ADIZ) in the East China Sea (ECS). After reclaiming land and building military bases on South China Sea (SCS) islands, ostensibly to help China's 'fishermen', Beijing continued its aggressive salami-slicing moves by asserting its claims more forcefully by instituting China's laws in non-Chinese territory.[7] There is great concern that China will claim an ADIZ over the South China Sea as well.

Xi laid some eggs to hatch in the South China Sea in April 2020 by announcing that Beijing created two new administrative districts – Xisha and Nansha. The Xisha district covers the Paracel Islands and Macclesfield Bank and is headquartered on Woody Island. Meanwhile, the Nansha district covers the Spratly Islands and is headquartered on Fiery Cross Island, though both Vietnam and the Philippines formally denounced these actions on their internationally-recognized territory.[8]

To be sure, Xi's meteoric ascent, personality cult, and authoritarian control are complex and a part of a larger trend that connects the present to the past. Xi was not the first to press forward with infrastructure investments, mass production, or a massive blue-water push outward to the seas in all directions. Yet, there is no doubt that he now controls the reigns and has pronounced China's grand vision like the 'Chinese dream', 'national rejuvenation', Made in China 2025, and Global Superpower push to 2050.[9]

---

5   Tanner Greer, "Xi Jinping Knows Who His Enemies Are," *Foreign Policy*, November 11, 2019, https://foreignpolicy.com/2019/11/21/xi-jinping-china-communist-party-francois-bougon/

6   EDX Courses, "Xi Jinping's Thought on Socialism with Chinese Characteristics for a New Era," *EDX Courses*, n.d., https://www.edx.org/course/xi-jinpings-thought-on-socialism-with-chinese-char?utm_source=sailthru&utm_medium=email&utm_campaign=triggered_shareit

7   Rachel Winston and Ishika Sachdeva, *Raging Waters in the South China Sea: What the Battle for Supremacy Means for Southeast Asia* (Irvine: Lizard Publishing, 2020).

8   Huong Le Thu, "Fishing While the Water is Muddy: China's Newly Announced Administrative Districts in the South China Sea," *Asia Maritime Transparency Initiative*, May 6, 2020, https://amti.csis.org/fishing-while-the-water-is-muddy-chinas-newly-announced-administrative-districts-in-the-south-china-sea/

9   Ting Shi, "Xi Jinping Lays Out Blueprint to Make China a Global Superpower by 2050," *National Post*, October 18, 2017, https://nationalpost.com/news/world/xi-jinping-lays-out-plan-to-make-china-a-global-superpower-by-2050

President Xi's Four Periods of Chinese History[10]

1. Ancient History – the disputed 5,000 years president Xi offers China's imperial past ending in the Qing dynasty (1644 – 1911).
2. The Century of Humiliation – The imperial powers take advantage of China with "unequal treaties".
3. The New China Era – Mao Zedong reigns (leader from 1949 – 1976) after the Chinese Civil War and creates the People's Republic of China (PRC).
4. The Era of Socialism with Chinese Characteristics – Beginning with Deng Xiaoping (leader from 1978 – 1989) to Xi Jinping's rule (2012 – Present).

Chinese President Xi Jinping's 2021 World Economic Forum Presentation Frames Collaboration

Xi Jinping's virtually-delivered speech to the World Economic Forum, traditionally held in Davos, Switzerland, was entitled "Let the Torch of Multilateralism Light Up Humanity's Way Forward". Intending to present China in the brightest light, Xi attempted to show the world China's benevolent leadership, humble heart, and multilateralist approach. Xi suggests that the world come together to solve its greatest problems, heal the economies, "abandon ideological prejudice and jointly follow a path of peaceful coexistence…with lasting peace, universal security, and common prosperity."[11] While this plan sounds like the step forward that the world has been hoping for from China, the reality is different. China's economic benevolence and aggressive People's Liberation Army Navy (PLAN) increasingly assert themselves into the global context.

The PRC constructed military enclaves in the South China Sea for observation posts though they have fortified them for war. Beijing took over Scarborough Shoal when they made an agreement with the United States to back off. They established "Special Administrative Districts" in disputed areas that the International Court of Justice said did not belong to them. China threatened to attack Taiwan and wholly took over Hong Kong without keeping its agreement with the United Kingdom. How do world leaders believe that China will keep these new agreements when they have not kept the ones they have made?

President Xi proclaimed, "the strong should not bully the weak." Taken at face value, Xi's sentiment is noble. Yet, these words are contrary to Beijing's actions in the South China Sea, East China Sea, Hong Kong, Taiwan, Tibet, Mongolia, India, Bhutan, Sri Lanka, Canada, and Australia, just to name a few regions bearing the brunt of Beijing's explosive anger and brutal torment. Albeit China 'claims' Hong Kong, Taiwan, Tibet, and Mongolia, but Beijing claims parts of a half dozen other states as well.

As an example, Xi's speech that proclaimed that states should remain "committed to international law and international rules instead of seeking one's own supremacy", is pure

---

10 Francois Bougon, *Inside the Mind of Xi Jinping* (Westland Limited, 2018).

11 Stephen M. Walt, "Xi Tells the World What He Really Wants," *Foreign Policy*, January 29, 2021, https://foreignpolicy.com/2021/01/29/xi-tells-the-world-what-he-really-wants/

fiction, as highlighted in the book *Raging Waters in the South China Sea* and China's loss of the *Philippines v. China* landmark case wherein the International Court of Justice ruled that China violated the United Nations Convention on the Law of the Sea (UNCLOS) to which Beijing was a signatory.

The Chinese Communist Party openly asserts its propaganda war on foreigners and dismisses foreign ideologies, including threatening and imprisoning foreign journalists. Xi's commitment to "openness" must refer to other countries since China continues to block information access to its people, silence Hong Kong activists, imprison Mongolians destroy churces, and 're-educate' the Uyghurs.

Coercion

China wants the world to be perfectly clear that they do not want any other country to interfere in its domestic affairs. Chinese Foreign Minister Wang Yi said in a text, "The most urgent task at the moment is that both sides should work together and remove all kinds of

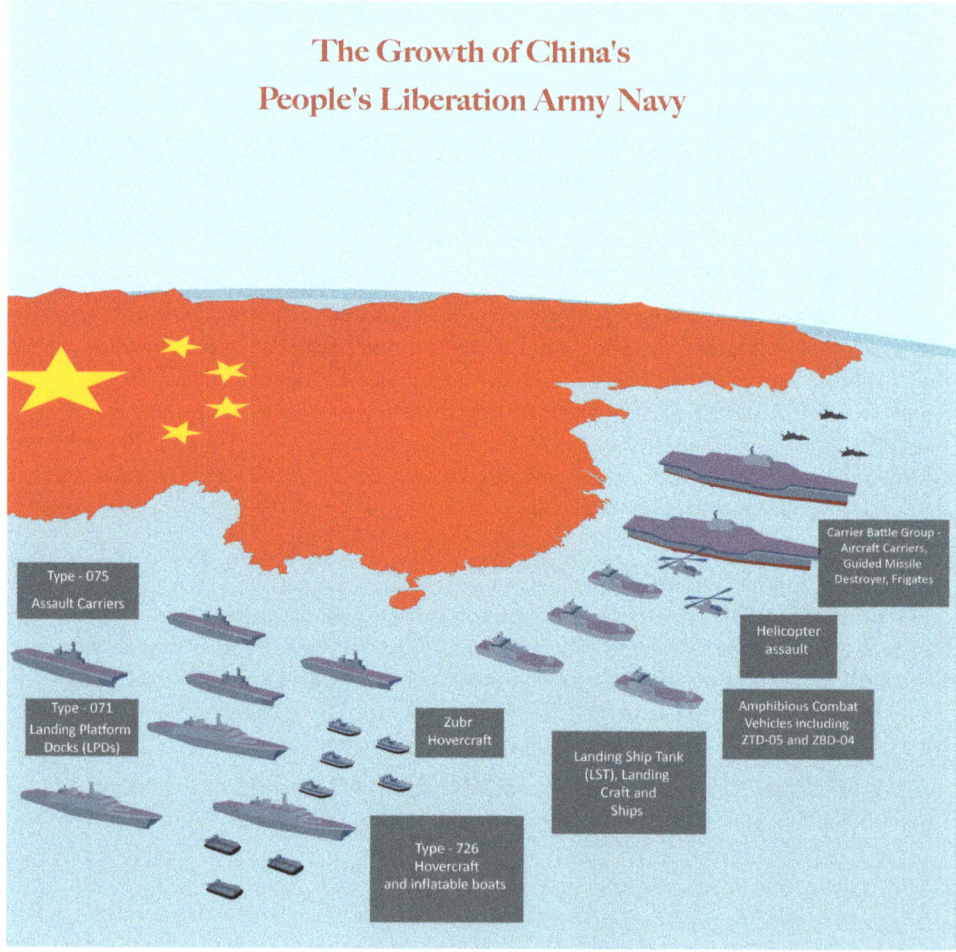

interference, to achieve a smooth transition of China-U.S. relations."[12] Meanwhile, China's coercion has been rampant in the international community. According to the Brookings Institution, Beijing's retrenchment on international, state-driven economic reform, tightening of technology-driven social controls, and external illiberal 'sphere of influence' through its Belt and Road Initiative has alarmed the business community and many others in Asia.[13]

China's stated goal, announced at its 19th Party Congress, is to become a global superpower by 2050. President Xi heralded China's 'new era of socialism with Chinese characteristics', cementing his PRC leadership well into the next decade while warning that there may be severe challenges to his road map. In a nearly 3.5-hour speech, Xi repeatedly exclaimed that China's development had entered a "new era", using the phrase 36 times.[14]

This "new era" is one that is proactive, insidious, and coercive. U.S. Senator Mitt Romney explained, "China has a comprehensive, rigorous strategy to achieve global domination and the tip of its spear today is economic aggression," furthering, "China lacks energy and raw materials. They are addressing these with their belt and road projects. China has a history of revolution. They are addressing this problem in ways reminiscent of repressive regimes in world history, but armed with modern technology,"[15]

In a June 2, 2020, *Washington Post* article, Charles Dunst described China's new interventionist foreign policy. China's coercion is not particularly new, though China continually promises that they will not infringe on the sovereignty of other countries. Brazilian Congressman Paulo Eduardo Martins shared a letter from the Chinese Embassy in Brasilia that asked for Brazil's congress to refrain from acknowledging Taiwanese President Tsai Ing-wen's election victory since China does not recognize Taiwan as a free and independent state.[16] Citizens throughout Brazil responded to the Chinese Community Party (CCPs) sovereignty intervention with their dissatisfaction, provoking a backlash with the Twitter hashtag #VivaTaiwan.[17]

Conclusion

During Deng Xiaoping's administration, China's foreign policy remained relatively free from interference as Beijing's leadership focused on China's economic growth. Deng

---

12 Evelyn Cheng, "China Foreign Minister Tells American CEOs He Hopes for Less U.S. 'Interference' in Chinese Affairs," *CNBC*, December 7, 2020, https://www.cnbc.com/2020/12/07/us-china-relations-chinese-foreign-minister-calls-for-less-us-interference.html

13 Tarun Chhabra and Ryan Hass, "Global China: Domestic Politics and Foreign Policy," *Brookings*, September, 2019, https://www.brookings.edu/research/global-china-domestic-politics-and-foreign-policy/

14 Ting Shi, "Xi Jinping Lays Out Blueprint to make China a Global Superpower by 2050," *National Post*, October 18, 2017, https://nationalpost.com/news/world/xi-jinping-lays-out-plan-to-make-china-a-global-superpower-by-2050

15 PTI, "China Most Likely to Become Sole Global Superpower by Mid-21st Century: Mitt Romney," *The Economic Times*, Updated December 6, 2019, https://economictimes.indiatimes.com/news/international/world-news/china-most-likely-to-become-sole-global-superpower-by-mid-21st-century-mitt-romney/articleshow/72396044.cms?from=mdr

16 Charles Dunst, "Welcome to China's New Interventionist Foreign Policy," *Washington Post*, June 2, 2020, https://www.washingtonpost.com/opinions/2020/06/02/welcome-chinas-new-interventionist-foreign-policy/

17 Taiwan News, "Brazilian Netizens Fight Back Against CCP Threats over Taiwan Support," *Taiwan News*, May 26, 2020, https://www.taiwannews.com.tw/en/news/3940533

Xiaoping said that China would "bide its time". The Chinese newspaper mouthpiece for the CCP, the *Global Times*, explained that Deng Xiaoping's suggestion translated 'properly' into English means "observe calmly, secure our position, cope with affairs calmly, hide our capacities and bide our time, be good at maintaining a low profile, and never claim leadership."[18]

Xi took a different path from hiding China's strength. He proudly shows off his military might and successes with loud hype. China's president has chosen not to bide time or move slowly and cautiously as he skips along the stones while he crosses the river, pushing his belt

---

18 Huang Youyi, "Context, Not History, Matters for Deng's Famous Phrase," *Global Times*, June 15, 2011, https://www.globaltimes.cn/content/661734.shtml

and road agenda worldwide. Finally, in terms of "never taking the lead," Xi tells countries that he knows the way and they should follow. If they cross his path, they will be sorry. More than a hundred countries have signed onto the BRI, including countries on nearly every continent. President Xi has amassed significant influence on the world stage and even with individual country's decision-making agendas.

What's at Stake?

First, a Harvard University Belfer Center for Science and International Studies article entitled, "Emperor Xi's China is Done Biding its Time", says it all.[19]

Second, while state leaders celebrate their big contracts with China, they should be careful of the champagne's bubbles. Other countries have celebrated too and now face the consequences. Astonishingly, extremely wealthy business leaders inside of China and political leaders outside of China have naively believed that nothing would happen to them. State leaders did not worry about their sovereignty until they, too, were nabbed in the CCP's web.

Third, while China's interventionist foreign policy has a stranglehold on governments worldwide, injecting its venom into political spheres, at some point, states may push back.

Fourth, China's 'digital authoritarianism' threatens the world in insidious ways that are often undetected until core aspects of each individual, community, business, or country are irreparably damaged.

---

19   Kevin Rudd, "Emperor Xi's China is Done Biding Its Time," *Harvard Kennedy School - Belfer Center for Science and International Affairs*, March 3, 2018, https://www.belfercenter.org/publication/emperor-xis-china-done-biding-its-time

Chapter 2
China's Belts and Roads
Wrapping Beijing's Arms Around the Planet

Introduction

While the Belt and Road Initiative (BRI) was a trumpet call to a wide range of projects that formalized Beijing's 2025 and 2050 global superpower objectives, the concept of infrastructure development in underdeveloped countries is not particularly new, not even for China. The World Bank and the International Monetary Fund have invested heavily in underdeveloped countries. However, in 1970, China's infrastructure investments were underway even during the Cultural Revolution when the Chinese built the TAZARA Line (Tanzania-Zambia Railway Authority), the third-largest infrastructure project ever undertaken in Africa by that time.[1] This was a significant undertaking, given China's financial status, commitment to the expansion of Chinese Communist ideologies, and determination to create a stakehold on Africa's continent. Though the railroad amounted to a boondoggle, failing to achieve its projected financial results, employing thousands of Chinese workers when Africans were out of work, and requiring tens of millions of dollars of additional capital resource infusion due to poor planning and disrepair, the TAZARA project is championed as a successful example of Chinese-African solidarity.[2] The railroad is considered by many to be a "perpetual loss-making company". Nonetheless, Chinese and African authorities highlight this "Freedom railway" effort as an example of anti-Western, anti-Imperialist success.[3]

Since Beijing's early investments a half-century ago, China has undertaken hundreds of projects across the continent of Africa and elsewhere, like a train connecting Chongqing to Duisburg, Germany, making China the biggest single-country investor on the planet. As of 2021, China continues to invest in Africa with new projects and signed agreements in continents worldwide. In Xi's 2013 speeches, China codified BRI's designated objective to solidify Xi Jinping's place in history. The cogs of China's financial machinery increased their speed as Beijing accelerated investment in countries that began long before Xi's tenure.[4]

President Xi's Initial Belt and Road Speeches

The massive Belt and Road Initiative (BRI), formerly called One Belt, One Road (OBOR), essentially began during Mao's era. Yet, President Xi wasted little time from the moment he took office to brand Beijing's global outreach and proclaim his commitment to expanding this effort. On September 7, 2013, in Kazakhstan, President Xi announced his "Silk Road Economic Belt" (SREB) in a speech entitled, "Promote People-to-People

---

1 Howard W. French, "The Next Empire," *The Atlantic*, May 2010, https://www.theatlantic.com/magazine/archive/2010/05/the-next-empire/308018/

2 Leandro Arenas, "21st Century Tazara – Expansion Amidst Irrelevance: Where is this Railway Headed?," *ArcGIS*, December 17, 2020, https://storymaps.arcgis.com/stories/c1994c733c364182bd4179271613a094

3 Ibid.

4 Cristina Constantinescu, Aaditya Mattoo, and Michele Ruta, "Policy Uncertainty, Trade, and Global Value Chains: Some Facts, Many Questions," *Policy Research Working Papers*, No. 9048, Retrieved from: https://openknowledge.worldbank.org/handle/10986/32657

Friendship and Create a Better Future".⁵ He explained that 2,100 years ago, Kazakhstan was a major stop on the transcontinental Silk Road where China cultivated cultural bridges, warm friendships, and peaceful relationships. With "unity and mutual trust, equality and mutual benefit, mutual tolerance and learning from each other, as well as cooperation and win-win outcomes," together, China and Kazakhstan can "unceasingly enhance mutual trust, to consolidate friendship, to strengthen cooperation, to push forward their common development and prosperity, and work for the happiness and well-being of the people in the regional countries."⁶

One month later, in Jakarta, Indonesia, President Xi Jinping announced the 21st Century Maritime Silk Road (MSR). During this October 3, 2013 speech to the Indonesian Parliament, Beijing's paramount leader suggested that China and Indonesia

Guanxi
How the Chinese Conduct Business

---

5   Ministry of Foreign Affairs of the People's Republic of China, "President Xi Jinping Delivers Important Speech and Proposes to Build a Silk Road Economic Belt with Central Asian Countries," *Ministry of Foreign Affairs of the People's Republic of China,* September 7, 2013, https://www.fmprc.gov.cn/mfa_eng/topics_665678/xjpfwzysiesgjtfhshzzfh_665686/t1076334.shtml

6   Ibid.

forge deeper bonds. As Xi explained, and the Chinese saying relays, "A big tree grows from a small seedling, and a nine-storeyed tower is built out of soil."[7] Furthermore, to ensure the leaves of the China-ASEAN friendship tree remain evergreen, the soil of social support should be compacted by upgrading the China-ASEAN Free Trade Area, expanding two-way trade to one trillion U.S. dollars by 2020.[8] China also proposed establishing the Asian Infrastructure Investment Bank (AIIB), giving priority to ASEAN countries.[9]

The Birth of the Belt and Road

Though the 2013 announcements were not new, they did reinforce China's commitment. Xi's statesmanship infused pomp and flair to Beijing's global reach. Past projects had been disparate entities. Xi's speeches breathed life into the diverse group of infrastructure investments, giving birth to an integrated Belt and Road Initiative. Codifying the unified plan, new projects were introduced and legitimacy was added.

China's determined commitment aided in the delivery of its products to other countries. Enhanced bilateral trade brought Chinese companies the raw materials they needed while adding an integrated solution to infrastructure development across Eurasia. China called this a win-win since other countries would pay for China's build-out while China benefitted from its transportation network. Chinese labor was required, which employed its citizens around the world. Simultaneously, countries would benefit from Chinese loans with fewer barriers to entry than multinational loan options. With a fast signature, energy, transportation, and communication projects were developed.

The magnitude of these projects was unlike any previous undertaking. China planned six economic corridors to link China with its subregions. The most important projects included port development so China could receive natural resources and raw materials from the Middle East and Africa and, in turn, deliver manufactured goods back to the African continent and other points abroad. To this end, China convinced Sri Lanka and Pakistan that they needed to pay for ports, holding out the carrot that these countries would have a significant return on their investments, though this never transpired. This unsurprising result left Sri Lanka having to give up its port to China in a 99-year lease.

Financing demands inspired China to create new banking institutions, including the Asian Infrastructure and Investment Bank (AIIB) and China's Export-Import Bank (EXIM) to go along with its institutions, Industrial & Commercial Bank of China, China Construction Bank Corp., Agricultural Bank of China, and Bank of China. A country's significant benefits to obtaining Chinese loans include a swift approval process, choice of investments, non-involvement in monetary allocation, and standardized procedures. Beijing wins in soft power projection, infusion of labor in multiple countries, the requirement of Mandarin on the job, and the use of China's RMB to eventually change the standard global currency from the USD to the RMB.

---

7   ASEAN-China Centre, "Speech by Chinese President Xi Jinping to Indonesian Parliament," *ASEAN-China Centre*, October 2, 2013, http://www.asean-china-center.org/english/2013-10/03/c_133062675.htm

8   Ibid.

9   Wu Jiao, "President Xi Gives Speech to Indonesia's Parliament," *China Daily*, Updated October 2, 2013, https://www.chinadaily.com.cn/china/2013xiapec/2013-10/02/content_17007915_2.htm

Conclusion

Beijing's rollout of the Belt and Road Initiative (BRI) added legitimacy to a bed of seedlings that had been watered, fertilized, and planned. Xi's announcement of a cohesive development plan took on increasingly greater proportions. Over time, each seedling grew. Today, the project is a fully grown agricultural enterprise of investments. Yet, most of the crops have not been harvested. Meanwhile, new pastures are being plowed for additional plantings.

From the very beginning, Beijing exuded the confidence of a benevolent financier who could provide quick results and opportunities that would reap significant rewards. Port, train, road, and power development projects have highlighted China's accomplishments as announced at the Second Belt and Road Forum held in 2019. There, Xi shared his "early harvests" that "opened up greater space for national and global economic growth, provided a platform for enhancing international cooperation, and made fresh contributions to building a community with a shared future for mankind."[10]

Billions of dollars in Asian Infrastructure and Investment Bank (AIIB) loans have been distributed. Chinese state-run media outlet, *Xinhua*, heralded China's dramatic results saying, "The AIIB's mission is financing infrastructure with sustainability at its core. Since beginning operations in January 2016, its membership has grown from 57 to 103. The cumulative approved investments grew from 1.69 billion U.S. dollars at the end of 2016 to 22.02 billion dollars at the end of 2020, and the number of cumulative approved projects from eight to 108."[11] As China heralds its remarkable success around the world, uncertainty underlies its projects.

What's at Stake?

First, Xi Jinping's two key speeches in 2013 set China ablaze with loan development and offered plentiful money for infrastructure projects. Though the cost may not be visible in upfront interest rates, buried on page 100 or so in small print, each country will give up some valuable resource or facility if they do not pay.

Second, since China refuses to be transparent with its interactions and contracts, myths are conjured. Curious people who do not want to fall into Beijing's trap want to know what lies within the pages of these agreements signed between CCP banking liaisons and the country's finance ministers and leaders.

Third, while some myths surrounding these contracts may be fabricated fantasy, actions speak louder than words. The consequences are devastating, as Sri Lanka can attest in losing its sovereignty and port to China. The Party line is that China "saved" Sri Lanka when

---

10 The Second Belt and Road Forum for International Cooperation, "Xi Jinping Chairs and Addresses the Leaders' Roundtable of the Second Belt and Road Forum for International Cooperation (BRF)," *The Second Belt and Road Forum for International Cooperation,* April 28, 2019, http://www.beltandroadforum.org/english/n100/2019/0429/c22-1392.html

11 Xinhua, "Xinhua Commentary: The AIIB's Five-Year Success Story," *Xinuha,* January 15, 2021, http://www.xinhuanet.com/english/2021-01/15/c_139669954.htm

the world was unwilling to step in, though China "sold" this contract in the first place. Sri Lanka was saved from whom? China? Other countries or international bodies whose loans were also due?

Fourth, by imposing its ruthless force on leaders inside and outside of China, the PRC's loans should come with a danger warning label to those who sign Beijing's contracts. If the contracts are not nefarious, why should China be so secretive?

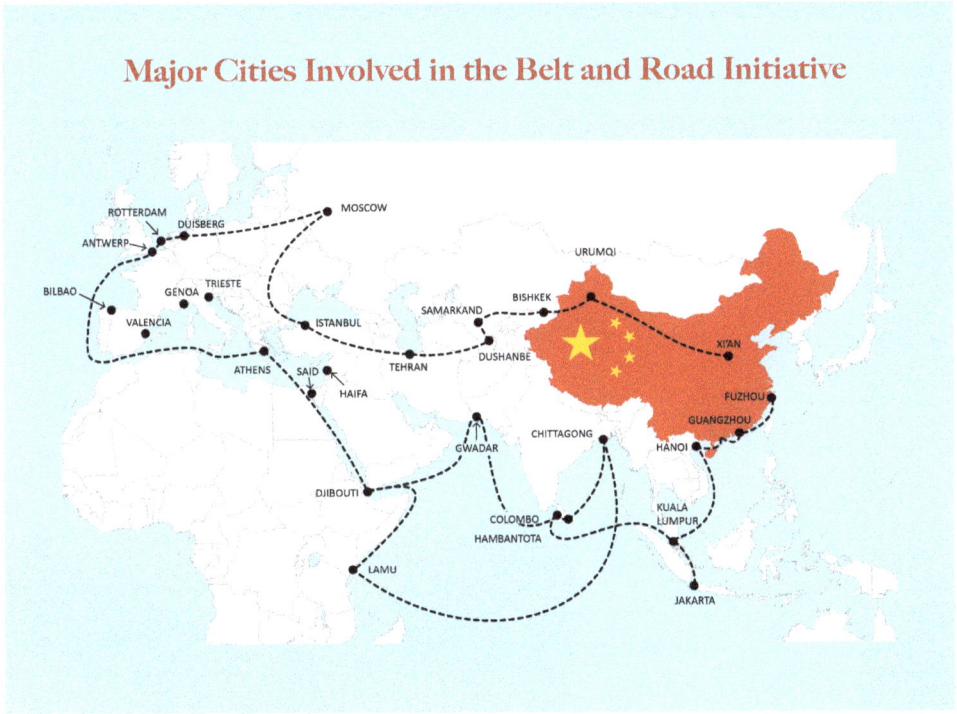

Chapter 3

A Match Made in Heaven

Offering No-Questions-Asked Loans to Developing Countries

Introduction

Africa and China are a match made in heaven. Africa is brimming with natural resources but needs money for infrastructure. China is brimming with cash and needs natural resources. The equation is simple; the transaction makes perfect sense.

The IMF and World Bank, as with virtually every commercial bank in the world, were willing to loan money to countries for viable projects where the revenue stream could pay off the loan. However, rules, laws, and environmental protections needed to be followed. Therefore, the IMF and World Bank were unwilling to loan money unless governments stabilized their economy, prevented human rights abuses, protected the environment, created transparent transactions, and set up stable political, economic, and social systems.

The amount of work needed to set up these financial transactions was often extensive. Ensuring and putting in place environmental protections also took so much time that countries felt it was unreasonable. Furthermore, government leaders did not want to be told how to run their country or have another governing body step in and take control.

As Western international institutions began to demand greater accountability for the money they lent, China stepped in to help, cut deals, and ask no questions. Chinese construction workers flowed into countries speaking Mandarin and setting up mini colonies within African states. Beijing enticed supporters, playing the empathy card, while telling developing countries that the Chinese understand what it is like to be poor. All the while, Beijing dangles financial support, thereby building relationships and ensuring votes in the international arena for its soon-to-come assumption of Taiwan and other roles in U.N. organizations and international order.[1]

In view of the perfect fit between money and need, China was seen as a savior. China offered money for infrastructure projects and asked no questions. No environmental protections were necessary; no transparency was required; and there would be no interference. Beijing's leadership did not intrude in how the money was spent, just that Chinese companies would provide the materials, labor, and development. Though the African countries would have preferred to employ their own workers and use their own material, this pairing seemed like the perfect match. China promoted its win-win diplomacy and eased citizen's fears through media, advertisements, propaganda and education, all while emphasizing that they are friendly neighbors offering brotherly cooperation and munificent generosity.

Supply and Demand

China is in great need. Chinese manufacturers need raw materials for its production lines and seeks alternative sources. Thus, the pairing is a logical engagement in projects on the African continent. Happily, it meets both its own needs and the needs of Africa for infrastructure development that would otherwise be unfunded.[2] African nations, wanting

---

1 Louisa Lombard, "Africa's China Card," *Foreign Policy,* April 11, 2006, https://foreignpolicy.com/2006/04/11/africas-china-card/

2 Rudolf Du Plessis, "China's African Infrastructure Projects: A Tool in Reshaping Global Norms," *South African Institute of International Affairs,* (2016), www.jstor.org/stable/resrep25976

to modernize, are determined to benefit from these transactions as does China, wanting to grow and seeing the benefits of unregulated markets.

As China's economy grew, its business leaders sought markets for Chinese products. Meanwhile, its citizens worldwide sought the benefits of cheap Chinese products, services, and technology. China is, now, "everywhere" in Africa with Chinese tech companies eager to expand into African markets, introducing products, services, and technology.[3] As Chinese companies entered African marketplaces, a diverse set of opportunities emerged for both Africa and China. Among them, Africa received telecommunications technology for Wi-fi, cell phones, and computer equipment to educate and expand its middle class.

In 2000, China established the Forum on China-Africa Cooperation (FOCAC) and, over time, expanded its functions to include subsectors:[4]

China-Africa People's Forum
China-Africa Young Leaders Forum
Ministerial Forum on China-Africa Health Cooperation
Forum on China-Africa Media Cooperation
China-Africa Poverty Reduction and Development Conference
FOCAC-Legal Forum
Forum on China-Africa Local Government Cooperation
China-Africa Think Tanks Forum

Early on, Hu Jintao announced to FOCAC that China would provide $20 billion in loans to African nations, double the amount he offered earlier. Beijing's no-questions-asked approach was fine for African leaders whose primary concern was not laws, human rights, viability, or environment, but rather the buildout of their country's infrastructure that desperately needed modernization. Trade with China also grew in dramatic fashion. The President of South Africa, Jacob Zuma, who served as the country's head of state for nine years, called for a greater balance of trade with China, commenting, "We certainly are convinced that China's intention is different to that of Europe, which to date continues to tend to influence African countries for their sole benefit."[5] China was benefitting, but when would Africa reap rewards?

FOCAC was developed on a multilateral basis to encourage dialogue between China and the African nations, though contracts are made on a bilateral basis. Simply put, in 2021, China signed agreements with 54 countries in Africa, one country at a time. These agreements have provided significant loan money. According to Johns Hopkins China-Africa Research Initiative, in 2019, China-Africa trade was $192 bn, up 3.8 percent from the previous year. That same year, "the largest exporter to China from Africa was Angola,

---

3   Justina Crabtree, " 'China is Everywhere' in Africa's Rising Technology Industry," *CNBC*, July 28, 2017, https://www.cnbc.com/2017/07/28/china-is-everywhere-in-africas-rising-technology-industry.html

4   Forum on China-Africa Cooperation, "FOCAC Mechanisms," *Forum on China-Africa Cooperation*, n.d., http://www.focac.org/eng/ltjj_3/ltjz/

5   Los Angeles Times, "China Promises $20 Billion in Loans to Africans," *HeraldNet*, July 19, 2012, https://www.heraldnet.com/news/china-promises-20-billion-in-loans-to-africans/

followed by South Africa and The Republic of Congo. In 2019, Nigeria was the largest buyer of Chinese goods, followed by South Africa and Egypt."[6]

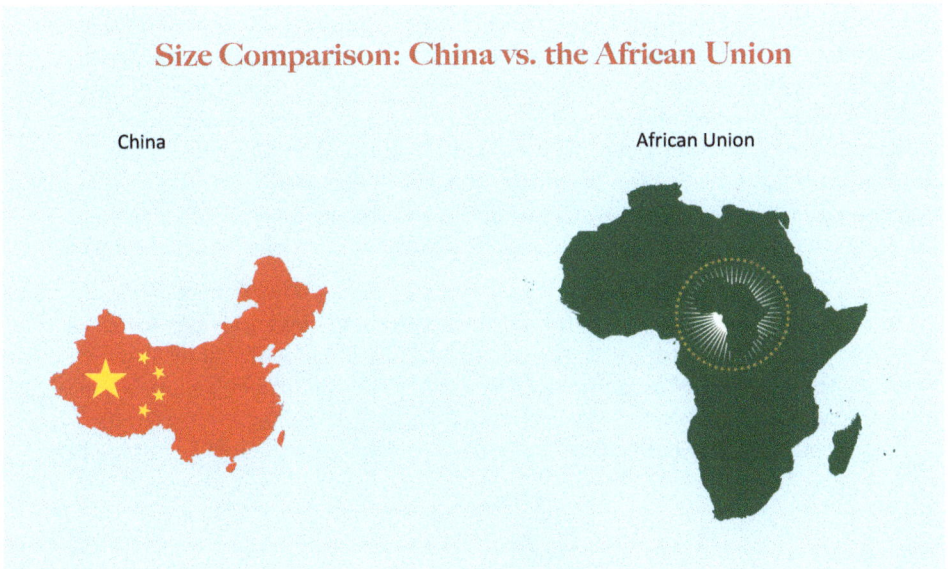

---

[6] China Africa Research Initiative, "Data: China-Africa Trade," *China Africa Research Initiative*, n.d., http://www.sais-cari.org/data-china-africa-trade

China overtook the U.S. as Africa's largest trading partner in 2009. Furthermore, a million Chinese are thought to have migrated to African countries. Africa supplies about 23 percent of the oil China needs primarily from Angola. Last year Li Keqiang, China's Prime Minister, unveiled an aid package for Africa worth at least $12 billion. That included a $10 billion cheap credit line on top of $20 billion in loans.[7]

China has turned its wealth into power with its state-owned enterprises (SOEs) funded by Beijing's vast resources.

> Never in world history has one government had so much control over so much wealth. It is no surprise, therefore, that Beijing is deploying its vast economic wealth to advance foreign policy goals. China is using economic statecraft more frequently, more assertively, and in more diverse fashion than ever before.[8]

Conclusion

China's quest to engage Africa's many authoritarian dictators in wide-ranging projects has resulted in opposition groups shouting dissenting views across Africa and seizing the opportunity to oppose China's infiltration. In the paper, "No Questions Asked?", Fodei Batty suggests that China's efforts may be counterproductive if the modernization theory holds true, postulating that with economic growth comes an educated middle class which aspires to have a free society.[9]

The concerning geopolitical challenge is that U.S. and international financial institutions often promote good governance. China competes as an international lender with no transparency, no concern for environmental damage, and less encumbered "assistance". Subsidized by the government, China's state-owned enterprises do not reveal underlying terms and conditions so that other entities can compete and are not accountable to shareholders. Thus, they can suffer short-term losses in order to obtain long-term strategic goals for the state. The "no-strings-attached" offers with looser terms are appealing to foreign governments who seek swift, efficient, and less intrusive solutions without the imposition of safeguards, international standards, human rights, or environmental protection.[10]

As opposed to most lender's caution, China's move into developing countries has been bold and intrepid with its no-questions-asked policy and with few up-front strings attached. From South Africa to the Mediterranean, China's model of lending is appealing to leaders whose arms are outstretched for infrastructure development without the stress and requirements of regulation. Free flowing money without the headaches of the liberal

---

7   Jerome Starkey, "China Hands Out Money to Africa with No Questions Asked," *The Times UK*, July 24, 2015, https://www.thetimes.co.uk/article/china-hands-out-money-to-africa-with-no-questions-asked-frm99fc3tzl

8   James Reilly, "China's Economic Statecraft: Turning Wealth into Power," *Lowy Institute*, November 27, 2013, https://www.lowyinstitute.org/publications/chinas-economic-statecraft-turning-wealth-power

9   Fodei Batty, "No Questions Asked? Development and the Paradox of China's Africa Policy," *Insight Turkey 21*, no. 1 (2019): 151-166, https://www.jstor.org/stable/26776052?seq=1

10 Congressional Research Service, "Tracking China's Global Economic Activities: Data Challenges and Issues for Congress," *Congressional Research Service*, Updated July 14, 2020, https://fas.org/sgp/crs/row/R46302.pdf

international order is welcome relief to developing countries. It is no wonder that Africa keeps asking and China keeps supplying.

What's at Stake?

First, China is now "everywhere" in Africa and changing the face of each country with its no-questions-asked loans. The swift flow of money into Africa has provided much-needed infrastructure. This match made in heaven has supplied countries with ports, roads, bridges, railroads, and dams. In some countries, China is the only player.

Second, since China uses millions of workers, either at low wages or imprisoned in hundreds of forced labor encampments, its production costs are lower. Other countries cannot compete. Thus, China can charge significantly lower prices for its products and services than the U.S. or Europe. This ease of market entry has made Chinese cell phone use prominent with telecommunications service providers, ZTE and Huawei leading the way.

Third, the no-questions-asked loans allowed Chinese and African leaders to ignore human rights, environment, or long-term implications. The downside of receiving funds from China is accepted as a small price to pay in the short-term since the African countries are unlikely to face ramifications or repercussions until a future leader takes the helm and is left attempting to resolve the resulting financial and environmental situation. Thus, many African leaders are impervious to Western criticism.

Chapter 4
China's Money Lending Benevolence

Introduction

China's dramatic economic growth in the 21st century has not only made it the second largest economy in the world but also a powerhouse in the flywheel of global growth.[1] Flooded with money entering the country worldwide from its global marketplace of cheap items and fueled by slave labor and foreign investment, China has grown so fast that Xi Jinping declared that he wiped out poverty during his tenure in office – a miracle that should "go down in history"[2]

Cheap goods were in high demand during the pandemic. Paper products of all types flew off the shelves at such a high rate that there were massive shortages in stores. Hospital gowns, ventilators, and computers were required for quick delivery. From March through December of 2020, China increased its trade balance by $52 billion dollars in facemasks alone, producing 224 billion masks, accounting to about forty masks for every single person in the world.[3]

Restructuring and Canceling Debt

With all of China's money surplus, Beijing continued its money lending benevolence by offering loans to governments around the world to be repaid at a later date. Although China wrote off a few small interest-free loans, the World Bank, IMF and G-20 asked China to write off African debts due to the coronavirus.[4] The loan forgiveness drumbeat increased during the pandemic since African nations could not pay back their loans and the alternative was to give up its infrastructure, natural resources, or sovereignty to China.

Attempts to ease the pressure from a gloomy economic outlook in African countries in 2020 was exacerbated by an increasingly unstable political climate. Industries closed, people were out of work, and the price of commodities plummeted. This price imbalance meant countries had to supply China with often double what they exported before, under the terms of the loan. Disruptions in employment, transportation, and productivity added to grwoing problems.

The IMF approved debt cancelation in 25 countries, yet without the participation of China, many economies remained at risk, since a significant amount of African government debt was owed to China.[5] Instead of loan forgiveness, China suggested that African debt may be suspended so that the poorest countries did not need to pay back

---

1   Center on Global Energy Policy, "Is China Still a Developing Country? And Why It Matters for Energy," *Columbia University*, July 23, 2020, https://blogs.ei.columbia.edu/2020/07/23/china-still-developing-country-matters-energy-climate/

2   Xinhua, "Xi Focus: Xi Hails China's Poverty Eradication Miracle," *Xinhua Net*, February 25, 2021, http://www.xinhuanet.com/english/2021-02/25/c_139766177.htm

3   Bloomberg News, "China Made 40 Face Masks for Every Person Around the World," *Bloomberg*, January 13, 2021, https://www.bloomberg.com/news/articles/2021-01-14/china-made-40-face-masks-for-every-person-around-the-world

4   Jevans Nyabiage, "China Asked to Write Off More African Debts as Coronavirus Hits Economies," *South China Morning Post*, April 3, 2020, https://www.scmp.com/news/china/diplomacy/article/3078333/china-asked-write-more-african-debts-coronavirus-hits

5   Yun Sun, "China and Africa's Debt: Yes to Relief, No to Blanket Forgiveness," *The Brookings Institute*, April 20, 2020, https://www.brookings.edu/blog/africa-in-focus/2020/04/20/china-and-africas-debt-yes-to-relief-no-to-blanket-forgiveness/

the loan until the end of 2020.⁶ Economies, though, still did not have the cash flow to pay China, causing significant tension. With other countries, China postponed payment, restructured debt, or swapped the debt with some kind of equity.⁷

China's Pivotal Role in Aid

China has played a pivotal role in rendering assistance to countries in need, primarily through loans and the execution of infrastructure projects. This benevolence, under normal circumstances, should be lauded and even emulated by other states. However, in the light of a state's inability to pay, the setback could result in debt-trap diplomacy. With this possibility and the potential loss of land, infrastructure, natural resources, or sovereignty, China's intentions are being second-guessed around the world.

Xi Jinping has been clear all along. In his 2017 address at the 19th National Congress, he said by 2049, China will "become a global leader in terms of composite national strength and international influence."⁸

> Whether it is the naval shipbuilding program that is churning out vessels at astonishing rate; the drive to control existing international organizations and build new ones; the projection of military power in the Arctic, the Indian Ocean and points beyond; the quest to dominate the world's high-tech industries; the ever-more system efforts to support authoritarian regimes and weaken democratic institutions; or the Belt and Road Initiative that encompasses multiple continents, China is hardly acting like a country that lacks a grand geopolitical design.⁹

Careful studies have been carried out regarding China's money lending. The unsavory results have given rise to grave concern. China's goals are being doubted. China's loans during the pandemic were accepted out of sheer desperation with a heavy dose of skepticism. Despite a leader's desire to create a better future for their country, an equally potent fear threateningly looms as states fall into a debt trap in each deal signed with the Chinese government.¹⁰

The World's Bank

China is the largest official creditor of developing countries and has the power to influence states' economic problems geopolitical norms and international decision-making.

---

6   Reuters, "China Supports the Suspension of Debt Payments to the Poorest Countries and will Make Due Contributions – Minister of Finance," *Reuters*, April 16, 2020, https://cn.reuters.com/article/china-mof-poor-country-debt-0416-idCNKCS21Y18Y

7   Yun Sun, "China and Africa's Debt: Yes to Relief, No to Blanket Forgiveness," *The Brookings Institute*, April 20, 2020, https://www.brookings.edu/blog/africa-in-focus/2020/04/20/china-and-africas-debt-yes-to-relief-no-to-blanket-forgiveness/

8   Xi Jinping, "Secure a Decisive Victory in Building a Moderately Prosperous Society in All Respects and Strie for the Great Success of Socialism with Chinese Characteristics for a New Era," *Xinhuanet*, October 18, 2017, http://www.xinhuanet.com/english/download/Xi_Jinping's_report_at_19th_CPC_National_Congress.pdf

9   Hal Brands, "What does China Really Want? To Dominate the World," *Bloomberg*, May 20, 2020, https://www.bloomberg.com/opinion/articles/2020-05-20/xi-jinping-makes-clear-that-china-s-goal-is-to-dominate-the-world

10 Weizhen Tan, "China's Lending to Other Countries Jumps, Causing 'Hidden' Debt," *CNBC*, July 12, 2019, https://www.cnbc.com/amp/2019/07/12/chinas-lending-to-other-countries-jumps-causing-hidden-debt.html

According to the World Bank's 2021 International Debt Statistics, "total external debt [to China] of DSSI-eligible countries climbed 9.5% to a record $744 billion."[11]

One of Beijing's concerns is default, though countries could give up sovereignty instead. Beijing seeks to prevent its debtor countries from defaulting on their loans. At the same time, China seeks to ensure that Chinese companies, working in these debtor countries on Chinese-financed infrastructure projects, do not end up with the short end of the stick and suffer losses.[12]

China's unrelenting "generosity" seems to serve a dual purpose. First, it helps to grow the Chinese economy in a roundabout way by establishing industries abroad and thereby creating opportunities for businesses in China to expand beyond its borders.[13]

Secondly, it helps to ensure that debtor countries not only seek to please the Chinese government, but also avoid making decisions that may potentially go against China's interests politically and economically.[14] In other words, the governments of these debtor countries, whether they like it or not, will do everything within their power to keep China happy and remain on its good side.

In an analyses of Beijing's money lending patterns, a trend has been discovered. Beijing has little interest in providing loans for projects that have little or no potential benefit for Chinese companies, especially in the event the borrowing country cannot pay back its loan. Thus, financing is typically offered for infrastructure or other tangible projects, rather than general budget support.[15]

Developed or Developing Country?

The issue of China being a developed country or a developing country often arises. While China's economy is number one in the world for purchasing power parity,[16] China prefers its status as a developing country since this designation comes with benefits within international institutions. The legitimate question arises: if China is able to loan money to more than a hundred countries, how does it have the right to economic benefits reserved for countries that are truly underdeveloped? The answer is in China's lack of transparency, manipulation of statistics, and ability to influence other countries for support.. One look at China's cities and anyone would be hard pressed to put China in the same category as some of the countries in sub-Saharan Africa.

---

11 World Bank Debt Data Team, "International Debt Statistics 2021: Debt Accumulation of Low- and Middle-Income Countries Surpassed $8 Trillion at end-2019," *World Bank Blogs*, October 12, 2020, https://blogs.worldbank.org/opendata/international-debt-statistics-2021-debt-accumulation-low-and-middle-income-countries

12 Tim Fernholz, "China Debt Trap: These Eight Countries are in Danger of Debt Overloads from China's Belt and Road Plans," *Quartz*, March 7, 2018, https://qz.com/1223768/china-debt-trap-these-eight-countries-are-in-danger-of-debt-overloads-from-chinas-belt-and-road-plans/amp/

13 Every CRS Report, "China's Economic Rise: History, Trends, Challenges, and Implications for the United States," *Every CRS Report*, June 25, 2019, https://www.everycrsreport.com/reports/RL33534.html

14 Brookings, "China and Africa's Debt: Yes to Relief, No to Blanket Forgiveness," *Brookings*, April 20, 2020, https://www.brookings.edu/blog/africa-in-focus/2020/04/20/china-and-africas-debt-yes-to-relief-no-to-blanket-forgiveness/

15 Alexandra O. Zeitz, "Emulate or Differentiate?," *The Review of International Organizations*, (2020).

16 Jeff Desjardins, "Visualizing the Composition of the World Economy by GDP (PPP)," *Visual Capitalist*, September 30, 2019, https://www.visualcapitalist.com/visualizing-the-composition-of-the-world-economy-by-gdp-ppp/

China views itself as both a developing and a developed country, depending on when the need arises. The usual criteria employed by international organizations to determine a country's development standing have become increasingly difficult to apply to China, given the dramatic changes it has undergone over the past several decades.[17] As such, China has become "developed" during Xi Jinping's tenure, while eradicating poverty, despite Beijing's crafted statistics. This situation is presently seen as extremely important in view of the Paris Agreement's provisions on global warming wherein China, together with other "developing countries" is released for many years from overall target objectives for carbon reduction, allowing it to become and remain the world's number one carbon polluter.[18]

---

17 Philippe Benoit and Kevin Tu, "Is China Still a Developing Country?," *Columbia/SIPA*, July 23, 2020, https://www.energypolicy.columbia.edu/research/report/china-still-developing-country-and-why-it-matters-energy-and-climate

18 Ibid.

Benevolent Loans to Laos

China not only provides loans but appears to also ensure that the debtor countries remain indebted for as long as possible. This is seen in the case of the Laotian railway.[19] The cost of the Chinese high-speed railway continues to rise as it makes its way from the capital of Laos, Vientiane, to the Chinese border.[20] The railway serves a dual purpose of linking China with Laos, and sinking the country further into debt.

Laos has a terrain that is predominantly mountainous, posing a problem with the whole railway system. This challenge however, has not deterred China in the least. Rather, both bridges and tunnels have been created to ensure that the project is a success with 417-kilometers of rail line, including 198 kilometers of tunnels and 61 kilometers of bridges at an astronomical cost.[21] The project is estimated to total a whooping sum of $6.2 billion, which is equivalent to around $15 million per kilometer.[22] This project is only one of hundreds that have raised concerns and is likely to keep Laos perpetually China's subject.

A study by the Lowy Institute estimated Laos' debt to China at 45 percent of Laos' GDP. Since the country is unable to pay its staggering debt, China basically owns Laos. Normally, this situation would lead Laotian leaders to contemplate their dependence on China and seek funding elsewhere. However, this is not the case. Although Laos could be eligible for help by the International Monetary Fund under its COVID-19 Financial Assistance and Debt Service Relief program, the government has stated that it would rather try to find a solution with China.[23]

The rising Chinese investment has slowly pulled Laos out of Vietnam's orbit, its traditional ally and patron, and into China's court.[24] This loan is likely to add fuel to the claims that China is employing "debt-trap diplomacy" to gain strategic advantage in countries overburdened with BRI infrastructure loans.

Conclusion

The clauses included in deals signed with China have been a source of constant tension and suspicion. The looming questions have spurred country's need to review the conditions under which China provides aid to the development of infrastructure and economies.[25]

---

19 Sebastian Strangio, "Laos Stumbles Under Rising Chinese Debt Burden," *The Diplomat*, September 7, 2020, https://thediplomat.com/2020/09/laos-stumbles-under-rising-chinese-debt-burden/

20 Eleanor Albert, "China Digs Deep in Landlocked Laos," *The Diplomat*, April 24, 2019, https://thediplomat.com/2019/04/china-digs-deep-in-landlocked-laos

21 Sebastian Strangio, "Laos Stumbles Under Rising Chinese Debt Burden," *The Diplomat*, September 7, 2020, https://thediplomat.com/2020/09/laos-stumbles-under-rising-chinese-debt-burden/

22 Ibid.

23 International Monetary Fund, "Questions and Answers: The IMF's response to COVID-19," *International Monetary Fund*, Updated January 29, 2021, https://www.imf.org/en/About/FAQ/imf-response-to-covid-19

24 Ralph Jennings, "Chinese Support Gives Laos an Edge Over Powerful Neighbor Vietnam," *VOA News*, October 12, 2019, https://www.voanews.com/east-asia-pacific/chinese-support-gives-laos-edge-over-powerful-neighbor-vietnam

25 Larry Hanauer and Lyle J. Morris, "China in Africa: Implications of a Deepening Relationship," *RAND Corporation*, 2014, https://www.rand.org/pubs/research_briefs/RB9760.html

President Xi continues to exude confidence. He promises countries around the world that China is a benevolent country with the intent to be cleaner, greener, and more transparent, though he acknowledges that there have been problems along the way in his billions of dollars in pledges and projects.[26] Nonetheless, China has not stopped and appears to only be picking up speed during the pandemic's great economic boom. Money is coming from across the globe for its cheap products which continues to enable its benevolent money lending.

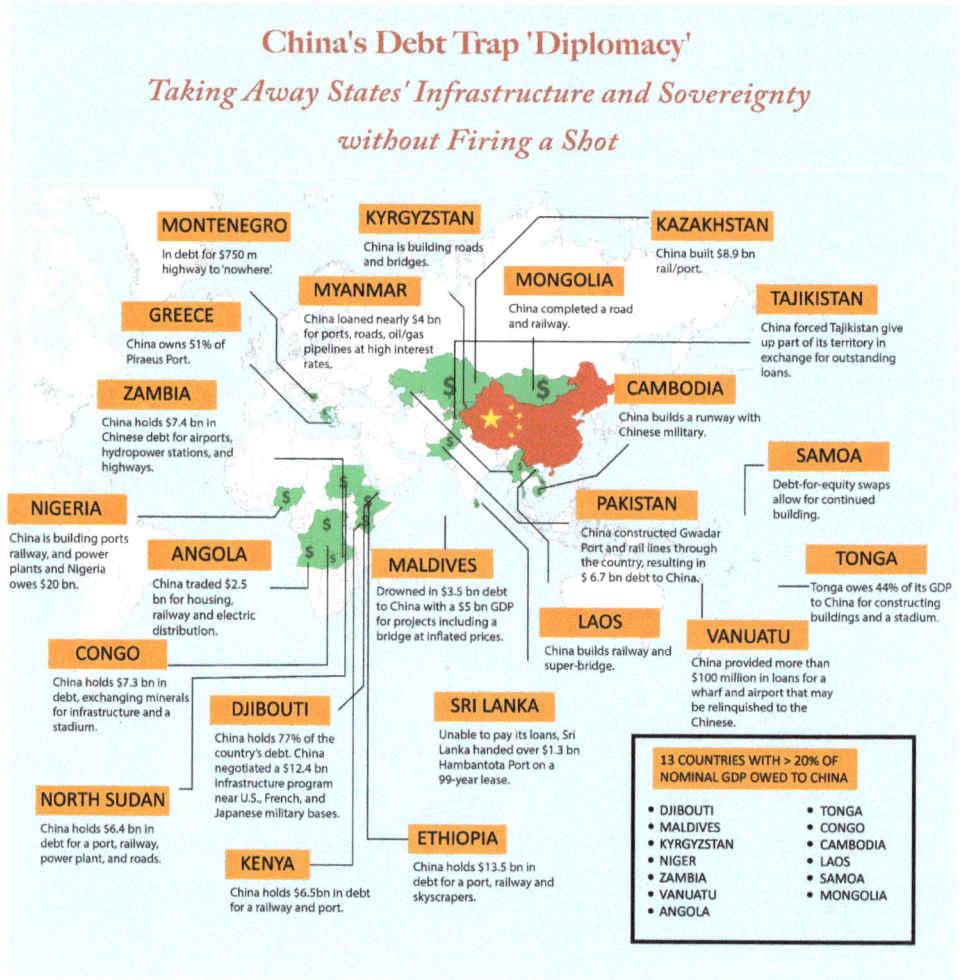

---

26 Catherine Trautwein, "All Roads Lead to China: The Belt and Road Initiative, Explained," *PBS*, June 26, 2019, https://www.pbs.org/wgbh/frontline/article/all-roads-lead-to-china-the-belt-and-road-initiative-explained/

What's at Stake?

First, despite the issues raised as to China's genuine intentions in lending to states dotted across the globe, these states continue to accept China's loans, and are complicit in building Chinese-owned companies and constructing Chinese city enclaves within their sovereign boundaries.

Second, several countries have fallen "victim" to China's "benevolence", spanning across continents.

Third, China combines significant characteristics of both developing and developed countries, Beijing is usually seen to view and project itself as a developing country in order to gain an unfair advantage.[27] Such dubious practices should instill a healthy dose of caution in countries still seeking China's assistance.

---

27 Every CRS Report, "China's Economic Rise: History, Trends, Challenges, and Implications for the United States," *Every CRS Report*, June 25, 2019, https://www.everycrsreport.com/reports/RL33534.html

Chapter 5

Not Technically A Debt-Trap

Sri Lanka's Former Hambantota Port

China's Loan, Debt Trap, and 99-Year Lease

Sri Lanka had big plans. The former Sri Lankan President, Mahinda Rajapaksa, envisioned a grand commercial project including a port, an airport, and railway infrastructure. The Hambantota Port was one of these projects, sitting on a strategic point in the Indo-Pacific, The location was prime real estate. Hundreds of boats passed nearby every day. In Rajapaksa's eyes, the potential seemed limitless. Sri Lanka counted the many opportunities. Little convincing was necessary when a Chinese state-owned enterprise (SOE) offered a loan to build out the infrastructure, relying on Sri Lankan officials to use their due diligence to acquire contracts and manage the infrastructure investment.

No Questions Asked

Ravi Ratnasabapathy, who reviewed the Hambantota deal commented, "With the World Bank or the Asian Development Bank, there are lots of checks and balances. They insist on open processes for tendering, and comprehensive reviews of a project. But with China, there are few conditions. So it's a lot easier to get approval and do projects with China than with these other international institutions." The Chinese "don't really ask you for proper assessments. They give you the loan and it's very easy to pad those contracts out — and make a lot of money."[1] Little is known about whose pockets were padded along the way. Today, Sri Lanka's debt continues to increase with China building a Port City to rival Dubai on land reclaimed from the Indian Ocean.[2]

The 99-Year Lease of Hambantota was NOT a Debt-Trap

Sri Lanka was provided a capital investment opportunity - a golden egg laid on its doorstep. China's SOE offered a no-questions-asked policy, though Chinese workers, housing, materials, and engineering were required. This loan signaled an economic revolution for one of Sri Lanka's poorest districts. However, when built, Hambantota's surplus capacity created an unsustainable economic condition.

Like many of China's other loans to countries whose mismanagement and underlying corruption created large gaps in their ability to pay, Sri Lanka looked for options. Authorities are quick to point out that this was not a debt-for-asset swap.[3] Thus, the project was not technically a debt-trap. Nonetheless, what went from being an optimistic undertaking to an economic catastrophe helped to plunge Sri Lanka's developing economy into short-term, high-interest debt.

While media reports hype that the lease was or was not a debt trap, there is an underlying story. China wants everyone to know that they did not lay a trap and Sri

---

1 NPR, "In Sri Lanka, China's Building Spree is Raising Questions About Sovereignty," *NPR*, December 13, 2019, https://www.npr.org/2019/12/13/784084567/in-sri-lanka-chinas-building-spree-is-raising-questions-about-sovereignty

2 Michael Safi, "Sri Lanka's 'New Dubai': Will Chinese-Built City Suck the Life out of Colombo?," *The Guardian*, August 2, 2018, https://www.theguardian.com/cities/2018/aug/02/sri-lanka-new-dubai-chinese-city-colombo

3 Lee Jones and Shahar Hameiri, "Debunking the Myth of 'Debt-Trap Diplomacy'," *Chatham House*, August 19, 2020, https://www.chathamhouse.org/2020/08/debunking-myth-debt-trap-diplomacy/4-sri-lanka-and-bri

Lanka wants everyone to know that they were not gullible enough to fall into the trap. Officially, there was no trap since the $1.12 billion did not pay off that loan but paid off othet staggering debt Sri Lanka had amassed. Whatever wording terms of agreement were politically correct or socially acceptable, Sri Lanka handed over land for 99 years and China is buying more chunks.

It would be remiss to forget Beijing's propaganda declarations. China explicitly reminds Sri Lanka and the world that it respects other states' sovereignty, noting in its embassy press release dated December 20, 2019, "China reiterates once again that it highly respects the sovereignty and territorial integrity of Sri Lanka."[4]

---

4   Embassy of the People's Republic of China in the Democratic Socialist Republic of Sri Lanka, "Press Release of the Embassy of China 2019/12/20," *Embassy of the People's Republic of China in the Democratic Socialist Republic of Sri Lanka*, December 20, 2019, http://lk.china-embassy.org/eng/xwdt/t1726458.htm

Feasibility, Job Creation, and Promises

Prior to the collapse of the Port of Hambantota investment, and China's willingness to turn the port into one of its military bases in the Indo-Pacific, Sri Lanka had seven seaports nationwide. According to various feasibility studies across the span of three decades,[5] the Port of Hambantota never had the potential to expand and thrive in the same capacity as the Port of Colombo, which was the largest in the country and, according to these studies, stood a better chance of expansion.

Despite the facts presented by the research, Sri Lanka, under the administration of President Mahinda Rajapaksa, was determined to carry out its plan of establishing a port in Hambantota. Expectations surrounding the presence of a functional port in the region were high and seemed achievable. In addition, new employment in that region would lift people out of poverty. Bhavani Fonseka, a lawyer in Colombo relayed, "If you go to any project site, it's the Chinese who have the jobs. Job creation hasn't come for locals. Will these [Chinese] workers settle here? Is this becoming a colony? Very few people are asking these questions."[6]

Flourishing trade and anticipated exponential revenue were significant driving factors pushing the project forward. This led Sri Lanka to take a $307 million loan from the Export-Import Bank of China for the first phase of the project at a 6.3% interest rate, considered high by all standards although[7] Sri Lanka opened a bid request for the project and, according to the Sri Lanka Ports Authority (SLPA), China had been the first to show open interest.

Recent reports, however, reveal that China was the only country willing to throw its weight behind the Hambantota project. By all indications, and with the benefit of hindsight this port project, had been an economic disaster waiting to happen. While political corruption may have been at the heart of the matter, this potential downfall led experts to believe that the action was a part of China's strategy to dominate its Asian neighbor using its financial and political influence.[8]

According to a 2018 *New York Times* report, several deals were sealed behind-the-scenes before the Hambantota project took off based upon delivering the "the biggest port constructed on land in the 21st century."[9]

---

5   Ship Technology, "The Story of Hambantota Port: A Flunking Token of Political Corruption," *Ship Technology*, September 18, 2018, https://www.ship-technology.com/features/hambantota-port-china-sri-lanka/

6   NPR, "In Sri Lanka, China's Building Spree is Raising Questions About Sovereignty," *NPR*, December 13, 2019, https://www.npr.org/2019/12/13/784084567/in-sri-lanka-chinas-building-spree-is-raising-questions-about-sovereignty

7   Dipanjan Roy Chaudhury, "New Chinese Loan May Further Plunge Sri Lanka into Debt Trap," *The Economic Times*, September 3, 2018, https://economictimes.indiatimes.com/news/international/world-news/new-chinese-loan-may-further-plunge-sri-lanka-into-debt-trap/articleshow/65659719.cms

8   Ship Technology, "The Story of Hambantota Port: A Flunking Token of Political Corruption," *Ship Technology*, September 18, 2018, https://www.ship-technology.com/features/hambantota-port-china-sri-lanka/

9   Kinling Lo, "Sri Lanka Wants its 'Debt Trap' Hambantota Port Back. But will China Listen?," *South China Morning Post*, December 7, 2019, https://www.scmp.com/news/china/diplomacy/article/3040982/sri-lanka-wants-its-debt-trap-hambantota-port-back-will-china

For years, the Port of Hambantota was deserted. With no shipping activity, its premises were haunted by wildlife roaming freely.[10] Between 2015 and 2016, Hambantota Port was the only port in Sri Lanka recording a negative growth rate and declining numbers of vessel traffic.[11] The port had $11.81 million in revenue and incurred expenses of $10 million.[12] Owing to its continued descent in shipping activities and its inability to sustain its revenue, the port eventually defaulted on the terms of its loan. Due to another loan's interest due, the Sri Lankan government handed over the majority of the port's ownership, including the surrounding land for 99 years.

The Sri Lanka Ports Authority busily deflected the blame, officials explained that the port's decline could be attributed to a global halt in shipping trade. This claim has been refuted by a collection of emails, cables, and intelligence files published on WikiLeaks which revealed that the outcome of a what was slated to be a buoyant port was influenced by factors more in-depth than the travails of tough economic times.[13]

The Plunge Downwards

Not only did the promises of economic wealth and increased trade fail to materialize, the port project threw Sri Lanka into debt. China's loans for 'white elephant' projects in crawling economies has been suspected by many to be a strategy for political and economic control, even though a *New York Times* report revealed that the collapse of the Hambantota port giveaway could have been preventable.[14]

The project was doomed from its inception. In 2010, a year after opening, shipping activities were limited as vessels were blocked by huge rocks. In 2012, activities picked up temporarily but only after additional capital outlays. Despite the money pumped into shoring up accessible shipping activities, the port attracted only thirty-four ships the entire year. According to the Ministry of Finance's annual report, the Chinese investments continued with further loan agreements signed and with accompanying price increases.[15]

After months of back-and-forth negotiations with the Chinese government, the new administration signed a 99-year lease for the port along with 15,000 acres of surrounding land, which it officially handed over in 2017. On the day of the handover, China's official news agency had made a tweet with the caption: "Another milestone along path

---

10 Eva Grey, "The Story of Hambantota Port: A Flunking Token of Political Corruption," *Ship Technology Global*, n.d., https://ship.nridigital.com/ship_oct18/the_story_of_hambantota_port_a_flunking_token_of_political_corruption

11 Central Bank of Sri Lanka, "Economic and Social Statistics of Sri Lanka," *Central Bank of Sri Lanka*, 2017, https://www.cbsl.gov.lk/sites/default/files/cbslweb_documents/statistics/otherpub/Economic_%26_Social_Statistics_of_SL_2017_e.pdf

12 Eva Grey, "The Story of Hambantota Port: A Flunking Token of Political Corruption," *Ship Technology Global*, n.d., https://ship.nridigital.com/ship_oct18/the_story_of_hambantota_port_a_flunking_token_of_political_corruption

13 Wikileaks, "Hambantota Port Complex: Will Sri Lanka Realize the Dream?," *Wikileaks*, February 9, 2010, https://wikileaks.org/plusd/cables/10COLOMBO103_a.html

14 Maria Abi-Habib, "How China Got Sri Lanka to Cough Up a Port," *The New York Times*, June 25, 2018, https://www.nytimes.com/2018/06/25/world/asia/china-sri-lanka-port.html

15 Ibid.

of #BeltandRoad",[16] a Chinese initiative to increase its market share, creating its global maritime trade routes and port facilities.

The Port of Hambantota lease sparked domestic protests and suspicion that Sri Lanka was trading its sovereignty for economic leverage.[17] Concerns also grew around the possibility of China's investment in other countries with weak economies as being a means to force these countries to become financially dependent in a way that can be exploited for economic and political control.[18]

However, Sri Lankan officials frequently came forward to reassure its citizens in the attempt to kill the rising suspicion and prevent wider protests.

Political Ambition

The Port of Hambantota loan was not a new idea. Several administrations considered it a part of Sri Lanka's official development campaign. Many of Sri Lanka's projects funded by China were unsolicited. However, in the case of the Port of Hambantota, Sri Lanka had publicly sought funding and China had stepped up. In the past decade, China has financed at least thirty-five ports globally, according to a *New York Times* analysis.[19]

Against the backdrop of several warnings by analysts on the consequences of granting China higher equity stakes, the Sri Lankan government insisted that the $1.1 billion Hambantota deal was imperative to chip away at its debt.[20] By extension, Hambantota's main problem came from within Sri Lanka itself.

A 2003 feasibility study on the port, done by a Canadian engineering firm, called SNC Lavalin, was presented to the Sri Lankan government which reviewed and eventually rejected the study.[21] The task force which was appointed to review the study faulted the finding for the lack of acknowledgment of the potential impact of the Port of Hambantota on the Colombo Port, which handles nearly 95 percent of the country's international trade.

Similarly, in 2006, barely three years after, a Danish consulting firm concluded a second feasibility study and was approved under the new administration of Rajapaksa who was elected president in 2005.[22] The second study took a more optimistic assessment of the port's potential. Traffic projections were based on Sri Lanka's future development and runoff from existing ports at Galle, Trincomalee, and Colombo. The study also projected that by

---

16   Jonathan E. Hillman, "Game of Loans: How China Bought Hambantota," *Centre for Strategic & International Studies*, April 2, 2018, https://www.csis.org/analysis/game-loans-how-china-bought-hambantota

17   Wade Shepard, "Violent Protests Against Chinese 'Colony' in Sri Lanka Rage On," *Forbes*, January 8, 2017, https://www.forbes.com/sites/wadeshepard/2017/01/08/violent-protests-against-chinese-colony-in-hambantota-sri-lanka-rage-on/?sh=43d3126c13dd

18   Maria Abi-Habib, "How China Got Sri Lanka to Cough Up a Port," *The New York Times*, June 25, 2018, https://www.nytimes.com/2018/06/25/world/asia/china-sri-lanka-port.html

19   Ibid.

20   Kai Schultz, "Sri Lanka, Struggling With Debt, Hands a Major Port to China," *The New York Times*, December 12, 2017, https://www.nytimes.com/2017/12/12/world/asia/sri-lanka-china-port.html

21   Jonathan E. Hillman, "Game of Loans: How China Bought Hambantota," *CSIS* April 2, 2018, https://www.csis.org/analysis/game-loans-how-china-bought-hambantota

22   Ralph Guldberg Bjørndal, "Feasibility Study for a New Major Seaport in Sri Lanka," *Ramboll*, n.d., https://ramboll.com/projects/group/hambantotaport

2040, the port would be managing about 20 million twenty-foot equivalent units (TEU), averaging the world's top five busiest ports in 2015.

Driven by Rajapaksa's overly optimistic assessment, an earlier project which he made as a part of his campaign promise, particularly to his home region of Hambantota, was devastated by the 2004 tsunami.[23] During Rajapaksa's tenure, a majority of Sri Lanka's high-ticket projects – including a cricket stadium, international conference center, an international airport, and the port - all used Chinese contractors, Chinese financing and Rajapaksa's name as a signatory.[24]

With hindsight, suspicions have developed concerning China's original intent in offering its financial aid.[25] The fact that there were no competing offers for the port when the government solicited for loans has been seen by many to have been an indication that no other potential lender considered the project as a worthy investment – a standpoint that reflected early studies and predictions made on the port.

Conclusion

Along the path, countries with weaker economies, like Sri Lanka, have found themselves accumulating insurmountable debt. At one time, officials revealed that Sri Lanka owed more than $8 billion to Chinese-controlled firms alone.[26] Placing political interests ahead of market demands, early plans for Hambantota, which focused on fuel distribution, were quickly adapted under the Rajapaksa administration to incorporate other activities, many of which were already carried out at the Port of Colombo.

In late 2020, China positioned itself on the path to build "a $13 billion city on Sri Lanka's seafront, as the island nation located near some of the world's most important shipping lanes deepens its ties with Beijing despite U.S. efforts to gain influence."[27] With billions more in debt, Sri Lanka will have an even greater responsibility to ensure solvency and safeguard sovereignty.

What's at Stake?

First, 'white elephant' deals are being made worldwide with short-term, high interest loans to countries where corruption, greed, and mismanagement are rampant. Thus, good intentions are lost, along with land or resources.

---

23 Patrick Barta, "In Sri Lanka's Post-Tsunami Rise, China is Key," *The Wall Street Journal*, December 18, 2014, https://www.wsj.com/articles/in-sri-lankas-post-tsunami-rise-china-is-key-1418938382

24 Bloomberg, "Trade and Debt: How China is Building an Empire Across New Silk Road," *Times of India*, Updated August 3, 2018, https://timesofindia.indiatimes.com/world/china/trade-and-debt-how-china-is-building-an-empire-across-new-silk-road/articleshow/65256563.cms

25 Maria Abi-Habib, "How China Got Sri Lanka to Cough Up a Port," *The New York Times*, June 25, 2018, https://www.nytimes.com/2018/06/25/world/asia/china-sri-lanka-port.html

26 Ship Technology, "The Story of Hambantota Port: A Flunking Token of Political Corruption," *Ship Technology*, September 18, 2018, https://www.ship-technology.com/features/hambantota-port-china-sri-lanka/

27 Saeed Shah and Uditha Jayasinghe, "China Regains Clout in Sri Lanka With Family's Return to Power," *The Wall Street Journal*, November 28, 2020, https://www.wsj.com/articles/china-regains-clout-in-sri-lanka-with-familys-return-to-power-11606568404

Second, following a *New York Times* investigation, when Sri Lankan government officials met with their Chinese counterparts in 2016 to renegotiate their loan to avoid default, China demanded a dominant equity stake be taken by a Chinese company in return. According to the final Concession Agreement, Chinese officials offered their Sri Lankan counterparts Chinese-ownership through China Merchants Port, signed July 29, 2017 with the Sri Lanka Port Authority.[28]

Third, though the 99-year lease on Hambantota Port cancelled over $1 billion in Sri Lanka's debt, other loans exist at much higher rates. Sri Lanka is now even further in debt.

Fourth, China continues to buy up Sri Lanka's land and beaches which has sparked alarm from those who see Sri Lanka losing its sovereignty one piece of land at a time.[29]

---

28 China Merchants Port Holdings Company Limited, "Sri Lanka," *China Merchants Port Holdings Company Limited*, n.d., http://www.cmport.com.hk/enTouch/business/Infor.aspx?id=10007513

29 NPR, "In Sri Lanka, China's Building Spree is Raising Questions About Sovereignty," *NPR*, December 13, 2019, https://www.npr.org/2019/12/13/784084567/in-sri-lanka-chinas-building-spree-is-raising-questions-about-sovereignty

Chapter 6

China's Name Controversy

Why Did China Change Its Name from OBOR To BRI?

Introduction

In 2013, Chinese President Xi Jinping introduced his glistening One Belt, One Road (OBOR). This project was not particularly new, but it was slated to be the hallmark of his administration. The goal of OBOR was to strengthen China's relationships and global interconnectivity, while ensuring a more stable, productive, and efficient economy.

During September and October visits to Kazakhstan and Indonesia, President Xi shined a light on his OBOR initiative.[1] The main goals were, "to construct a unified large market and make full use of both international and domestic markets, through cultural exchange and integration, to enhance mutual understanding and trust of member nations, ending up in an innovative pattern with capital inflows, talent pool, and technology database."[2]

What started as Beijing's avenue to restructure and redevelop China's railway, land and sea routes both in and around the Asian continent evolved into a global endeavor. The OBOR's infrastructure, banking, and development projects cater to its initial proposed set of supporting countries, revised now to include about 140 countries,[3] broadening the goals to include grassroots-level development, infrastructural innovations, and noteworthy acts of humanitarianism.[4]

Name Change from OBOR to BRI

In 2016, Beijing had a public relations problem. The word "One" seemed to mean 'China-centered'. Secondly, there was a Silk Road, a Maritime Road, an Arctic Road, a Digital Road, and other roads, "One" made little sense to outsiders. With the confusing name and numerous misinterpretations, regional partners questioned whether OBOR was designed to create competition along the one road. Negative perceptions and criticisms over "China-centered institution building" led China to change the name from the One Belt, One Road (or OBOR strategy) to the Belt and Road Initiative (BRI).[5] The change, as reported, was due to a consideration of its many meanings that an emphasis on the moniker would evoke – some of which would be harmful to the overall image.[6]

---

1 Xinhua, "Chronology of China's Belt and Road Initiative," *The State Council – The People's Republic of China*, Updated March 28, 2015, http://english.www.gov.cn/news/top_news/2015/04/20/content_281475092566326.htm

2 UNV, "The Belt and Road Initiative," *UNV*, September 29, 2018, https://en.uniview.com/News/News/201809/804999_169683_0.htm

3 James Griffiths, "Just What is This One Belt, One Road Thing Anyway?," *CNN*, Updated May 11, 2017, https://www.cnn.com/2017/05/11/asia/china-one-belt-one-road-explainer/index.html

4 Hong Yu, "Motivation Behind China's 'One Belt, One Road' Initiatives and Establishment of the Asian Infrastructure Investment Bank," *Journal of Contemporary China 26,* no. 105 (2016): 353–368.

5 Una Aleksandra Bērziņa-Čerenkova, "BRI Instead of OBOR – China Edits the English Name of its Most Ambitious International Project," *Latvian Institute of International Affairs*, July 28, 2016, https://web.archive.org/web/20170206061842/http://liia.lv/en/analysis/bri-instead-of-obor-china-edits-the-english-name-of-its-most-ambitious-international-project-532

6 Nadège Rolland and Brad Carson, "The Geo-Economic Challenge of China's Belt and Road Initiative," *War on the Rocks*, March 5, 2019, https://warontherocks.com/2019/03/jaw-jaw-the-geo-economic-challenge-of-chinas-belt-and-road-initiative/

Regional Partners Worried

1. China aimed to create only one route to Beijing's success. This objective seemed less collaborative and favorable to all parties involved since all countries seek success in the import-export business.[7]

2. The OBOR would create unnecessary competition among the countries. Thus, China substituted the 'strategy' for 'initiative', emphasizing that the project is as transparent as it is inclusive.

3. The overall project would create animosities and place a wrench in the plans of countries supposedly working together.

4. The word 'strategy' could mean literally anything from a simple plan to a complex program with interconnected parts like the Belt and Road Initiative (BRI).[8]

5. The outcome might be sinister like toppling the global political hierarchy and China's subsequent ascent to the top of the food chain in every way that matters.[9] Theories described how China's ascent could be a threat.[10]

6. With China's economic output and global push, Beijing's program was slated to overtake the U.S. by 2032.[11]

7. What China is doing now is a thinly veiled strategy to secure the rise to power of Modern China along with an encyclopedia of 'proof' to support its claims.[12]

Moving Forward

Although the name was changed to the Belt and Road Initiative (BRI), doubt still remained. Mutual growth and interconnectedness remined the goal though some questioned the overarching political implications. The European Council on Foreign Relations continued to be concerned in 2017. A meeting was called for the 65 member countries to gather; only 29 member countries were in attendance. Japan and India are two countries which have not been quiet in expressing their skepticism regarding China's

---

7 HKTDC Research, "The Belt and Road Initiative," *HKTDC Research*, January 21, 2016, https://beltandroad.hktdc.com/sites/default/files/imported/beltandroadbasics/hktdc_1X0K715S_en.pdf

8 Lee Jones and Jinghan Zeng, "Understanding China's 'Belt and Road Initiative': Beyond 'Grand Strategy' to a State Transformation Analysis," *Third World Quarterly 40*, no. 8 (2019), https://www.tandfonline.com/doi/abs/10.1080/01436597.2018.1559046?journalCode=ctwq20

9 Jeffrey Frankel, "Is China Overtaking the US as a Financial and Economic Power?," *The Guardian*, May 29, 2020, https://amp.theguardian.com/business/2020/may/29/is-china-overtaking-the-us-as-a-financial-and-economic-power

10 Ali Wyne, "Can China Use the Pandemic to Displace the US?," *Defense One*, May 5, 2020, https://www.defenseone.com/ideas/2020/05/can-china-use-pandemic-displace-us/165168/

11 Frank Tang, "China to Overtake US as World's Top Economy in 2032," *South China Morning Post*, September 2, 2020, https://amp.scmp.com/economy/china-economy/article/3099951/china-overtake-us-worlds-top-economy-2032-despite-washington

12 Richard Pendlebury, "China Is Desperate to Overtake America As the World's Economic Superpower," *Daily Mail*, Updated April 21, 2020, https://www.dailymail.co.uk/news/article-8238399/amp/China-desperate-overtake-America-worlds-economic-superpower-stop-it.html

genuine intentions about the BRI.[13]

During the People's Republic of China's (PRC) seventy-plus years, the Chinese Communist Party (CCP) has sought to build internally, while expanding its ideology and influence outwardly. Beijing's leadership set a target for seventy countries originally earmarked for the OBOR project and leaped over that amount with real estate property spanning several areas already in use for this initiative. As of January 2021, China's OBOR included 140 countries.[14] In March 2021, China's Ministry of Foreign Affairs said that the construction of the "Belt and Road" has contributed to China's plan for world development and human rights.[15]

The One Belt, One Road was the brainchild of the Chinese Communist Party (CCP) leadership with President Xi at the helm. OBOR was originally designed to provide a head start for China's grand plan. This strategy sought to boost import dependency for other countries, while encouraging internal development, trade, and domestic production - all of which are components of the country's dream of establishing diplomacy in all matters relating to China's economic strides.

China's aim is to illuminate underdeveloped markets and to connect them with major commercial opportunities and nations seeking their products. In addition to greatly increasing community participation and human resource development and connectivity (a key goal of Modern China and the BRI), these efforts created additional economic and trade activity with the heretofore underdeveloped areas.

The OBOR offered much needed increases in the number of existing markets for Chinese merchandise. This link was designed to help China's economy to thrive, restoring the power to the world's global manufacturing center. Beijing could then select and dictate methods and routes to increase access, speed delivery, and prevent product losses.[16]

Questions have been raised about the environmental implications of the initiative's infrastructure projects. Since international efforts commit to saving the environment, China's devastating deforestation, water rerouting, and drowning out farmland is seen as destructive. Many are concerned that the world cannot suffer additional environmental hazards that may trigger another bout of catastrophes resulting from global warming.

Efforts to introduce infrastructure and other major projects in the European Union have been met with hesitation and feet-dragging as some members of the EU fear the distressing effects from a substitution of Europe's social and environmental standards with China's loosely-worded entries on preserving a sustainable environment. China can simply hire a no-questions-asked company to produce a green-lit feasibility study that does not hamper a

---

13   Angela Stanzel, "China's Belt and Road – New Name, Same Doubts?," *European Council on Foreign Relations*, May 19, 2017, https://www.ecfr.eu/amp-article/commentary_chinas_belt_and_road_new_name_same_doubts

14   Green Belt and Road Initiative Center, "Countries of the Belt and Road Initiative (BRI)," *Green Belt and Road Initiative Center*, n.d., https://green-bri.org/countries-of-the-belt-and-road-initiative-bri/

15   Belt and Road Portal, "Ministry of Foreign Affairs: The Joint Construction of the 'Belt and Road' has Contributed to China's Plan for World Development and Human Rights," *Belt and Road Portal*, March 10, 2021, https://www.yidaiyilu.gov.cn/xwzx/gnxw/166850.htm

16   Shobhit Seth, "One Belt One Road (OBOR)," *Investopedia*, Updated September 28, 2020, https://www.investopedia.com/terms/o/one-belt-one-road-obor.asp

projects's development. With the ball in another country's court, states can just look away from EU rules and requirements or blame it on the Chinese contracting company.

Although the BRI is geared towards global emancipation, the initiative stems, in part, from Eurasian and Maritime sovereign states along the Silk Road. Another angle to consider regarding China's haste and enthusiasm is what they stand to gain. A careful study of China's population has shown that a larger population of Chinese citizenry is rapidly ageing. Therefore, this cohort's contribution to the economy is declining steadily. In a bid to combat this, China is investing in developing countries around the Silk Road axis, channeling excess local capacity and output to these areas to train and incorporate states' much younger workforce.[17]

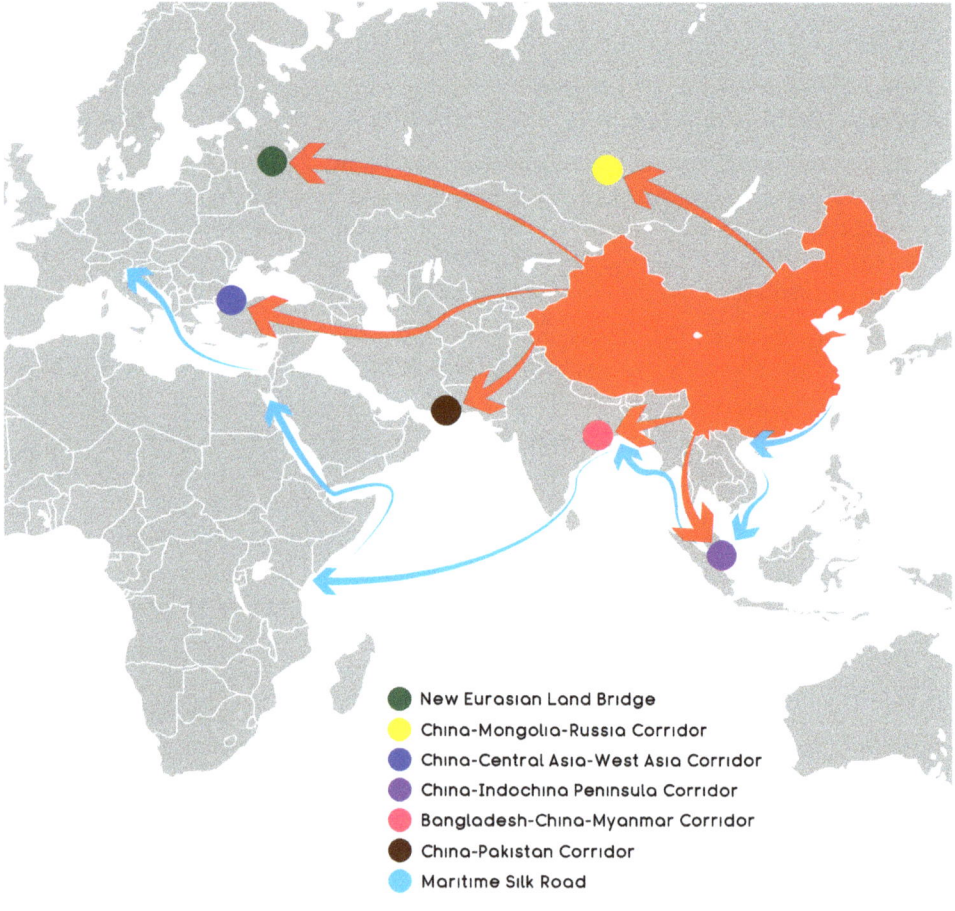

- New Eurasian Land Bridge
- China-Mongolia-Russia Corridor
- China-Central Asia-West Asia Corridor
- China-Indochina Peninsula Corridor
- Bangladesh-China-Myanmar Corridor
- China-Pakistan Corridor
- Maritime Silk Road

---

17 Lauren A. Johnston, "The Belt and Road Initiative: What is in it for China?," *Asia & The Pacific Policy Studies 6*, no. 1 (2019): 40-58, https://onlinelibrary.wiley.com/doi/full/10.1002/app5.265

Conclusion

Despite the global population's skepticism about China, the amount of money Beijing is offering is too enticing for countries to pass up. Even countries threatened by the People's Liberation Army are accepting China's loans.

Furthermore, the coronavirus outbreak from Wuhan, China that paralyzed the globe has increased each country's need. China's propaganda arms have successfully pacified the angry public with money. Consider also that China infiltrated and influenced the World Health Organization to lessen its COVID-19 public relations nightmare and pandemic scandal.

By changing the name from One Belt, One Road (OBOR) to Belt and Road Initiative (BRI), after widespread criticism of the fact that China's self-centeredness lacked inclusion, China has done itself some good in laying to rest doubts about its global authoritarian control and state's loss of sovereignty.

Other doubts remain. Beijing's One Road show has injected tempered hesitation and thought-provoking questions about China's intentions, political discourse, and takeover on the international level.[18]

What's at Stake?

First, China's Ministry of Foreign Affairs stated that Beijing's plan is to develop the entire world. This effort is happening with Chinese labor, materials, and control. This worldwide development may be benign or it may be nested with its other goals of collecting every person's DNA, installing surveillance systems in every country, and keeping track of movements on a global scale.

Second, Beijing pronounced in March 2021 that it championed human rights. That should worry everyone concerned about freedom and choice. If Xi Jinping thought this proclamation was true, the CCP should do a reality check by asking the millions in Xinjiang's torture and slave labor camps what the rest of the world might look like with China's definition of human rights.

Third, in most countries where infrastructure has been developed by the PRC, devastating ecological disaster has wiped out farmland, animals, and livelihoods without concern for the environment.

---

18 Una Aleksandra Bērziņa-Čerenkova, "BRI Instead of OBOR – China Edits the English Name of its Most Ambitious International Project," *Latvian Institute of International Affairs*, July 28, 2016, https://web.archive.org/web/20170206061842/http://liia.lv/en/analysis/bri-instead-of-obor-china-edits-the-english-name-of-its-most-ambitious-international-project-532

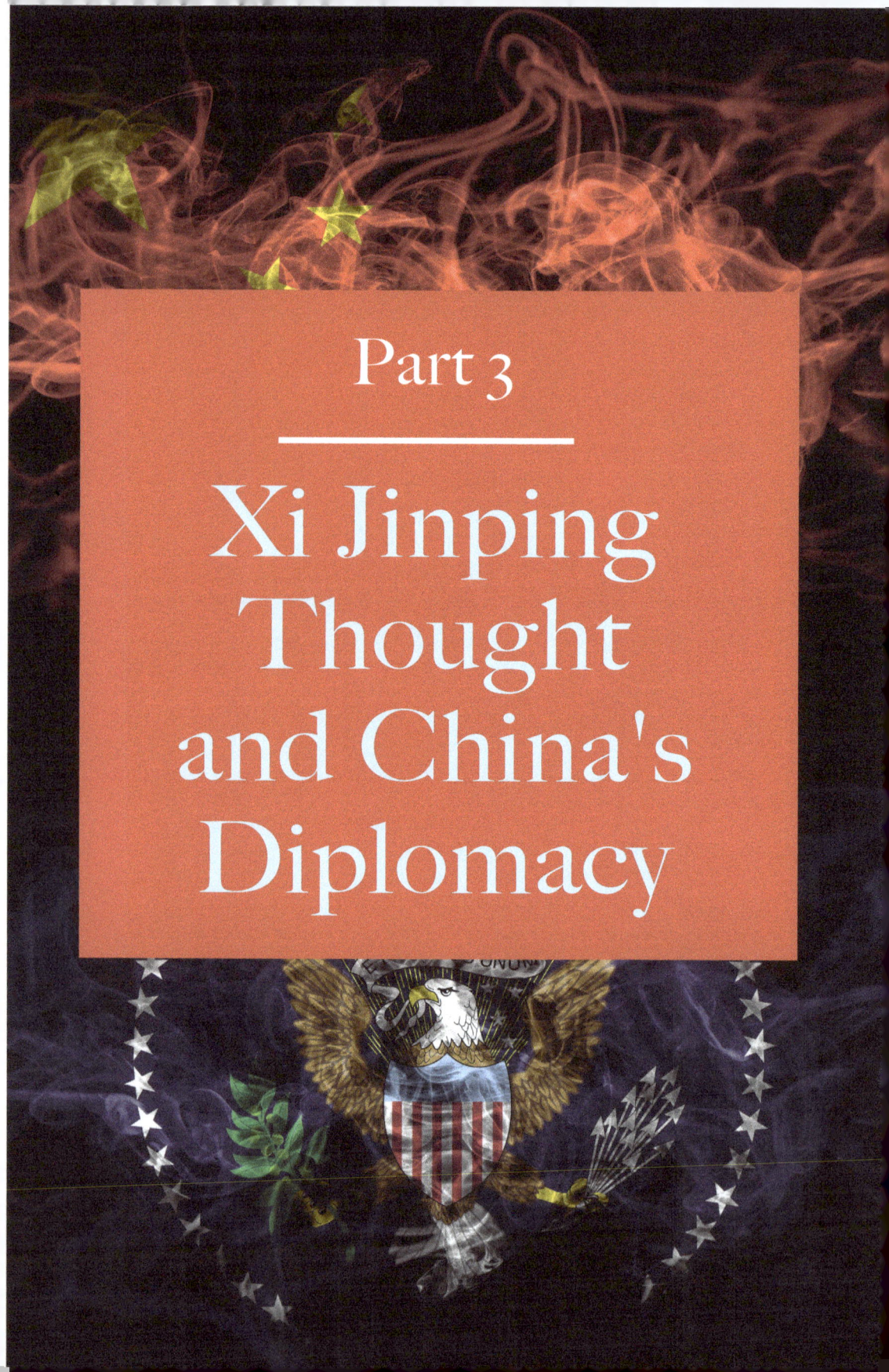

Part 3
Xi Jinping Thought and China's Diplomacy

China's Cooperation, Rhetoric, & Competition

"The destiny of humankind is in the hands of Xi Jinping along with China's development of the whole world," so says Yang Jiechi, former Foreign Minister of the PRC, in his 2017 statement, thereby shedding light on Xi Jinping's thought and the importance of China's global push for diplomacy. In 2049, the People's Republic of China will celebrate its 100-year anniversary under CCP rule. It will also celebrate the realization of "the Chinese dream of national renewal". Human progress will unfold, executing 'external work' with Chinese characteristics – reflecting Marxist socialism enriched with diplomatic thinking and strategy having far-reaching significance as a New China emerges.

When Xi Jinping appeared on the historic stage, he painted himself as the ideal leader in a world hungering for leadership. Conducting state visits in his first years of office in dozens of countries, Xi has repeatedly called for peace and cooperation, presenting himself as:[1]

- Well-learned and culturally refined
- A benevolent ruler
- Evoking nationalism and legitimacy
- Desiring cooperation with Western countries as an equal partner
- Offering a sense of historical knowledge
- Expressing gratitude

China's diplomatic relations must be secured strategically and pointedly. The Wolf Warrior was born out of a need to protect China's image and sharpen words to strike down anyone who speaks ill about China. Economic diplomacy was extended through loans given to 140 countries. Health diplomacy, facemask diplomacy, and vaccine diplomacy were deployed in 2020 and 2021 when the world needed China to step up to the plate and help. However, hostage diplomacy put fear in the minds of journalists and travelers who worried that they would also be imprisoned to teach countries a lesson. To push back, Taiwan introduced its own brand of diplomacy – Death Metal Diplomacy.

In constructing a New China that embraces the world with benevolence, the CCP offers money to all who want to be under China's communist umbrella. Few countries have been able to pass up China's generous benevolence and slickly delivered diplomacy.

---

1 Xing Lu, "Rhetorical Construction of the Ideal Chinese Leader in President Xi Jinping's Overseas Speeches," *China Media Research* 13, no. 1 (2017): 74.

Chapter 1

Win-Win Diplomacy

China's Soft Power Sprinkling the Planet

Introduction

The 2015 Boao Forum, entitled, "Asia's New Future: Towards a Community of Common Destiny" began with President Xi Jinping's keynote speech, "Towards a Community of Common Destiny and A New Future for Asia". President Xi spoke about a unified world where peace and cooperation are complemented with win-win diplomacy as each state seeks stability, common development, and a tranquil international environment.[1]

On March 14, 2013, Xi Jinping was elected President of China.[2] From the early moments of his presidency, Xi began promoting his Chinese Dream and Win-Win Diplomacy. On March 23, 2013, "Xi called on the international community to build a new type of international relations with win-win cooperation at the core and stressed that China will unswervingly follow the path of peaceful development and steadfastly develop its comprehensive strategic partnership of coordination with Russia."[3] Xi continued by telling the audience at the Moscow State Institute of International Relations that the world was changing and needed a new future with converging interests between China and Russia.

In September of 2013, he continued traveling from country to country starting with Turkmenistan, Kazakhstan, Uzbekistan, and Kyrgyzstan promoting his Chinese Dream and Win-Win Diplomacy with China's "national rejuvenation and the world dream of lasting peace and common prosperity."[4] By the end of 2013, President Xi had met with dozens of world leaders sharing his vision and offering his hand in cooperation.

In December 2013, Foreign Minister Wang Yi reaffirmed China's win-win model of cooperation between China and the United States, suggesting that both countries "abandon bearish expectations on their relations and foster confidence in their prospects. Mutual respect is the basic principle. If this principle is not followed, the two countries will not be able to seek common ground while shelving differences, accumulate consensus while addressing differences, and live with each other in harmony. Win-win cooperation is the only way forward.[5]

---

1 China.org.cn, "Full Text of Chinese President's Speech at Boao Forum for Asia," *China.org.cn*, March 29, 2015, http://www.china.org.cn/business/2015-03/29/content_35185720.htm

2 John Ruwitch, "Timeline – The Rise of Chinese Leader Xi Jinping," *Reuters*, March 16, 2018, https://www.reuters.com/article/us-china-parliament-xi-timeline/timeline-the-rise-of-chinese-leader-xi-jinping-idUSKCN1GS0ZA

3 Ministry of Foreign Affairs of the People's Republic of China, "Xi Jinping Calls for the Building of New Type of International Relations with Win-Win Cooperation at the Core in a Speech at the Moscow State Institute of International Relations," *Ministry of Foreign Affairs of the People's Republic of China*, March 23, 2013, https://www.fmprc.gov.cn/mfa_eng/topics_665678/xjpcf1_665694/t1024781.shtml

4 China Daily, "Xi's Trip to Promote Win-Win Cooperation," *China Daily*, August 28, 2013, http://www.chinadaily.com.cn/china/2013xivisitcenterasia/2013-08/28/content_16931629.htm

5 Ministry of Foreign Affairs of the People's Republic of China, "Embark on a New Journey of China's Diplomacy," *Ministry of Foreign Affairs of the People's Republic of China*, December 16, 2013, https://www.fmprc.gov.cn/mfa_eng/wjb_663304/wjbz_663308/2461_663310/t1109943.shtml

South China Sea

In 2012, Beijing showed the world what win-win diplomacy meant when China "hoodwinked" the United States by reneging on a deal between President Barak Obama's negotiators and Xi Jinping's counterparts.[6] Philippine President Benigno Aquino III compared China's takeover of Scarborough Shoal to Nazi Germany's annexation of Czechoslovakia.[7]

> In June of 2012, a group of U.S. diplomats led by Assistant Secretary of State Kurt Campbell thought they had successfully mediated a resolution that required both China and the Philippines to withdraw from the area and negotiate a peaceful settlement. However, while the Philippines kept its end of the deal, China never left—a move Philippines president Benigno Aquino would compare, albeit with some hyperbole, to Nazi Germany's annexation of the Sudetenland in 1938. The following month China further escalated the crisis by blockading a portion of the shoal where Filipinos have fished for generations. It then proceeded to issue a fifteen-mile fishing ban around the area in question.[8]

In 2013, China further demonstrated its win-win diplomacy when Beijing's People's Liberation Army Navy (PLAN) began reclaiming land and militarizing islands in the South China Sea. In 2016, the International Court of Justice (ICJ) Permanent Court of Arbitration (PCA) determined that China did not have grounds for its claims in the South China Sea. Against the law and despite the court's ruling China put surface-to-air missiles on the islands it overtook.

In 2018, China sent bombers into the South China Sea.[9] China threatened Philippine fishermen, rammed Philippine boats, and sank Philippine vessels, stopping them from fishing in Philippine waters.[10] In addition to threatening Malaysian and Vietnamese oil exploration in 2020,[11] China attacked and sunk Vietnamese vessels.[12]

---

6   Financial Times, "Obama Forced Xi to Back Down over South China Sea Dispute," *Financial Times,* July 11, 2016, https://www.ft.com/content/c63264a4-47f1-11e6-8d68-72e9211e86ab

7   Keith Bradsher, "Philippine Leader Sounds Alarm on China", *The New York Times,* February 4, 2014, https://www.nytimes.com/2014/02/05/world/asia/philippine-leader-urges-international-help-in-resisting-chinas-sea-claims.html?_r=0

8   Peter Navarro, "The Obama-Clinton Legacy: A More Aggressive China," *The National Interest,* July 14, 2016, https://nationalinterest.org/feature/the-obama-clinton-legacy-more-aggressive-china-16959

9   People's Daily, China (@PDChina), "Chinese bombers including the H-6K conduct takeoff and landing training on an island reef at a southern sea area," *Twitter,* May 18, 2018, 1:00AM, https://twitter.com/PDChina/status/997386306660384768

10   Ben Westcott and Brad Lendon, "Duterte Threatens 'Suicide Mission' if Beijing Oversteps in South China Sea," *CNN,* Updated April 5, 2019, https://www.cnn.com/2019/04/05/asia/south-china-sea-duterte-beijing-intl/index.html

11   Ivy Kwek and Chiew-Ping Hoo, "Malaysia's Rationale and Response to South China Sea Tensions," *Asia Maritime Transparency Initiative,* May 29, 2020, https://amti.csis.org/malaysias-rationale-and-response-to-south-china-sea-tensions/

12   Shashank Bengali and Vo Kieu Bao Uyen, "Beijing's Aggressive South China Sea Expansion Shows its Willingness to Defy International Laws for President Xi Jinping's Visions of Power," *Los Angeles Times,* November 12, 2020, https://www.latimes.com/world-nation/story/2020-11-12/china-attacks-fishing-boats-in-conquest-of-south-china-sea

Xi Jinping Thought and China's Diplomacy | Part 3

This kind of win-win cooperation continued through 2021 when China declared administrative districts over other country's territory and began imposing Chinese laws in the South China Sea on other country's people. China's new law allows its navy to fire on foreign vessels while in their own sovereign territory.[13]

China's brand of aggressive and deadly win-win diplomacy is being felt throughout Asia.

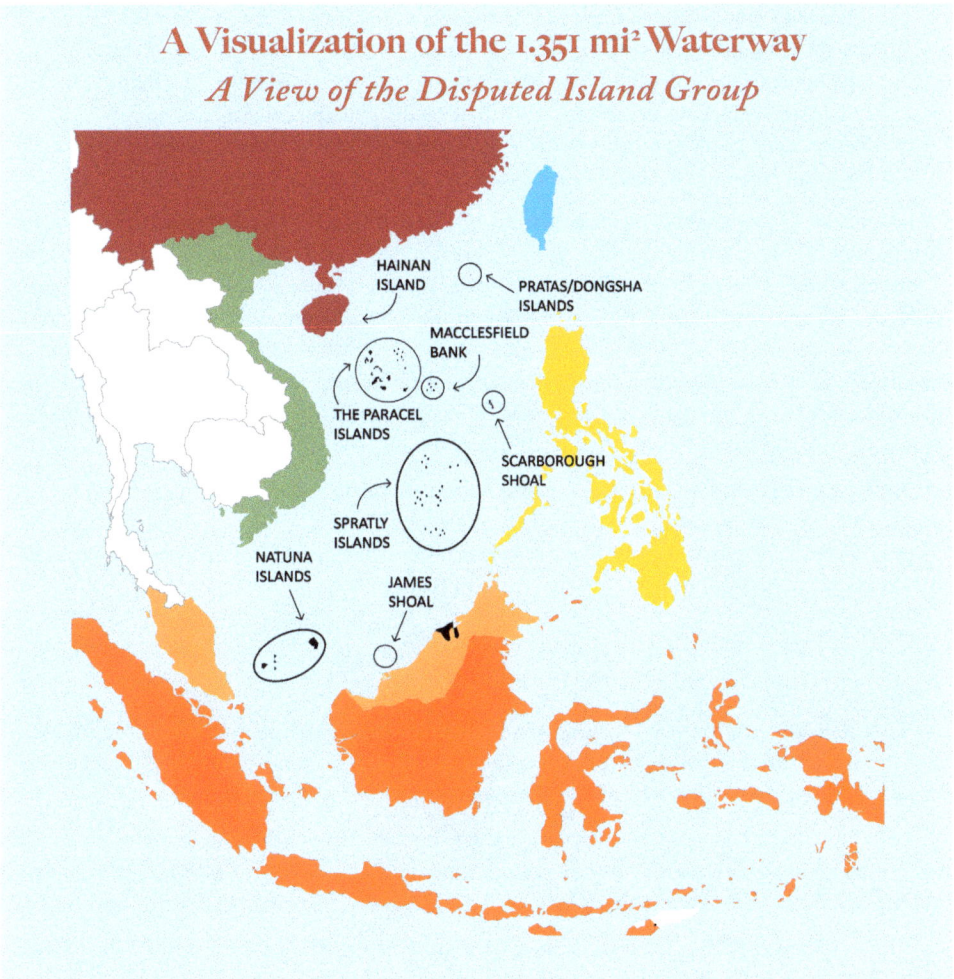

Conclusion

At the 2015 Boao Forum, President Xi's offered lotus flowers, flowing water, and open arms of friendship in a speech that was truly a work of art. Additionally, the warmth and delivery of his presentation was worthy of an award.

---

13   Bloomberg News, "China Adopts Law Letting Coast Guard Fire on Foreign Vessels," *Bloomberg*, January 22, 2021, https://www.bloomberg.com/news/articles/2021-01-23/china-adopts-law-letting-coast-guard-fire-on-foreign-vessels

Turbulence or war runs against the fundamental interests of the Chinese people. The Chinese nation loves peace and has, since ancient times, held high such philosophies that "harmony is the most valuable", "peace and harmony should prevail" and "all men under heaven are brothers". China has suffered from turbulence and war for more than a century since modern times, and the Chinese people would never want to inflict the same tragedy on other countries or peoples. History has taught us that no country who tried to achieve its goal with force ever succeeded. China will be steadfast in pursuing the independent foreign policy of peace, the path of peaceful development, the win-win strategy of opening-up, and the approach of upholding justice while pursuing shared interests. China will work to promote a new type of international relations of win-win cooperation and will always remain a staunch force for world peace and common development.[14]

President Xi's win-win diplomacy would be a welcome gift. However, his actions tell a completely different story. Members of Chinese Communist Party (CCP) have imprisoned, tortured, raped, or murdered millions of people. Beijing's leaders have locked up millions in forced labor camps. The CCP's arm reached into Hong Kong and both silenced and imprisoned the masses. China's People's Liberation Army Navy (PLAN) moved into the South China Sea, taking other country's land, preventing countries from drilling, sinking ships, and violating international law. China's PLAN aggressively encroached on Taiwan, Japan, Korea, and waters in the Arctic, South America, and the Indo-Pacific.

In the game Rock-Paper-Scissors, paper covers the rock, but there is no flowery, poetic rhetoric that covers the rock hard campaign Beijing has waged on its neighbors. Xi Jinping's words of win-win diplomacy and brotherly friendship are diametrically opposite the coercion, torture, and genocide that exist in reality.

What's at Stake?

First, China has promoted its win-win diplomacy across the planet. While the rhetoric is pleasant, warm, and friendly, China's actions are far from friendly and have dangerously crossed the line from aggressive to murderous.

Second, China has violated international law and declared that its laws are the only laws to which it will adhere. With this behavior, it appears that win-win diplomacy means that as long as China wins, everyone will win. If China loses, China will still win.

Third, China does not keep all of its agreements except when they are in China's favor. What is at stake is the gullibility of countries to believe China, as the United States did when it brokered the agreement over the Scarborough Shoal. The question is whether or not the Biden administration will remember what happened in 2012 when Biden was the U.S. Vice President.

Fourth, India had a chance to experience China's win-win diplomacy as well. In 2020, China built encampments on the India-China Line of Actual Control and attacked and

---

14 China.org.cn, "Full Text of Chinese President's Speech at Boao Forum for Asia," *China.org.cn,* March 29, 2015, http://www.china.org.cn/business/2015-03/29/content_35185720.htm

killed Indian soldiers.[15] Countries throughout the world are being faced with win-win diplomacy and will have to make decisions about how they view China's rhetoric versus China's actions.

The Chinese Dream
Promoted by Xi Jinping Since 2013

---

15 BBC News, "India-China Clash: 20 Indian Troops Killed in Ladakh Fighting," *BBC News*, June 16, 2020, https://www.bbc.com/news/world-asia-53061476

Chapter 2
Vaccine Diplomacy
The Pandemic and Vaccine Rollout

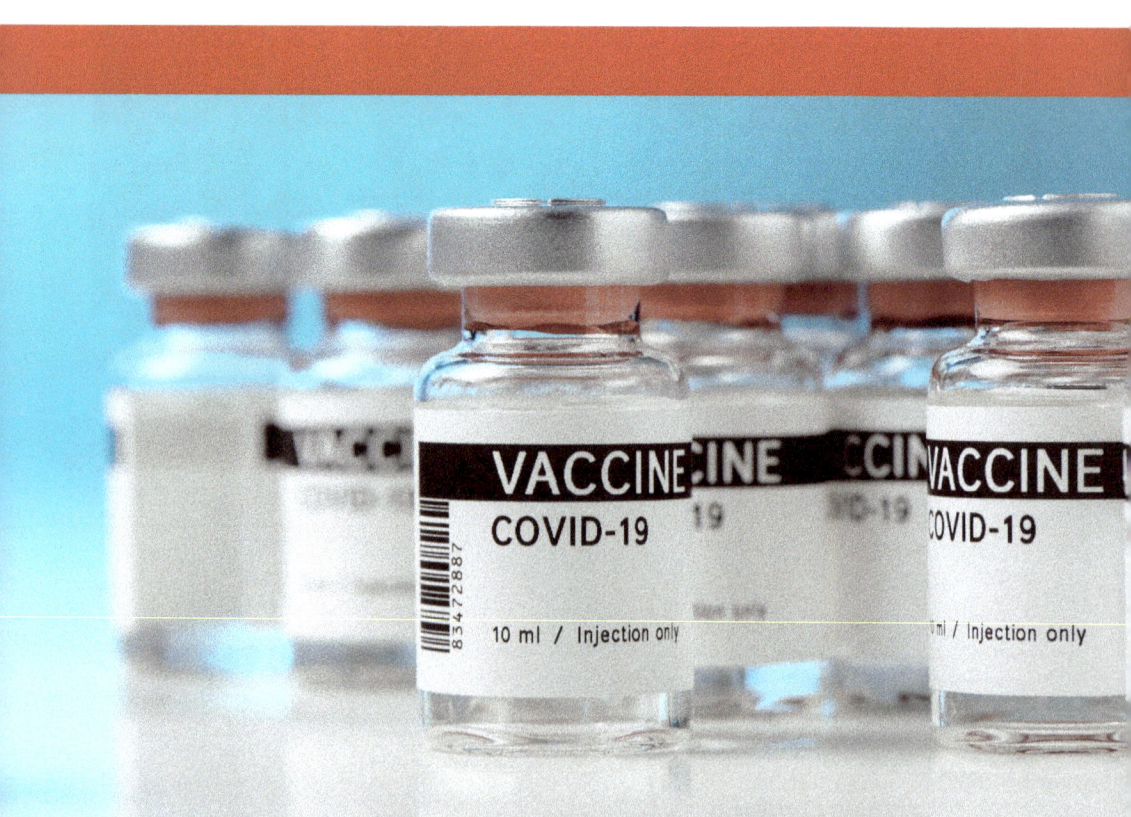

Introduction

States seek many objectives to achieve prosperity, among them to employ, produce, and trade. Alliances help keep economies moving, while financial, political, and military challenges impede relationship-building and cooperation. Although countries can use hard power - force, coercion, and threats – they can also facilitate soft power – goodwill, cultural exchanges, and financial support. Soft power interchanges like language, education, movies, and television can also inspire and excite the public. While COVID-19 started in Wuhan, China, it spread to the rest of the world, leaving global citizens vulnerable. In return, using "Vaccine Diplomacy," China offered to aid countries with its Sinovac and Sinopharm COVID-19 inoculations to help compensate for its failed "Mask Diplomacy" roll out.[1]

Repairing Its Reputation

When China began its "Vaccine Diplomacy" Beijing went on the "Charm Offensive" as Rand Corporation political scientist, Jeffrey W. Hornung, put it.[2] China sought to "repair its reputation damaged by Beijing's alleged cover-up of the COVID-19 outbreak in the early days.[3] Early on, China provided defective equipment and masks, suffering from a lack of quality control and poorly articulated propaganda which tarnished Beijing's efforts to portray itself as generous and willing to supply the world with effective rather than just cheap products.[4] President Xi called countries in March 2020, expressing his concern and vowing to prioritize aid to countries through the China Belt and Road Initiative, the "Health Silk Road".[5]

The Pandemic

With approximately three million deaths, the COVID-19 pandemic will live on in recorded history as one of the world's great health crises. In the United States alone, there were about six hundred thousand deaths. China, preferring to appear unblemished and telling other countries that Chinese socialism was a better system, did not fully report its statistics. Thus, there are likely to be many hundreds of thousands more unreported deaths that we will never know about. Meanwhile, numerous nefarious issues regarding the COVID-19 pandemic have been exposed.

---

1   James Walker, "China's Mask Diplomacy Fails to Improve Europe's Opinion of Beijing," *Newsweek*, June 29, 2020, https://www.newsweek.com/china-mask-diplomacy-fails-improve-european-opinion-beijing-1514129

2   Jeffrey W. Honrnung, "Don't be Fooled by China's Mask Diplomacy," *RAND Corporation*, May 5, 2020, https://www.rand.org/blog/2020/05/dont-be-fooled-by-chinas-mask-diplomacy.html

3   Jane Li, "China's Coronavirus Vaccine Diplomacy has Already Begun," *Quartz*, December 8, 2020, https://qz.com/1942494/indonesia-is-a-major-front-in-chinas-covid-19-vaccine-diplomacy/

4   Yanzhong Huang, "Vaccine Diplomacy is Paying Off for China," *Foreign Affairs,* March 11, 2021, https://www.foreignaffairs.com/articles/china/2021-03-11/vaccine-diplomacy-paying-china?utm_medium=newsletters&utm_source=twofa&utm_campaign=The%20Pandemic%20That%20Won%E2%80%99t%20End&utm_content=20210312&utm_term=FA%20This%20Week%20-%20112017

5   Ministry of Foreign Affairs of the People's Republic of China, "President Xi Jinping Talked with Italian Prime Ministry Giuseppe Conte over the Phone," *Ministry of Foreign Affairs of the People's Republic of China*, March 16, 2020, https://www.fmprc.gov.cn/mfa_eng/zxxx_662805/t1756887.shtml

First, from the start, if a whistleblower, and later a villainized doctor, in Wuhan, had not revealed the outbreak, less would have been known in its earlier phases. China's slowed revelation of the dynamics of this catastrophe led to a faster spread of the virus with many more deaths in the early months of its hyper-speed spread. Second, China's lack of transparency has prevented the world from understanding the true nature of the pandemic. A researcher from the WHO global response team emerged from the Wuhan Institute of Virology saying, "Very interesting. Many questions."[6] Except for official rhetoric, few still know the truth. However, the events that unfolded exposed profound issues yet to be examined as well as the present threat to the underlying principles of freedom, transparency, and rule of law that people in the free world heretofore took for granted.

Individuals worldwide quietly acquiesced to giving up their freedoms amidst a noisy concert of media. Officials urged citizens with a unifying, pervasive discourse of 'quarantine, follow orders, and change your way of life for the good of society'. This mandate was complemented with additional governmental dictums. The resulting tsunami of closures and job losses financially drowned small stores, restaurants, and service industries in debt. Meanwhile, the severest impact was, all along, predominantly a single, older age group of the population. With trillions of dollars in financial disbursements, the pandemic's wake will be felt for many years to come. Businesses shuttered, churches closed, and schools effectively stopped teaching. Restrictions led millions into psychological trauma, resulting in destructive behaviors (drugs, alcohol, and domestic violence) of catastrophic proportions many time beyond the millions worldwide who died. The human impact is incalculable.

Hypocrisy took a front seat as massive street protests were allowed while prayer in church was denied. People sat back, fearful for their lives and for the lives of those they love, all the while complying uneasily with mandated, and policed personal behaviors. Businesses went overboard denying access to outdoor activities, schools fired coaches who let players touch a ball, and put college students on probation for taking photographs without a mask. In a massive set of college policing actions, thousands of students across the United States were reprimanded, suspended, or dismissed for vague COVID-related infractions.[7] Restrictions often resulted in behaviors that were categorically mean, abrasively vindictive, or unusually slothful. Meanwhile, as a reality check, according to the Centers for Disease Control (CDC), only 4.4% of the deaths in the United States attributed to COVID-19 occurred in individuals under 50-years-old as of May 2021.[8]

Media bias and social media overreach were exacerbated by the loss of academic freedom and internet shut offs aiming to subdue the population. In 2019, there were 25 documented instances of partial or total internet shutdowns worldwide, compared with 20 in 2018 and 12 in 2017, according to Access Now, an independent monitoring group.[9]

---

6   VOA News, "'Many Questions' After WHO Team Visits Wuhan Virology Lab," *VOA News*, February 3, 2021, https://www.voanews.com/covid-19-pandemic-many-questions-after-who-team-visits-wuhan-virology-lab

7   Elizabeth Redden, "COVID Conduct," *Inside HigherEd*, February 23, 2021, https://www.insidehighered.com/news/2021/02/23/colleges-wield-codes-conduct-enforce-compliance-covid-policies

8   CDC, "COVID-19 Mortality Overview," *CDC*, n.d., https://www.cdc.gov/nchs/covid19/mortality-overview.htm

9   Christopher Giles and Peter Mwai, "Africa Internet: Where and How Are Governments Blocking It?," *BBC News*, January 14, 2021, https://www.bbc.com/news/world-africa-47734843

By 2021, in addition to the shutdowns in China, there were 29 other cases of internet shutdowns.[10] In the United States, social media giants took down social media accounts from individuals all the way up to the U.S. president. A *Forbes* article explains that even before the election, Facebook and Twitter had censored the president.[11]

Through all of the closures, restrictions, and curfews, the spread continued while threatening health screening, education, and the economy. Many people decided to forego necessary testing and treatment thereby adding to the insecurities. Instances of mental illnesses increased as did suicides, alcoholism, drug use, and video game addiction. Frustration, isolation, disillusionment, and unemployment went along with the loss of sports, activities, travel, and social interactions. Instances of domestic violence will not be fully determined until after the pandemic when health studies will assess the landscape.

Vaccine Diplomacy
Eradicating the World of COVID-19

---

10 Al Jazeera, "Mapping Internet Shutdowns Around the World," *Al Jazeera*, March 3, 2021, https://www.aljazeera.com/news/2021/3/3/mapping-internet-shutdowns-around-the-world

11 John Brandon, "Facebook and Twitter Keep Censoring President Trump as a Way to Prepare for the Upcoming Election. Here's Why I'm Worried," *Forbes*, June 25, 2020, https://www.forbes.com/sites/johnbbrandon/2020/06/25/facebook-and-twitter-keep-censoring-president-trump-as-a-way-to-prepare-for-the-upcoming-election-heres-why-im-worried/?sh=d6cdd004db34

Conclusion

"Vaccine Diplomacy" may be China's saving grace from its lack of transparency and its public relations nightmare regarding the spread of COVID-19 and the sending of defective ventilators. As China continues to help countries while propagating defamatory information about other vaccines, Beijing charges ahead on the warpath to discredit Western-made vaccines and spread conspiracy theories.[12]

China's 'Wolf Warrior' diplomacy went in full swing in early 2021. Credibility is essential and cannot be obtained if China hides its vaccine data and does not provide transparency in its laboratory results.[13] Without this, "Vaccine Diplomacy" is a flying leap of faith in the arms of a country that covers up everything it does.

In addition to the global health crisis, freedom, truth, and human rights all took a huge hit in 2020. The United States was infiltrated with propaganda as were many other democratic countries. Hong Kong fell prematurely to China in a dramatic defeat of freedom and nearly immediate subjugation. The pandemic provided the perfect cover as few countries were prepared or willing to prevent the toppling of a city and dissolution of liberties. Voices across the planet cried out.

The tragedy of COVID-19 on all fronts will forever remain with everyone who lived through the pandemic. The policy of stopping the virus at any cost set a dangerous precedent for all nations, since this will not be the last virus or mutation. Yet, the politicization of healthcare, lies told for political purposes, and lack of transparency put individuals, countries, and the world in jeopardy. Truth was the loser in these battles.

What's at Stake?

First, regarding the propagation of lies told to the global public about the pandemic, we should never succumb to the infamous declaration attributed to Nazi propagandist Joseph Goebbels, "A lie told once remains a lie, but a lie told a thousand times becomes the truth." The pandemic should not have been about public relations or convenient conquest, but about saving lives and preventing this kind of event from ever happening again.

Second, soft power can invite, attract, and shape the beliefs of people through culture, friendship, and cooperation. However, soft power can be used to control, influence, and co-opt citizens and their governments through tactical persuasion. Yet, as Joseph Nye who coined the term "soft power" explained, "in an Information Age in which credibility is the scarcest resource, the best propaganda is *not* propaganda."[14] Today, China is at work shaping

---

12 Gerry Shih, "China Turbocharges Bid to Discredit Western Vaccines, Spread Virus Conspiracy Theories," *The Washington Post*, January 20, 2021, https://www.washingtonpost.com/world/asia_pacific/vaccines-coronavirus-china-conspiracy-theories/2021/01/20/89bd3d2a-5a2d-11eb-a849-6f9423a75ffd_story.html

13 Eyck Freymann and Justin Stebbing, "China Must Stop Hiding its Vaccine Data," *Foreign Affairs*, February 26, 2021, https://www.foreignaffairs.com/articles/china/2021-02-26/china-must-stop-hiding-its-vaccine-data

14 Joseph S. Nye, Jr., "China's Soft Power Deficit," *The Wall Street Journal*, May 8, 2012, https://www.wsj.com/articles/SB10001424052702304451104577389923098678842

long-term attitudes and preferences. However, "Nye's message is that U.S. security hinges as much on winning hearts and minds as it does on winning wars."[15]

Third, the public does not trust Chinese vaccines because its scientists do not provide complete data. Sinovac's obfuscation is not just bad science, it is also bad politics for Beijing. By becoming a leading vaccine supplier, China hoped to show off its high-tech capabilities and burnish its international reputation after a damaging 2020. But its approach to vaccine data has hardly helped Beijing put the past behind. If China learned nothing else in Wuhan last January, the obvious lesson would seem to be that evading uncomfortable truths can do more damage than confronting them. Yet Chinese vaccine companies have taken an approach to data that is at best sloppy and at worst misleading.[16]

Coronavirus

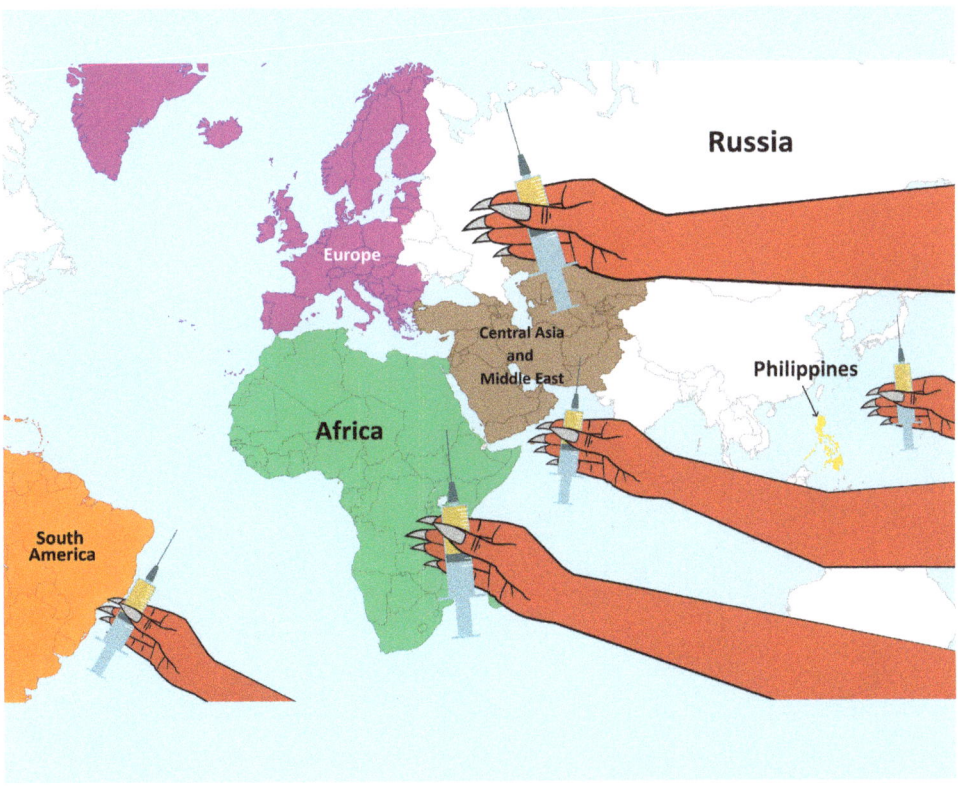

---

15 Joseph S. Nye, Jr., "Soft Power: The Means to Success in World Politics," *Foreign Affairs*, May/June 2004, https://www.foreignaffairs.com/reviews/capsule-review/2004-05-01/soft-power-means-success-world-politics

16 Eyck Freymann and Justin Stebbing, "China Must Stop Hiding its Vaccine Data," *Foreign Affairs*, February 26, 2021, https://www.foreignaffairs.com/articles/china/2021-02-26/china-must-stop-hiding-its-vaccine-data

Chapter 3

Facemask Diplomacy

China's PPE Generosity, Failures, and Economic Enrichment

Introduction

The COVID-19 outbreak confronted global leaders with monumental and unprecedented challenges. Governments were forced to 'flatten the curve', reduce the number of cases, and prevent the disease's spread. From elected leaders to industry administrators, all levels were impacted. Every health-related industry sector faced bottlenecks in the delivery of services. Across all industries, staff became ill, positions were cut, and employees were furloughed. The quarantine locked down the majority of the population for a year. While innovation did resume virtually through platforms such as Zoom, Skype, GoToMeeting, and Webex, there were numerous hiccups along the way. Education reinvented itself as teachers adapted to the online environment after bouts of anxiety, a steep learning curve, and a period of uncertainty. Life as people knew it transitioned to a new normal as people worked from home and virtual interactions replaced in-person meetings.

Decision-making was disrupted by constantly changing data, inconsistent rules, and a lack of transparency. Furthermore, fear and uncertainty were palpable given the need for protection, scarcity of medical equipment, and the very real possibility of contracting the virus. Meanwhile, in the ever-shifting quagmire of information quicksand, leaders created and enforced constantly-adapted policies without any certainty.

Protection Directive

One of the rules or requirements was to wear facemasks. Some experts believed that by covering the mouth and nose with a facemask, there was a high probability of lessening the spread of the respiratory virus. By June 2020, using personal protective equipment (PPE) became mandatory worldwide in an effort to reduce the coronavirus death toll.[1] The U.S. Food & Drug Administration (FDA) defines PPE as "surgical masks, face shields, respirators, gowns, and gloves" used for protection.[2]

With a firm reliance on PPE to depress the number of COVID-19 cases, facemasks became a commodity in high demand. Thus, with its manufacturing capacity, China rose to the challenge of supplying PPE globally, creating what President Xi Jinping deemed the new 'Health Silk Road'.[3]

With this 'Health Silk Road', China paved the path for a new diplomatic agenda, engaging in 'facemask diplomacy' as they shipped facemasks worldwide. Through the Chinese Communist Party's 'facemask diplomacy' efforts, Beijing pledged to send aid to nations and '*gift*' these masks to countries in need. However, while President Xi's generosity was most assuredly welcomed, Beijing sent billions of these '*presents*', while

---

1   Al Jazeera, "Which Countries Have Made Wearing Face Masks Compulsory?," *Al Jazeera*, August 17, 2020, https://www.aljazeera.com/news/2020/04/countries-wearing-face-masks-compulsory-200423094510867.html

2   U.S. Food and Drug Administration, "Coronavirus (COVID-19) and Medical Devices," *U.S. Food and Drug Administration*, n.d., https://www.fda.gov/medical-devices/emergency-situations-medical-devices/coronavirus-covid-19-and-medical-devices

3   Alan Crawford, Peter Martin, and Bloomberg, "'Health Silk Road:' China Showers Europe with Coronavirus Aid as Both Spar with Trump," *Fortune*, March 19, 2020, https://fortune.com/2020/03/19/china-europe-coronavirus-aid-trump/

requiring that the recipient countries paid the bill for their PPE shipments. To the dismay of government procurement officials, both the PPE were defective and the antigen/antibody test kits purchased were inaccurate, rendering them completely useless.

Test Kits

Defective products and incorrect test results caused chaos and sent ripples of frustration through global governing bodies needing to resolve the crises. Red flags were raised regarding China's COVID-19 'benevolent' merchandise. Numerous deficiencies were discovered in Chinese-manufactured COVID-19 antigen and antibody test kits. Testing for COVID-19 was crucial during the pandemic; countries needed to test millions of people per day to detect COVID-19 in symptomatic as well as asymptotic persons who may be spreading the virus.[4] Antigen test kits were supposed to determine whether a patient has contracted coronavirus, while antibody test kits revealed if a patient had previously acquired the virus and had built up immunities.[5] With both of these tests, many nations reported Chinese kits recorded 'low accuracy rates'. Medical experts spoke out against antigen and antibody tests' reliability, and some even reported accuracy rates as low as 5%.[6]

In early April 2020, Spain, Slovakia, Turkey, Britain, and the Czech Republic announced that they had spent millions of dollars purchasing faulty Chinese antigen and antibody test kits.[7] While some countries canceled their orders when they found out the testing was defective, others simply sacrificed the millions of dollars they spent.

These complaints were not independent incidents. The *Jerusalem Post* reported that just one technician out of hundreds found over 10,000 defective Chinese test kits from a single shipment.[8] In experimental testing to determine Chinese test kit accuracy, scientists conducted trials on patients already diagnosed with coronavirus. When the results indicated that test-positive patients were negative for the virus, they knew the tests were inaccurate.

Public statements from countries that were sold unreliable test kits alerted others, making them wary of purchasing antigen and antibody test kits from China. Georgia canceled its agreement with Chinese companies for facemasks and began purchasing test kits from South Korea.[9] Malaysia followed Georgia's footsteps, opting to purchase test kits

---

4   Michael Le Page, "Why Countries Should Start Weekly COVID-19 Testing for Key Workers," *NewScientist,* May 6, 2020, https://www.newscientist.com/article/mg24632812-700-why-countries-should-start-weekly-covid-19-testing-for-key-workers/

5   Mayo Clinic, "How do COVID-19 Antibody Tests Differ From Diagnostic Tests?," *Mayo Clinic,* August 19, 2020, https://www.mayoclinic.org/diseases-conditions/coronavirus/expert-answers/covid-antibody-tests/faq-20484429

6   BBC News, "Coronavirus: India Cancels Order for 'Faulty' China Rapid Test Kit," *BBC News*, April 28, 2020, https://www.bbc.com/news/world-asia-india-52451455

7   Alice Su, "Faulty Masks. Flawed Tests. China's Quality Control Problem in Leading Global COVID-19 Fight," *Los Angeles Times*, April 10, 2020, https://www.latimes.com/world-nation/story/2020-04-10/china-beijing-supply-world-coronavirus-fight-quality-control

8   Maayan Jaffe-Hoffman, "As Many as 10,000 Coronavirus Test Kits from China Found Faulty," *The Jerusalem Post*, April 23, 2020, https://www.jpost.com/israel-news/as-many-as-10000-coronavirus-test-kits-from-china-found-faulty-625517

9   Agenda, "Georgia Suspends Agreement with Chinese Company for Rapid Coronavirus Tests," *Agenda*, March 27, 2020, https://agenda.ge/en/news/2020/953

from South Korea as well.[10] Meanwhile, PPE orders were also canceled after determining their similar low quality. Inaccuracy in test kits not only posed health crises but also created strains within and between governments.

During the spring and summer of 2020, India and China engaged in several high-stakes border conflicts that escalated tensions. In early April 2020, India purchased 500,000 antibody test kits from China in an initiative to increase their testing potential. India reported 29,000 cases of defective test kits in April[11] and, by July 1, 2020, the instances skyrocketed to over 600,000.[12]

---

10 Minderjeet Kaur, "Georgia Suspends Agreement with Chinese Company for Rapid Coronavirus Tests," *Free Malaysia* Today, March 27, 2020, https://www.freemalaysiatoday.com/category/nation/2020/03/27/malaysia-to-test-south-korean-covid-19-test-kits-tonight/

11 Anjana Pasricha, "China Slams India's Decision to Stop Using 'Faulty' Chinese Rapid Test Kits," *VOA News,* April 28, 2020, https://www.voanews.com/covid-19-pandemic/china-slams-indias-decision-stop-using-faulty-chinese-rapid-test-kits

12 The New York Times, "India Coronavirus Map and Case Count," *The New York Times,* August 25, 2020, https://www.nytimes.com/interactive/2020/world/asia/india-coronavirus-cases.html

Shortly after the purchase, the Indian Council of Medical Research (ICRM) ran tests using China's equipment on patients already test-positive for coronavirus. The results indicated those who were already COVID-19-positive presented negative for the virus. The ICRM's findings, deeming these kits' faulty',[13] indicated that Chinese testing equipment was unreliable and erroneous. India canceled an order of half a million antibody test kits from China and refused to purchase more.[14]

In response to the annulled order and India's public statements, Chinese Embassy spokesperson Ji Rong in New Delhi stated, "It is unfair and irresponsible for certain individuals to label Chinese products as 'faulty' and look at issues with pre-emptive prejudice." While border disputes continued, including military skirmishes that killed Indian troops, India's withdrawal from purchasing Chinese test kits enraged Beijing, feeding fuel to an already fiery dragon.

The Cases of Defective Masks

At the same time that antigen and antibody test kits were scrutinized on the world stage, nations questioned the safety of Chinese-manufactured facemasks. Local Chinese news in Beijing reported that on March 12, 2020, State Council officials announced the seizure of 80 million counterfeit or faulty masks as well as 370,000 false or defective disinfectants in February alone.[15] The Chinese people also suffered from significant health risks resulting from counterfeit PPE equipment, yet they continued shipping these damaged products worldwide, receiving political backlash from the international community.

In April 2020, a coalition of nations released statements on Chinese mask defects due to poor manufacturing. The Netherlands returned 600,000 Chinese facemasks due to inadequate filters and sizing.[16] Australian border officials seized around 800,000 faulty or counterfeit masks from China.[17] The Dutch health ministry recalled 600,000 facemasks from China with a quality assurance certificate that still had defective filters and incorrect sizing.[18]

The Czech Republic alone paid $600,000 for masks from China,[19] and 80% of those

---

13   BBC News, "Coronavirus: India Cancels Order for 'Faulty' China Rapid Test Kit," *BBC News,* April 28, 2020, https://www.bbc.com/news/world-asia-india-52451455

14   Anjana Pasricha, "China Slams India's Decision to Stop Using 'Faulty' Chinese Rapid Test Kits," *VOA News,* April 28, 2020, https://www.voanews.com/covid-19-pandemic/china-slams-indias-decision-stop-using-faulty-chinese-rapid-test-kits

15   Ding Tian, "In the Past Month, More Than 80 Million Fake and Inferior Masks Were Seized Nationwide," *Beijing News,* March 12, 2020, http://www.bjnews.com.cn/news/2020/03/12/702723.html

16   Stuart Lau, "Netherlands Recalls 600,000 Face Masks from China due to Low Quality," *South China Morning Post,* March 29, 2020, https://www.scmp.com/news/china/diplomacy/article/3077428/netherlands-recalls-600000-face-masks-china-due-low-quality

17   Andrew Greene, "Australia Seizes Faulty Coronavirus Protective Equipment Imported from China," *Australia Broadcasting Corporation News,* March 31, 2020, https://mobile.abc.net.au/news/2020-04-01/coronavirus-chinese-ppe-border-force-intercepted/12085908

18   BBC News, "Coronavirus: Countries Reject Chinese-Made Equipment," *BBC News,* March 30, 2020, https://www.bbc.com/news/world-europe-52092395

19   Charles Dunst, "How China's Mask Diplomacy Backfired," *The American Interest,* April 15, 2020, https://www.the-american-interest.com/2020/04/15/how-chinas-mask-diplomacy-backfired/

masks were defective.[20] Even so, the Czechs were still charged for these masks. These failures were replicated in the Philippines, Italy, Spain, the United Kingdom, Indonesia, Hungary, Northern Ireland, Azerbaijan, Turkey, Brazil, Japan, Mexico, Qatar, Serbia, Austria, and dozens of other countries who were purchasing China's "gifts" to the world.[21]

The United States also jumped on the bandwagon of purchasing Chinese PPE, despite its continuous criticism of China's response to the coronavirus outbreak. In early April 2020, President Donald Trump announced his plans to buy millions of facemasks, gloves, and gowns from China.[22] However, the FDA pulled the authorization to use Chinese facemasks, writing in a letter that the masks "may not provide consistent and adequate

---

20 Keoni Everington, "80% of Coronavirus Test Kits 'Gifted' to Czechs by China Faulty," *Taiwan News*, March 25, 2020, https://www.taiwannews.com.tw/en/news/3903937

21 Charles Dunst, "How China's Mask Diplomacy Backfired," *The American Interest*, April 15, 2020, https://www.the-american-interest.com/2020/04/15/how-chinas-mask-diplomacy-backfired/

22 Jackie Northam, "U.S. Buys Masks From China While Criticizing It For COVID-19," *NPR*, April 1, 2020, https://www.npr.org/2020/04/01/825056981/u-s-buys-masks-from-china-while-criticizing-it-for-covid-19

respiratory protection to health care personnel exposed to Covid-19."[23]

Still, a few U.S. states sent millions, even billions, of dollars to Chinese companies to purchase their masks. Illinois Governor J.B. Pritzker spent $1.7M to buy masks and gloves from China.[24] California Governor Gavin Newsom struck a $1B deal with China to purchase PPE from Chinese companies. Due to delivery delays, California received a $247M refund.[25] These states chose to outsource to Chinese companies rather than select and hire in-state manufacturing companies to produce this equipment.

Conclusion

Though Chinese manufactured personal protective equipment (PPE) was shipped in incorrect sizes with faulty filters, defective straps, and flimsy material, Chinese state media, *Xinhua*, reported China made 'donations' to over 100 countries and produced a daily output of 116 million units of facemasks since February 29, 2020.[26] Though many nations rebuked these Chinese products, some continued to purchase millions of dollars of masks throughout the pandemic and fund Chinese manufacturing companies. Despite the noble intentions of leaders who valiantly believed they were 'serving and protecting', counterfeit and faulty PPE have posed serious health threats for billions of citizens and put people at high risk for catching the coronavirus.

What's at Stake?

First, since facemasks were deemed a requirement by the World Health Organization, billions needed to be made quickly. China came to the rescue as the world's manufacturer of cheap products. China offered this 'gift' at a price.

Second, sending faulty products was unwelcome by countries worldwide. Making countries pay for the PPE, further added salt to the wound.

Third, diplomacy is loosely termed and should have been replaced with 'cutthroat capitalism', though that word does not sit well in China's communist-socialist playbook. In this instance, it looks a lot like an outright case of bait and switch.

---

23   Anna Edney, "U.S. Pulls Authorization for Use of Face Masks Made in China," *Bloomberg*, May 7, 2020, https://www.bloomberg.com/news/articles/2020-05-07/u-s-pulls-authorization-for-use-of-face-masks-made-in-china

24   Casey Leins, "Gov. Pritzker Spends $1.7 Million to Fly Masks, Gloves From China to Illinois," *U.S. News & World Report*, April 15, 2020, https://www.usnews.com/news/best-states/articles/2020-04-15/illinois-purchases-millions-of-gloves-masks-from-china

25   U.S. News & World Report, "California to Get $247M Refund as Masks Face Delivery Delay," *U.S. News & World Report*, May 6, 2020, https://www.usnews.com/news/business/articles/2020-05-06/california-gov-newsoms-billion-dollar-mask-deal-hits-snag

26   Xinhua, "Xinhua Headlines: Rumor Buster: Six facts About China's Fight Against COVID-19," *Xinhua Net*, April 9, 2020, http://www.xinhuanet.com/english/2020-04/09/c_138961792.htm

Xi Jinping Thought and China's Diplomacy | Part 3 | III

Chapter 4

Wolf Warrior Diplomacy

China's Aggressive Verbal Attacks, Institutionalized During the Pandemic

Introduction

Chinese representatives have unloaded salvos of confrontational rhetoric. These sharply worded jabs through Twitter and press conferences dramatically contrast with the previously respectful Chinese diplomacy. These attachés have come to be called "Wolf Warriors", a term taken from a series of Chinese film blockbusters where "Rambo-style" aggressors defeat a team led by a U.S. Navy Seal turned mercenary.[1]

The Film *Wolf Warrior II*

Wolf Warrior 2, the highest-grossing film in China by that time, was released in 2017. In the movie, the protagonists defend China both at home and abroad. The tagline of *Wolf Warrior 2* reads, "Even though far away, anyone who affronts China will pay."[2] At the end of the movie, the cover of the People's Republic of China (PRC) passport is displayed along with text reading "Citizens of the PRC: When you encounter danger in a foreign land, do not give up! Please remember, at your back stands a strong motherland."[3]

The term, Wolf Warrior, became a buzzword during the COVID-19 pandemic.[4] Some European nations have expressed surprise over the change in Chinese foreign relations' narrative from one of collaboration to that of confrontation.[5] 'Wolf Warrior' diplomacy adds to Beijing's increasingly aggressive foreign policy initiatives under Xi, while also contradicting former CCP philosophy.

'*Wolf Warrior*' diplomacy is the antithesis to the kind of diplomacy that China showcased for decades - that of keeping a low profile. This philosophy was exemplified by the then leader Deng Xiaoping, who proclaimed, "Hide your strength, bide your time, never take the lead." For decades, Chinese foreign policy incorporated a calculated risk approach and emphasized state sovereignty, institutionalized collective decision making, and Deng Xiaoping's famous term 'crossing the river by feeling the stones.'[6]

'Fighting Spirit' Instructed by President Xi

In September 2019, President Xi Jinping told Chinese diplomats to promote Beijing's viewpoints across the world more aggressively with a 'fighting spirit'.[7] Ambassadors

---

1. Ben Westcott and Steven Jiang, "China is Embracing a New Brand of Foreign Policy. Here's What Wolf Warrior Diplomacy Means," *CNN*, Updated May 29, 2020, https://www.cnn.com/2020/05/28/asia/china-wolf-warrior-diplomacy-intl-hnk/index.html

2. Ibid.

3. Abdul Rasool Syed, "Wolf Warriors: A Brand New Force of Chinese Diplomats," *Modern Diplomacy*, July 14, 2020, https://moderndiplomacy.eu/2020/07/14/wolf-warriors-a-brand-new-force-of-chinese-diplomats/

4. Earl Wang, "How Will the EU Answer China's Turn Toward 'Xi Jinping Thought on Diplomacy'?," *The Diplomat*, July 31, 2020, https://thediplomat.com/2020/07/how-will-the-eu-answer-chinas-turn-toward-xi-jinping-thought-on-diplomacy/

5. Kathrin Hille, "'Wolf Warrior' Diplomats Reveal China's Ambitions," *Financial Times*, May 11, 2020, https://www.ft.com/content/7d500105-4349-4721-b4f5-179de6a58f08

6. The Soufan Center, "IntelBrief: The Rise of 'Wolf Warrior' Diplomacy from China," *The Soufan Center*, July 17, 2020, https://thesoufancenter.org/intelbrief-the-rise-of-wolf-warrior-diplomacy-from-china/

7. Bloomberg News, "China's Xi Warns Party Needs 'Fighting Spirit' to Overcome Risks," *Bloomberg*, September 3, 2019, https://www.bloomberg.com/news/articles/2019-09-03/china-s-xi-urges-party-to-prepare-for-long-term-struggle

and representatives set up Twitter accounts to go on the offensive to meet the challenge presented by Xi Jinping.[8] According to a February 2021 Associated Press report, "Chinese diplomatic accounts have more than tripled on Twitter and more than doubled on Facebook" since the beginning of the pandemic.[9]

Major proponents of the Wolf Warrior diplomacy are two top spokespeople of the Chinese Foreign Ministry, Hua Chunying and Zhao Lijian. These individuals have launched groundless conspiracy theories and dragged other countries through the mud over their handling of the coronavirus pandemic. With the help of the Atlantic Council's Digital Forensic Research Lab, the Associated Press conducted a nine-month investigation including China's disinformation campaign called the "Anatomy of a Conspiracy". This report explained how the Chinese weaponized their propaganda going through "millions of social media postings and articles on Twitter, Facebook, V.K., Weibo, WeChat, YouTube, Telegram and other platforms."[10]

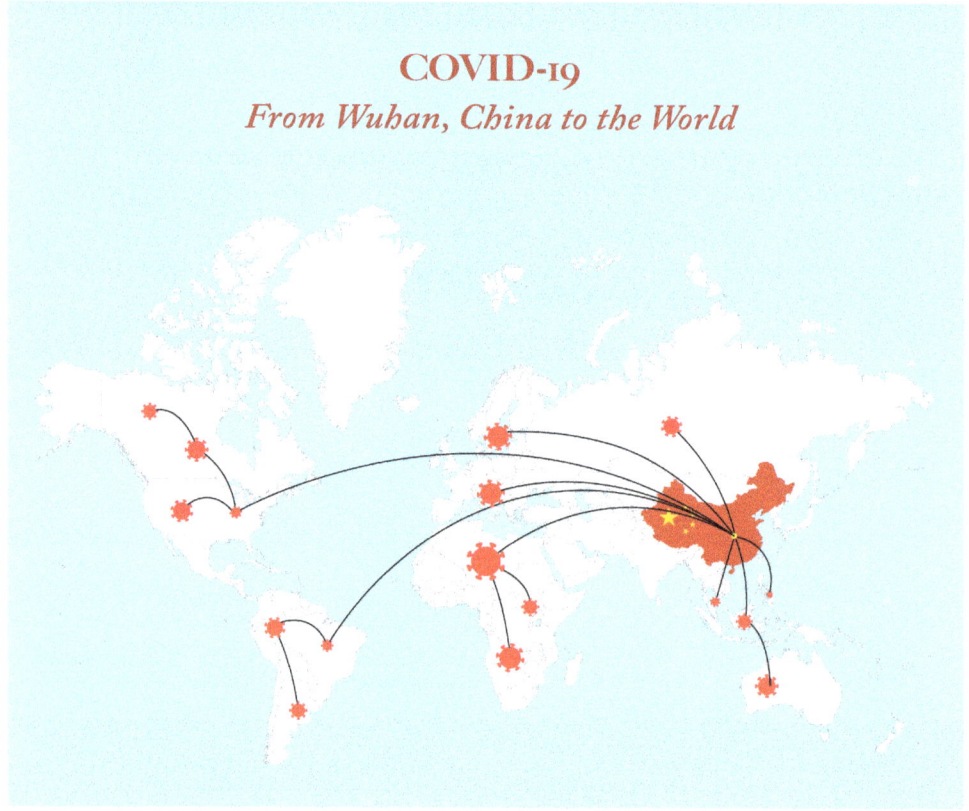

COVID-19

From Wuhan, China to the World

---

8   Reuters Staff, "China Demands 'Fighting Spirit' from Diplomats as Trade War, Hong Kong Protests Simmer," *Reuters*, December 3, 2019, https://www.reuters.com/article/us-china-diplomacy/china-demands-fighting-spirit-from-diplomats-as-trade-war-hong-kong-protests-simmer-idUSKBN1Y80R8

9   Erika Kinetz, "Anatomy of a Conspiracy: With COVID, China Took Leading Role," *AP News*, February 14, 2021, https://apnews.com/article/pandemics-beijing-only-on-ap-epidemics-media-122b73e134b780919cc1808f3f6f16e8

10 Ibid.

Wolves on the Attack

In March 2020, as tensions continued to soar between the U.S. and China over the origin of the COVID-19, Zhao Lijian tweeted a fabricated story, "It might be the U.S. army who brought the epidemic to Wuhan," though later, Twitter posted a fact check tag.[11] Twitter, banned for nearly all people in mainland China, plays a prominent role in spreading China's outfacing propaganda. Yet, given the CCP's authoritarianism, state control, and hostile public posturing, it is inconceivable that 'Wolf Warrior' messaging could be disseminated without, at a minimum, tacit permission from China's highest leadership.[12]

In May 2020, Hua Chunying responded to the U.S. Department of State's support for Hong Kong protesters by saying, also on Twitter, "I can't breathe."

> Shanghai resident Hu Jian-Guo said, "I can't breathe at all. I am living in terror every single day…I have friends around me who can't breathe either, and many of them don't even have food and shelter." Another resident from Wuhan said, "We can't breathe, we can't even say anything and if we do, the police come and find us. The families of those who died of the Wuhan pneumonia cannot even speak out. They wanted to hold the government accountable but were not allowed to hold up signs or go out of their houses. So, can the Wuhan people breathe? Right now, people in Wuhan have no food to eat. Why isn't there anyone stepping in to help?"[13]

In an attempt to redirect the attention of Washington off China back home and just after President Donald J. Trump signed a bill to sanction China over the oppression of Uyghur Muslims in Xinjiang in June, Hua again took to Twitter to say, "The U.S. should enact an African American Human Rights Policy Act instead."[14]

These reactions are ironic since Twitter is, as a matter of fact, banned in China. "Long gone are the days when China is at the mercy of other countries," said Zhang Xiaoming, Deputy Director of the Hong Kong and Macau Affairs Office, at a press conference discussing the new national security laws imposed on Hong Kong in July 2020. When Zhang was asked about U.S. sanctions on Chinese officials, he replied, "This is the logic of bandits. It will give us an opportunity to show our determination and capacity to fight back."[15]

In response to Australia's investigation into the origin of the pandemic, the Editor-in-Chief of China's tabloid *Global Times* said on his Weibo account, "I feel it is a bit like

---

11   Zhao Lijian (@zlj517), "CDC was caught on the spot. When did patient zero begin in the US? How many people..." Twitter, March 12, 2020, 7:37 AM, https://twitter.com/zlj517/status/1238111898828066823

12   The Soufan Center, "IntelBrief: The Rise of 'Wolf Warrior' Diplomacy from China," *The Soufan Center*, July 17, 2020, https://thesoufancenter.org/intelbrief-the-rise-of-wolf-warrior-diplomacy-from-china/

13   Epoch Video, "Chinese Netizens to CCP: 'We Can't Breathe Any Better Either,'" *The Epoch Times*, June 11, 2020, https://www.theepochtimes.com/chinese-netizens-to-ccp-we-cant-breathe-any-better-either_3385024.html

14   Hua Chunying (@SpokespersonCHN), "The US should enact an African American Human Rights Policy Act instead of the Uyghur Human Rights Policy Act," Twitter, June 18, 2020, 2:50 AM, https://twitter.com/spokespersonchn/status/1273553545715789824?lang=en

15   Michael Smith and Emma Connors, "China's Wolf Warriors Take on the World," *Financial Review*, July 3, 2020, https://www.afr.com/world/asia/china-s-wolf-warriors-take-on-the-world-20200702-p558bs

chewing gum stuck to the soles of China's shoes. Sometimes you have to find a stone to rub it down."[16]

China's actions have further strengthened the West's determination to stand together. Members of the Five Eyes intelligence alliance (U.S., U.K., Canada, Australia, and New Zealand) have jointly criticized China's proposed national security law in Hong Kong.[17] NATO has also aptly noted that "China is coming closer to Europe's doorstep."[18]

The Chinese ambassador to the United Kingdom, Liu Xiaoming, another Wolf Warrior, had said the term "Wolf Warrior" was only a misunderstanding of Beijing's "independent foreign policy of peace." He tweeted, "Where there is a 'wolf', there is a warrior."[19]

Wumao and Google Censorship

Another term that has emerged and is used against China is Wumao, which literally translates as "fifty cents". "Wumao" describes the comments of the legions who post and follow other posts on social media.[20] Popular opinion suggests that Wumao refers to people paid by the Chinese Communist Party (CCP) to comment on China in a positive way, though PRC officials claim that the term is derogatory and is only used because the user cannot bear to see China in a positive light.[21]

On May 26, 2020, Palmer Luckey joined a few other observant internet users and announced to the world that YouTube was, in fact, deleting comments that contained the word Wumao. He made this known via his Twitter handle when he asked, "Who at Google [YouTube's parent] decided to censor American comments on American videos hosted in America by an American platform that is already banned in China?"[22] U.S. Senator Ted Cruz labelled the phenomenon as "very disturbing" and also asked why YouTube deemed it fit to be "censoring Americans on behalf of the CCP."[23]

In what has been called "the case of the vanishing comments," *Business Insider* also reported the same occurrence and even tested how fast they were deleted. They found that inserting the phrases "共匪" ("Communist Bandit") or "五毛" ("50 Cent Party") in

---

16   Tom Flanagan, "Chinese State Media Lashes Australia over Calls for Coronavirus Investigation," *Yahoo News Australia*, April 28, 2020, https://au.news.yahoo.com/coronavirus-chinese-state-media-slams-australia-over-investigation-calls-233415455.html

17   Sarah Zheng, "Why is the Five Eyes Intelligence Alliance in Beijing's Crosshairs?," *South China Morning Post*, June 20, 2020, https://www.scmp.com/news/china/diplomacy/article/3089564/why-five-eyes-intelligence-alliance-beijings-cross-hairs

18   DW, "NATO's Jens Stoltenberg Sounds Warning on China's Rise," *DW*, June 13, 2020, https://www.dw.com/en/natos-jens-stoltenberg-sounds-warning-on-chinas-rise/a-53795384

19   Liu Xiaoming (@AmbLiuXiaoMing), "Where there is a 'wolf', there is a 'warrior'," *Twitter*, May 24, 2020, 4:42 PM, https://twitter.com/AmbLiuXiaoMing/status/1264703262722273280

20   Renée DiResta, "For China, the 'USA Virus' Is a Geopolitical Ploy," *The Atlantic*, April 11, 2020, https://www.theatlantic.com/ideas/archive/2020/04/chinas-covid-19-conspiracy-theories/609772/

21   Keith Lamb, "What About 'Whataboutism' and 'Wumao'?," *CGTN*, September 7, 2020, https://news.cgtn.com/news/2020-09-07/What-about-whataboutism-and-wumao--TAJ7FJORkQ/index.html

22   The Economist, "Google's Removal of Anti-Beijing Comments Raises Political Eyebrows," *The Economist*, May 28, 2020, https://www.economist.com/united-states/2020/05/28/googles-removal-of-anti-beijing-comments-raises-political-eyebrows

23   Ted Cruz (@tedcruz), "This is very disturbing. Why is Google/Youtube censoring Americans....", Twitter, May 26, 2020, 7:58 AM, https://twitter.com/tedcruz/status/1265296230281854980?lang=en

comments caused them to be automatically deleted in under 30 seconds.[24]

When *Business Insider* reached out to the YouTube representative Ivy Choi, she responded saying, "This appears to be an error in our enforcement systems and we are investigating." It is crystal clear from all of these oddities that Beijing would stop at nothing to spread far and wide the policies of the CCP, even if that required force or censorship in another country. Google finally acknowledged that it was deleting comments made about the Chinese Communist Party.[25]

Conclusion

The strident voices of hostility spread by China's 'Wolf Warrior' diplomats have not helped increase China's standing. An October 2020 Pew Research study showed "Disapproval of how China has handled the COVID-19 pandemic also colors people's confidence in Chinese President Xi Jinping. A median of 78% say they have not too much or no confidence in him to do the right thing regarding world affairs, including at least seven-in-ten in every country surveyed."[26]

In Africa, the result is not much different. A recent analysis from the Global Engagement Center (GEC) suggests that Chinese COVID-19 disinformation in Africa pushed by CCP officials, was negatively received and rejected by the intended audience.[27] 'Wolf Warrior' diplomacy adds to Beijing's antagonism by other states. Beijing's methods make clear that the CCP would rather influence-pedal by interjecting itself into other states' media and immersing itself into international structures rather than respecting other states' sovereignty and following the rule of law.

What's at Stake?

First, Xi Jinping's 'fighting spirit' continues with rabid, and sometimes racist remarks. While some police are abusive, and suspected criminals have been killed, this also happens in China as well and is very different than forcibly rounding up and torturing millions of people.

Second, legions of civilian 'Wolf Warriors', inspired by their diplomatic counterparts, are emerging as China's heroes as they fire off scathing posts.

Third, if Google and other media giants are complicit in censorship coerced by China's leadership, our society has a much bigger problem.

---

24 Ben Gilbert, "YouTube has been Auto-Deleting Comments about China's Government-Sponsored Hacker Army, but Says it is 'An Error in our Enforcement Systems'," *Business Insider*, May 26, 2020, https://www.businessinsider.com/youtube-deleting-comments-china-government-sponsored-hacker-army-2020-5

25 Prasham Parikh, "YouTube Acknowledges Deleting Comments Made on China's Communist Party," *Mashable India*, n.d., https://in.mashable.com/tech/14289/youtube-acknowledges-deleting-comments-made-on-chinas-communist-party

26 Laura Silver, Kat Devlin, and Christine Huang, "Unfavorable Views of China Reach Historic Highs in Many Countries," *Pew Research Center*, October 6, 2020, https://www.pewresearch.org/global/2020/10/06/unfavorable-views-of-china-reach-historic-highs-in-many-countries/

27 The Soufan Center, "IntelBrief: The Rise of 'Wolf Warrior' Diplomacy from China," *The Soufan Center*, July 17, 2020, https://thesoufancenter.org/intelbrief-the-rise-of-wolf-warrior-diplomacy-from-china/

Chapter 5

Hostage Diplomacy and Extradition Treaties

Showing Who's Boss by Taking Foreigners Hostage

Introduction

China has taken an aggressive stance on the global stage that belies its 'win-win', 'responsible power' rhetoric, and insistence that Beijing is working in unity with other states. In January 2021, President Xi declared at the World Economic Forum, "We have been shown time and again that to beggar thy neighbor, to go it alone, and to slip into arrogant isolation will always fail. Let us all join hands and let multilateralism light our way toward a community with a shared future for mankind."[1] That statement sums up Xi's idea of a 'shared future' as long as it is under his authoritarian control.

The Chinese Communist Party (CCP) has seized and detained internal dissenters, journalists, and foreign nationals. In response, press organizations pulled most of their staff. Any remaining journalists were forced out of China and unable to photograph and report eyewitness news. With imprisonments, lack of transparency, and 'Wolf Warrior' rhetoric an alarm has sounded, questioning Beijing's 'benign' stance and spate of new national security laws.

Hostage Diplomacy

Hostage diplomacy is the act of taking prisoners for diplomatic purposes. Typically, hostages are taken and detained on charges that lack substance, like "threat to national security" and then used as pawns between countries as a bargaining chip. During instances of hostage diplomacy, little is known about why the individuals are chosen, though typically they are high enough profile for the country to take note. Simultaneously, a diplomatic dispute must be occurring between the country of the victim's citizenship and the hostage taker's country.

According to Lien-sheng Yang in the *Harvard Journal of Asiatic Studies*, hostage diplomacy, *zhizi*, was integral to ancient Chinese foreign relations approximately 2,500 years ago.[2] Although China has not used hostage diplomacy in each of its dynasties, recently its practice has gone hand-in-hand with its more assertive approach to foreign policy.

The Canadian Poster Examples

Although former Canadian diplomat, Michael Kovrig, has done nothing wrong, he has been held in a Beijing cell for more than 900 days as of June 2021. Though the reason for his arrest and that of his compatriot, Michael Spavor, Director of Paektu Cultural Exchange in North Korea, have not been stated, they appear to be hostages in an international dogfight related to the detention of Meng Wanzhou, business leader and Chief Financial Officer of the Chinese technology giant Huawei. The fates of these individuals are held in a nebulous balance where justice does not prevail and does not exist.

---

1   Economic Forum, "President World Xi Jinping's Speech at Davos Agenda is Historic Opportunity for Collaboration," *World Economic Forum*, January 25, 2021, https://www.weforum.org/press/2021/01/president-xi-jinping-s-speech-at-davos-agenda-is-historic-opportunity-for-collaboration/

2   Lien-Sheng Yang, "Hostages in Chinese History," *Harvard Journal of Asiatic Studies 15*, no. 3/4 (1952): 507–521, doi:10.2307/2718238

In December 2018, the "two Michaels" were taken into custody and later charged with spying.[3] While Meng is 'imprisoned' in her $15 million mansion, the two Michaels are in a moldy plaster cell, eating dirt-filled mush, designed to force confessions and crush the human spirit, all violating "international treaties such as the UN conventions on torture and on the minimum standards of treatment for prisoners, as well as China's own laws and the Chinese constitution."[4]

The Canadian government released a statement,[5]

> The arbitrary arrest or detention of foreign nationals to compel action or to exercise leverage over a foreign government is contrary to international law, undermines international relations, and has a negative impact on foreign nationals traveling, working and living abroad. Foreign nationals abroad are susceptible to arbitrary arrest and detention or sentencing by governments seeking to compel action from other States. The purpose of this Declaration is to enhance international cooperation and end the practice of arbitrary arrest, detention or sentencing to exercise leverage over foreign governments.

The Chinese Embassy in Canada responded to more than fifty countries decrying China's aggression saying that an "attempt to pressure China by using 'Megaphone Diplomacy' or ganging up is totally futile and will only head towards a dead end."[6]

Australians

Australians Yang Hengjun, an author and researcher, and Cheng Lei, Australian news anchor, were also caught in China's hostage diplomacy sting.

Australia's Minister of Foreign Affairs, Marise Payne, released a statement in February 2021 saying,[7]

> Today Australia stands with more than 55 of our international partners in our strong support for universal human rights and reiterates our resolute opposition to the use of arbitrary detention, arrest and sentencing to influence state-to-state relations.
>
> The practice of arbitrary detention is against international law. States must uphold all of their international human rights obligations, and that includes those owed to foreign and dual nationals within their jurisdictions.

---

3   The Economist, "Hostage Diplomacy – Only America can Break the Deadlock between Canada and China," *The Economist*, March 8, 2021, https://www.economist.com/the-americas/2021/03/08/only-america-can-break-the-deadlock-between-canada-and-china

4   Peter Humphrey, "The Cruel Fate of Michael Kovrig and Michael Spavor in China," *The Diplomat,* December 10, 2019, https://thediplomat.com/2019/12/the-cruel-fate-of-michael-kovrig-and-michael-spavor-in-china/

5   Government of Canada, "Declaration Against Arbitrary Detention in State-to-State Relations," *Government of Canada,* n.d., https://www.international.gc.ca/news-nouvelles/arbitrary_detention-detention_arbitraire-declaration.aspx?lang=eng

6   Embassy of the People's Republic of China in Canada, "Chinese Embassy Spokesperson's Remarks," *Embassy of the people's Republic of China in Canada,* February 16, 2021, http://ca.china-embassy.org/eng/sgxw/t1854178.htm

7   Minister for Foreign Affairs Senator the Hon Marise Payne, "Canada's Declaration Against the Use of Arbitrary Detention in State-to-State Relations," *Minister for Foreign Affairs,* February 15, 2021, https://www.foreignminister.gov.au/minister/marise-payne/speech/canadas-declaration-against-use-arbitrary-detention-state-state-relations

Australia will hold countries to account for their international commitments and their obligation to comply with international laws and practices.

We will continue to work with our international partners to counter this malicious activity.

Held Without Cause or With Trumped Up Charges

However, China is making it dangerous for any foreigner to travel to its cities. A few other cases of hostage diplomacy include Richard O'Halloran of Ireland, Nobu Iwatani of Japan, Kai Li and Sandy Phan-Gillis from the United States.

China warned the United States that its people visiting China were in danger. "China started issuing the warning this summer after the U.S. began arresting a series of Chinese scientists, who were visiting American universities to conduct research, and charged them with concealing from U.S. immigration authorities their active duty statuses with the People's Liberation Army."[8] John Demers, Justice Department's national security division noted, "If China wants to be seen as one of the world's leading nations, it should respect the rule of law and stop taking hostages."[9]

Conclusion

The United States closed China's Houston's consulate in July 2020 to stop military scientists and researchers from coordinating activities through the facility.[10] President Xi has cracked down in return. Other instances of China's reach include the pro-democracy movement in Hong Kong, Uyghur minority group dissenters, and anyone who might challenge Xi's authority or that of the Chinese Communist Party.[11]

What's at Stake?

First, hostage diplomacy is not compatible with international rule of law.

Second, China's shoot-from-the-hip 'Wolf Warrior' diplomacy is antithetical to its spoken commitment to inclusiveness and cooperation. The combination of collaborative propaganda and virulent bombastic speech continues as the CCP carries a carrot in one hand and a stick in the other.

Third, concerns regarding theft of intellectual property by People's Liberation Army (PLA) members led to the closure of China's Houston consulate. Countries have warned the CCP to stop their IP theft. The U.S. Embassy in Beijing warned Americans that any action taken on Chinese soil (for example, VPNs are illegal) could put them in danger.

---

8   Kate O'Keeffe and Aruna Viswanatha, "China Warns U.S. It May Detain Americans in Response to Prosecutions of Chinese Scholars," *The Wall Street Journal*, Updated October 17, 2020, https://www.wsj.com/articles/china-warns-u-s-it-may-detain-americans-in-response-to-prosecutions-of-chinese-scholars-11602960959

9   Edward Wong, "China Threatens to Detain Americans if U.S. Prosecutes Chinese Scholars," *The New York Times*, October 18, 2020, https://www.nytimes.com/2020/10/18/us/politics/china-us-threats-detain.html

10 Kate O'Keeffe and Aruna Viswanatha, "Chinese Diplomats Helped Military Scholars Visiting the U.S. Evade FBI Scrutiny, U.S. Says," *The Wall Street Journal*, August 25, 2020, https://www.wsj.com/articles/chinese-diplomats-helped-visiting-military-scholars-in-the-u-s-evade-fbi-scrutiny-u-s-says-11598379136

11 Stephen M. Walt, "Why 'Hostage Diplomacy' Works," *Foreign Policy*, February 17, 2021, https://foreignpolicy.com/2021/02/17/why-hostage-diplomacy-works/

Chapter 6

Economic Diplomacy
China's Spider Web in Africa Interwoven with Soft Power

Introduction

At a time when the International Monetary Fund and World Bank sought safe investments with long-term growth and profit potential and demanded austerity measures, China provided monies to African countries even when projects were not viable. African nations championed these loans as they eagerly looked to their new benevolent trading partner. Not wanting to be barred from capital investment, African countries sought avenues to gain strength and compete on the global market. African 'freedom' was often tied to the sentiment, "The fight against extreme poverty has become part of a wider objective in the fight against financial exclusion."[1] Thus, the China-Africa partnership was born.

China's Early Investment into Africa

While most analysts point to Beijing's emergence onto the world stage as an event occurring in the 21st-century, the People's Republic of China (PRC) expanded its influence much earlier. China took a significant step on the African continent in the 1970s when it agreed to finance the TAZARA Railway, stretching from Dar es Salaam, Tanzania to Kapiri Mposhi, Zambia, where its mines contained zinc, lead, and copper.[2] International banking institutions refused to finance this project because of its risk and no clear pathway to repay.

From 1964 – 1985, anti-colonialist Julius Nyerere served as the president of Tanzania, instituting socialism to counter Western democracy. As socialist-style work was initiated in Tanzania, productivity decreased. Socialism dis-incentivized hard work.

> The majority of the people did not want to work on communal farms because they had traditionally worked on their own farms owned by themselves or by individual families. The people did not work hard in ujamaa villages as much as they did on their own farms because they did not feel that the farms belonged to them but to the community…People expect to get profit from their investment in terms of labour and capital. Everything belonged to the community.[3]

In communal ujamaa villages, the people did not work as hard since everyone obtained the same return even when they did not contribute to the effort. When the government took away rights to own farmland and restricted private ownership, the goal of social equality might have been noble, but the people lost the desire to produce. Tanzania's goal of becoming a socialist society also led the West to limit foreign aid. This aid had also created dependencies that actually stifled self-reliance efforts.

Meanwhile, Nyerere negotiated with Chinese leaders who agreed to stay out of states' internal political and decision-making business and did not mind if repayment was made in natural resources, access to shipping, lucrative trade deals, and soft power. At the same

---

1   Mario La Torre and Gianfranco A. Vento, *Microfinance* (Basingstoke, England; New York: Palgrave Macmillan, 2006).

2   Mindat.org, "Carmarnor Mine, Kapiri Mposhi District, Central Provinec, Zambia," *Mindat.org*, n.d., https://www.mindat.org/loc-207411.html

3   Godfrey Mwakikagile, *Tanzania Under Mwalimu Nyerere: Reflections on an African Statesman* (New Africa Press, 2006).

time, China ensured that its human capital was used in the infrastructure building process. This requirement had many benefits for China, including:

1. allowing the PRC to train and deploy its people who needed jobs
2. solidifying the use of Chinese workers in its construction plans; African workers either needed to learn Chinese or be hired as laborers
3. allowing Beijing to plant seeds in countries in Africa with its soft power
4. providing China with resource, transportation, and market needs
5. exporting its loan process to countries worldwide when states were unlikely to return the investment in cash
6. offering countries with the newfound opportunity to develop their infrastructure

In Tanzania and Zambia, some even heralded the TAZARA Railway as "The Great Uhuru Railway"[4] or freedom railway in Swahili.[5] A *Wall Street Journal* article entitled "Red Guard Line Chugging into Africa" suggested that Mao Zedong's Communist Red Guards were descending into Africa to build the railroad.[6] They did, and China's link to Africa was chiseled. The loan deal was sealed in an agreement, and land-locked Zambians now

---

4   BBC News, "Letter from Africa: The Great Train Safari from Tanzania to Zambia," *BBC News*, November 18, 2019, https://www.bbc.com/news/world-africa-50420129

5   Ibid.

6   R. Vicker, "Red Guard Line Chugging into Africa", *Wall Street Journal*, September 29, 1967.

had access to a much-needed port. This method proved successful, as China found ways to reach out to countries with opportunities that were almost impossible to refuse.

In recent times, China found its way into Africa, making roots in various African countries.[7] Even now, though some say that the TAZARA is as 'slow as a bicycle', the legacy of the railroad and the commitment of China to trust African leaders is not lost. Many consider the railway the continent's opening, an opportunity for freedom and emancipation, though as it 'jolts and shakes', and is not widely used.[8]

China's 'soft power' reach has accumulated immense successes. Rather than using military interventions, invasive involvements, or politically-oriented requirements, China, instead, has taken a gentler tack through cooperation. These methods include international assistance, cultural exchanges, language training, media programming, and win-win diplomacy.[9]

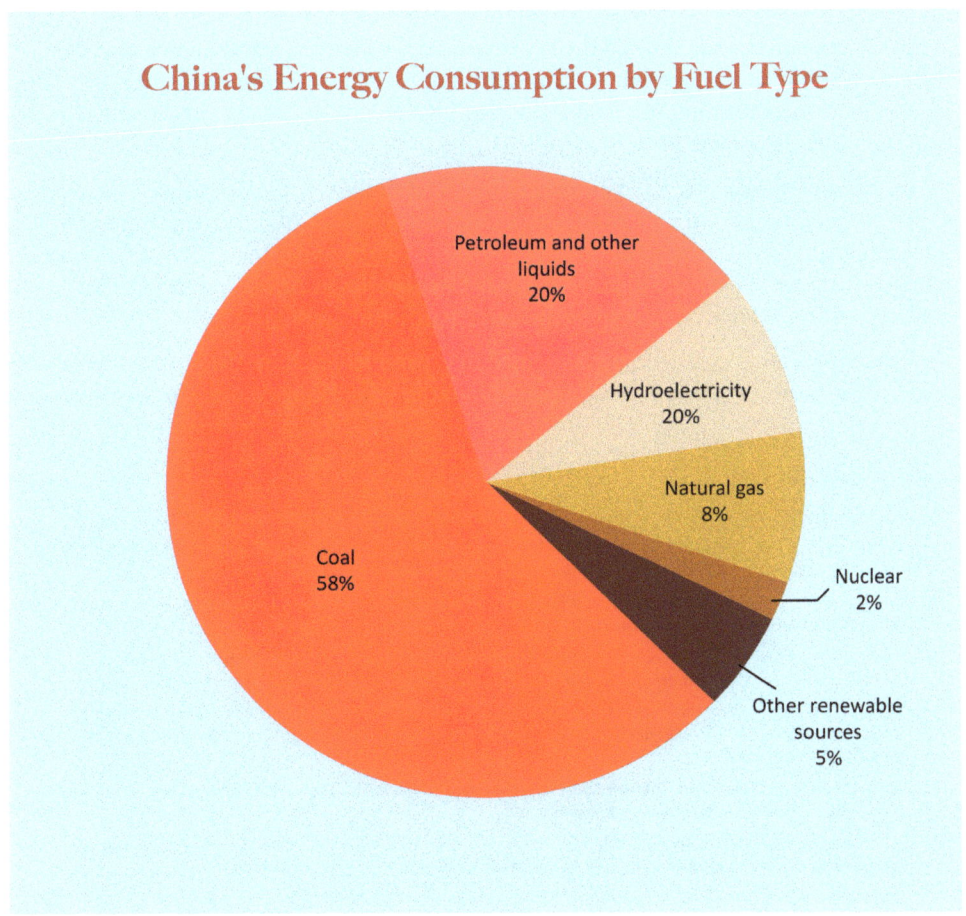

---

7   Chris Alden, "China in Africa," *Survival 47*, no. 3 (2006): 147-164.
8   BBC News, "Letter from Africa: The great train safari from Tanzania to Zambia," *BBC News,* November 18, 2019, https://www.bbc.com/news/world-africa-50420129
9   Michael Barr, *Who's Afraid of China?: The Challenge of Chinese Soft Power* (Zed Books, 2011).

Diplomatic channels were opened through social media as well. China made a place for itself on Twitter, choosing to hold some diplomatic talks and interviews on social media, rather than over CCTV.[10] This new avenue created tension between Chinese ambassadors and some African ministers on social media by late 2019.[11]

Outside of social media, Chinese private corporations sought avenues to boost Beijing's soft power in Africa and other regions.[12] One Chinese corporation uses the satellite TV provider, StarTimes, through its 10,000 Villages Project, which distributes satellite TV to impoverished communities in East, West, and Southern Africa.[13]

Another example of China's soft power tools in Africa is in the area of sustainable energy. Since Africa seeks dependable sources of electricity for its citizens, China has begun to exploit this need. Chinese state-owned corporations have built coal-powered plants to solve Africa's electricity problems, which has proven to be detrimental to the environment.[14]

In Kenya, citizens have voiced their concerns and made their stand known that they would not allow their environment to be destroyed by pollution from these proposed power plants. Some local communities and a group of NGOs have defeated a proposed Chinese-funded coal-fueled power plant.[15]

In the last few decades, China intensified its relationships with African states through the creation of the Forum on China Africa Cooperation (FOCAC).[16] According to The State Council of the People's Republic of China,[17] in 2014, more than 53% of Chinese foreign assistance funds were directed towards 51 countries in Africa and the African Union.[18] China became Africa's biggest trading partner in 2009.

Language is another tool that China used to expand its reach in Africa. In states across Africa, Mandarin is extensively incorporated into the school curriculum.[19] In Lakewood

---

10   Dan Hart and Asaf Siniver, "The Meaning of Diplomacy," *International Negotiation 1*, (2020): 1-25.

11   Cobus van Staden, "China-Africa 2020: Three Trends to Watch," *The ChinAfrica Project*, January 3, 2020, https://chinaafricaproject.com/analysis/china-africa-in-2020-three-trends-to-watch/

12   Wei Liang, "China's Soft Power in Africa: Is Economic Power Sufficient?," *Asian Perspective 36*, no 4 (2012): 667-692, https://www.jstor.org/stable/42704810

13   Jenni Marsh, "How China is Slowly Expanding its Power in Africa, One TV Set at a Time," *CNN Business*, Updated July 24, 2019, https://www.cnn.com/2019/07/23/business/startimes-china-africa-kenya-intl/index.html

14   Christoph Nedopil Wang, "Kenya's Lamu Coal Fired Power Plant," *Green Belt and Road Initiative Center*, 2019, https://green-bri.org/kenyas-lamu-coal-fired-power-plant-lessons-learnt-for-green-development-and-investments-in-the-bri

15   Alastair Leithead, "Row Over Chinese Coal Plant Near Kenya World Heritage Site of Lamu," *BBC News*, June 5, 2019, https://www.bbc.com/news/uk-48503020

16   Luka Powanga and Irene Giner-Reichl, "China's Contribution to the African Power Sector: Policy Implications for African Countries," *Journal of Energy*, (2019), https://doi.org/10.1155/2019/7013594

17   The State Council, The People's Republic of China, "China's Foreign Aid (2014)," *The State Council The People's Republic of China*, Updated July 10, 2014, http://english.www.gov.cn/archive/white_paper/2014/08/23/content_281474982986592.htm

18   China International Development Cooperation Agency, "China's Foreign Aid (2014)," *China International Development Cooperation Agency*, Updated August 9, 2018, http://en.cidca.gov.cn/2018-08/09/c_261152.htm

19   Aanu Adeoye and Idris Mukhtar, "China's Influence in Africa Grows as More Young People Learn to Speak Mandarin," *CNN Travel*, Updated April 10, 2019, https://www.cnn.com/travel/article/mandarin-language-courses-africa-intl/index.html

Premier School, Nairobi, Kenya, Mandarin is taught to the school children as a part of their subjects.[20]

Children in these countries will be joined by scores of those throughout the continent. Learning Mandarin is a move to help the Africans obtain jobs with Chinese companies and projects that have expanded throughout the continent. Mandarin is taught in schools across Kenya, integrated into the South African curriculum, and will be a compulsory subject in Uganda.[21] Teachers and trainers are trained at Confucius Institutes, a non-profit organization with the aim of promoting the Chinese language and culture around the world.

According to Illaria Carrozza, a researcher on China-Africa relations at the London School of Economics and Political Science, "The continued expansion of Chinese cultural institutes on the continent is part of the country's strategy to increase its influence in Africa through 'soft power'," adding that "Soft power, if successful, may lead to more influence -- as a matter of fact, it is more than just influence and rather works through persuasion and attraction."[22]

She warned that African leaders would do well to keep an eye on Chinese institutions as they spread throughout Africa and quickly both detect and curb any possible problems that may arise in the future. "Without degenerating into a witch-hunt, this is something African governments and institutions need to carefully consider in each individual case," Carrozza said.[23]

The presence of COVID-19 has proven to be another opportunity for China to cement its name in Africa. As African countries arm themselves against the virus, China has offered to be a reliable support system,[24] though defective equipment has proven to be a diplomacy problem as the inferior and ineffective PPE sent to Africa was in the news for weeks.[25] On the other hand, China is attempting to regain its status. In Ethiopia and Burkina Faso, the Chinese are working as advisers to the countries in the fight against the pandemic.[26]

At the same time, in Guangzhou, racism and discrimination against Africans were rampant. Video footage of mistreatment shown on the African continent offered a high-profile public relations catastrophe that confounded efforts to increase economic

---

20 Ibid.

21 Lynsey Chutel, "Mandarin is Putting in Extra Work to Catch Up with European Languages in South African Classrooms," *Quartz Africa*, February 5, 2019, https://qz.com/africa/1538828/south-africa-schools-now-taking-mandarin-chinese-language-lessons/

22 Aanu Adeoye and Idris Mukhtar, "China's Influence in Africa Grows as More Young People Learn to Speak Mandarin," *CNN Travel*, Updated April 10, 2019, https://edition.cnn.com/travel/article/mandarin-language-courses-africa-intl/index.html

23 Ibid.

24 Kwasi Gyamfi Asiedu, "China Wants to Help Africa Fight Coronavirus but Not Everyone is Welcoming," *Quartz Africa*, April 8, 2020, https://qz.com/africa/1834670/chinese-medical-aid-for-covid-19-in-africa-gets-mixed-support/

25 Jevans Nyabiage, "Could Quality Problems Unravel China's Coronavirus Mask Diplomacy in Africa?," *South China Morning Post*, August 11, 2020, https://www.scmp.com/news/china/diplomacy/article/3096908/africa-chinas-mask-diplomacy-will-rise-or-fall-quality-those

26 Kwasi Gyamfi Asiedu, "China Wants to Help Africa Fight Coronavirus but Not Everyone is Welcoming," *Quartz Africa*, April 8, 2020, https://qz.com/africa/1834670/chinese-medical-aid-for-covid-19-in-africa-gets-mixed-support/

engagement.²⁷ Africans were forcibly evicted from their homes and Chinese-owned McDonald's did not permit Black people to dine in their restaurant.²⁸ The Economic Freedom Fighters (EFF) included this statement:

> We condemn in the strongest possible terms the abuse and racist mistreatment of Africans living and working in China; particularly at a time when we should be supporting one another to recover from the Coronavirus pandemic. As the international community we must come together to fight the spread of Covid-19 instead of engaging in racial discrimination based on unfounded claims that Africans are spreading the virus.²⁹

Despite the xenophobic attacks on Africans living in China, it seems Africa is left with no choice but to embrace China's generous help in combating the global pandemic. Beijing's loans and soft power have gone a long way to win China a place in the heart of Africa's economy.

What's at Stake?

First, China constructed a spider's web over Africa, weaving its way into social, economic, and political circles. This interwoven entanglement will not go away and most Africans both want the infrastructure investment and are leery about the potential dangers.

Second, despite China's xenophobia, as long as countries vote with China in the United Nations, cooperate on trade policies, and push back against the West, each of these countries will be benefactors of vaccines, loans, and happiness with 'Chinese characteristics'.

Third, Chinese language, television, and cultural exchanges are deepening Beijing's commitment to the African continent. This societal interconnection will solidify over time, and relationships with the West will need to be strengthened or become less relevant.

---

27 Yun Sun, "COVID-19, Africans' Hardships in China, and the Future of Africa-China Relations," *Brooking Institute*, April 17, 2020, https://www.brookings.edu/blog/africa-in-focus/2020/04/17/covid-19-africans-hardships-in-china-and-the-future-of-africa-china-relations/

28 Ineke Mules, "African Expats Accuse China of Xenophobic Response to COVID-19 Resurgence Fears," *DW*, April 14, 2020, https://www.dw.com/en/african-expats-accuse-china-of-xenophobic-response-to-covid-19-resurgence-fears/a-53120697

29 Vuyani Pambo, "EFF Statement on China's Treatment of African Nationals," *PoliticsWeb*, April 12, 2020, https://www.politicsweb.co.za/politics/chinas-treatment-of-african-nationals-inhumane--ef

Xi Jinping Thought and China's Diplomacy | Part 3 | 129

Chapter 7

Death Metal Diplomacy

Taiwan's Sovereignty, Energy, and Not-So-Chinese Characteristics

Introduction

Power and influence do not emanate from state leaders. Young people have always been a powerful force for change. Culture wars emerge from groups who see a different way forward in attitudes, beliefs, and styles. Many of these cultural influences arise from the next awakened generation who see a new future for their tomorrow. In Taiwan, Korea, and Japan, artists, designers, anime creators, and vocalists offer expressive interpretations for the way forward.

In Taiwan, young people hold the key to their future. They will have a large stake in whether they are willing to fight for freedom and remain independent of China or be assimilated underneath China's social control and legal structure. Taiwanese citizens 15 to 30 years of age will be the ones primarily on the front lines of defense when China invades and declares war on the independent state. The question of assimilation into China or all-out war is not if, but when.

Taiwan, Independence, and Unification

In 1949, after the Chinese Civil War, one faction of Chinese leaders, the Kuomintang (KMT), left China's mainland for the island of Formosa, known as Taiwan where a new government was established. Taiwan has since grown into a prosperous country with thriving industries. Though the Taiwanese speak Chinese, there are numerous differences in culture and lifestyle. Yet, China claims Taiwan is part of its territory.

Chinese State Councilor and Defense Minister, Wei Fenghe, asserted, "If anyone dares to split Taiwan from China, the Chinese military has no choice but to fight at all costs for national unity."[1] For years, the Chinese Communist Party (CCP) has continuously threatened Taiwan through intimidation, provocative naval activities, and warplane overflights, warning that Taiwanese independence means war.[2] Yet, at the same time, according to *Reuters*, "Most Taiwanese people have shown no interest in being ruled by autocratic China, and have also strongly supported anti-government protests in Chinese-run Hong Kong."[3]

Death Metal Diplomacy

Freddie Lim is an elected politician by day and a vocal sensation by night. His following of young, exuberant Taiwanese are attracted to the messages contained in his songs. Lim is bright, charismatic, and patriotic, but additionally, he is the lead vocalist in the death metal band Chthonic, presenting his followers with the hope of Taiwanese independence.[4]

---

1   Chen Zhuo, "China Must Be and Will Be Reunified: Chinese Defense Minister," *China Military,* June 2, 2019, http://eng.chinamil.com.cn/view/2019-06/02/content_9520799.htm

2   Tony Munroe and Yew Lun Tian, "China Sharpens Language, Warns Taiwan that Independence 'Means War'," *Reuters*, January 8, 2021, https://www.reuters.com/article/us-china-taiwan/china-sharpens-language-warns-taiwan-that-independence-means-war-idUSKBN29X0V3

3   Reuters Staff, "China Says Will Deter Taiwan Independence but Seek Peaceful Ties," *Reuters*, March 4, 2021, https://www.reuters.com/article/us-china-parliament-taiwan/china-says-will-deter-taiwan-independence-but-seek-peaceful-ties-idUSKBN2AX05B

4   ABC, "Death Metal Diplomacy," *ABC*, Updated August 21, 2019, https://www.abc.net.au/foreign/death-metal-diplomacy/11409672

A captivating singer and political leader, he energizes his audiences in powerful concerts. He proclaims optimism while living in the shadow of an old enemy, one bent on war and operating on a war footing and proclaims: "Only if Taiwanese are united can we overcome all difficulties!"[5]

Taiwan is under increasing pressure to assimilate under China's umbrella as Beijing tightens its grip, strips Hong Kong of its independence, and declares its dominance in the South China Sea. Freddie Lim's band is banned from playing in Hong Kong due to his political messages.

Freddie Lim explains to Australia's news station broadcasters, "We have no choice. We can't give up because Taiwan is our home. We have nowhere to escape. We just have to try to protect our way of life."[6] Freddie Lim does this as a heavy metal vocalist, bringing power and cultural exchanges to energetic crowds to set the mood, while being a level-headed politician at the same time.[7]

Freddie Lim won his second legislative term in 2020 and was a founding leader of the New Power Party (NPP). From 2010 to 2014, Lim served as the chair of Amnesty International Taiwan.

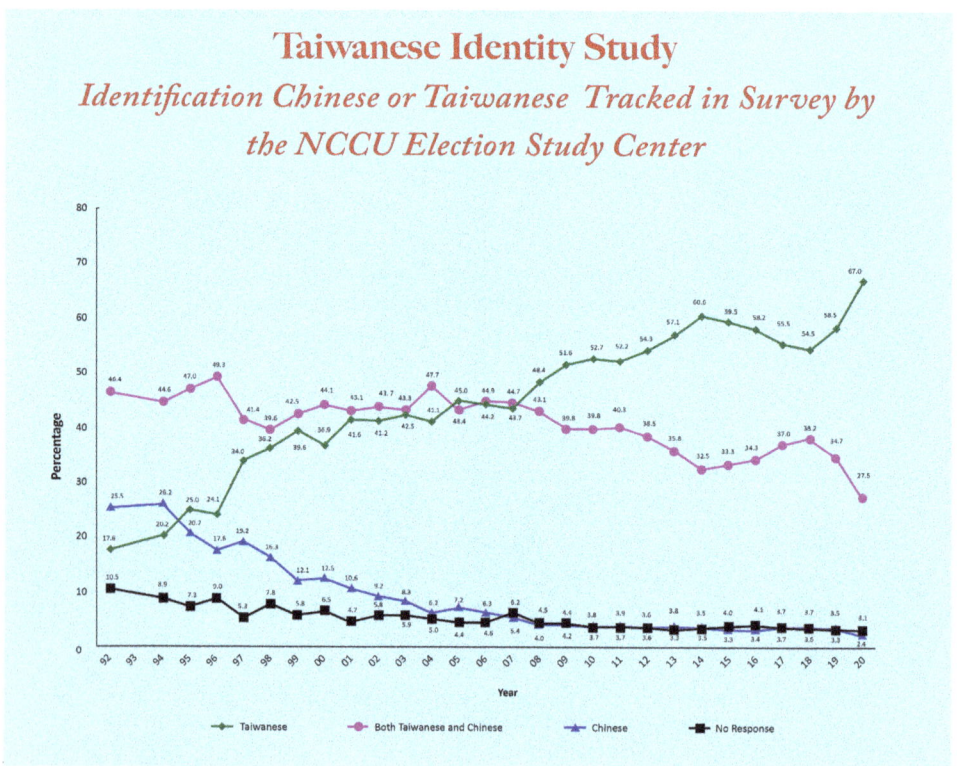

5 ABC, "Death Metal Diplomacy," *ABC*, Updated August 21, 2019, https://www.abc.net.au/foreign/death-metal-diplomacy/114096722

6 CHTONIC, "Australia ABC News Interview with CHTHONIC," *CHTONIC*, August 21, 2019, https://chthonic.tw/en/australia-abc-news-interview-with-chthonic/

7 Nelson Moura and Athena Chen, "Meet Freddy Lim, Taiwan's Heavy Metal Politician," *Vice*, December 10, 2015, https://www.vice.com/en/article/rkqx5e/meet-freddy-lim-taiwans-metal-politician

Conclusion

According to the National Chengchi University of Taiwan's Election Study Center January 25, 2021 research data, 64.3% of the people in Taiwan see themselves as Taiwanese only, while 29.9% see themselves as Taiwanese and Chinese, and 2.6% see themselves as Chinese only.[8] Freddie Lim is a vocal leader for Taiwan's freedom. The masses who attend his concerts energize a cultural movement that has inspired masses of Taiwanese citizens.

The future for Taiwan is uncertain. However, the people's sense of Taiwanese identity is growing. In large part, this is due to the cultural shifts on the island and China's abusive destruction to Hong Kong's lifestyle, liberty, and economy. The Taiwanese people, witnessing what is happening to Hong Kongers, do not desire to live in that kind of imprisonment, one marked by dictatorial and totalitarian social control.

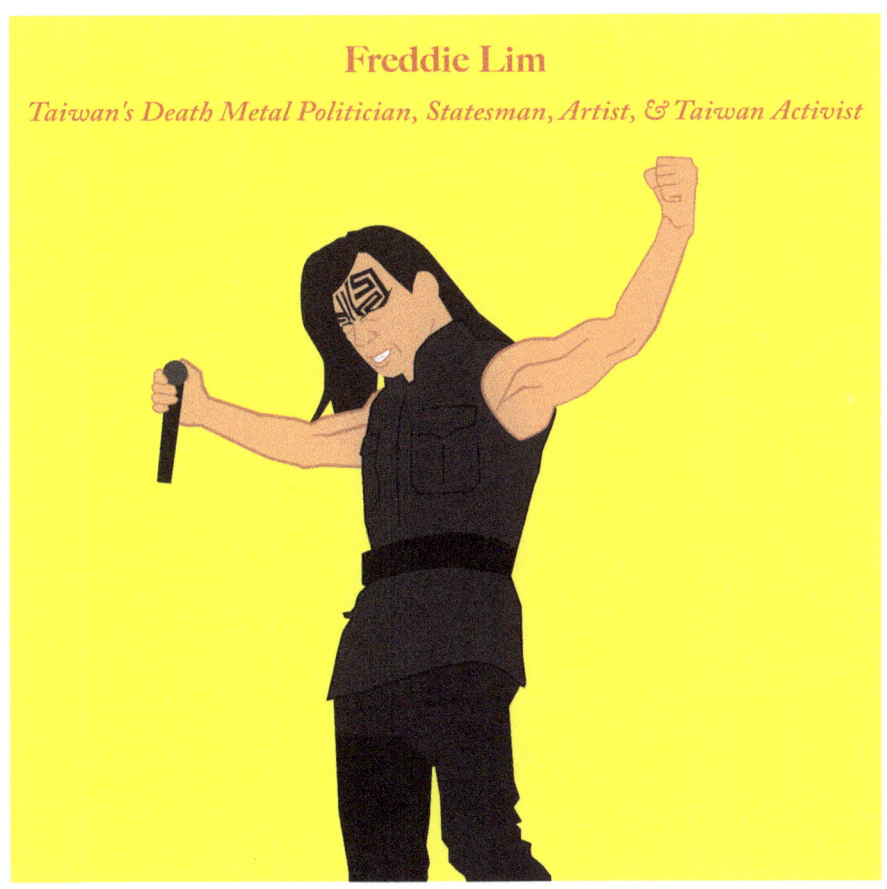

Freddie Lim
Taiwan's Death Metal Politician, Statesman, Artist, & Taiwan Activist

---

8 Election Study Center, National Chengchi University, "Changes in the Taiwanese/Chinese Identity of Taiwanese as Tracked in Surveys by the Election Study Center, NCCU (1992~2020.12)," *Election Study Center, National Chengchi University*, n.d., https://esc.nccu.edu.tw/upload/44/doc/6961/People202012.jpg

One person who voted for President Tsai Ing-wen in her 2020 landslide election win said, "If there's no Taiwan, I feel it will be very hard to have another place in Asia that has this degree of freedom…Only Taiwan that allows you to be that free for saying [what you want to say]."[9] In an October 2020 poll, released by The Taiwan Center for International Strategic Studies and the Taiwan International Studies Association, "More than 77 percent of Taiwanese say they are willing to fight for the nation in the event of an invasion by China."[10]

What's at Stake?

First, with China's disinformation campaign wielding fake news, the Chinese Communist Party is intent on shaping Taiwan's political discussion in any way it can.

Second, China's People's Liberation Army (PLA) has flown into Taiwan's airspace and sailed within its boundaries. The intimidation is unlikely to let up soon. Military experts suggest that within the decade, China will takeover Taiwan one way or another.

Third, the Death Metal Diplomacy of Freddie Lim and the youth of Taiwan will decide Taiwan's future as they question the costs required for their freedom and the freedom of all who come afterward.

---

9   Randy Mulyanto, "Generation Next: How the Young are Changing Taiwan's Politics, *Al Jazeera*, March 27, 2020, https://www.aljazeera.com/news/2020/3/27/generation-next-how-the-young-are-changing-taiwans-politics

10 Ibid.

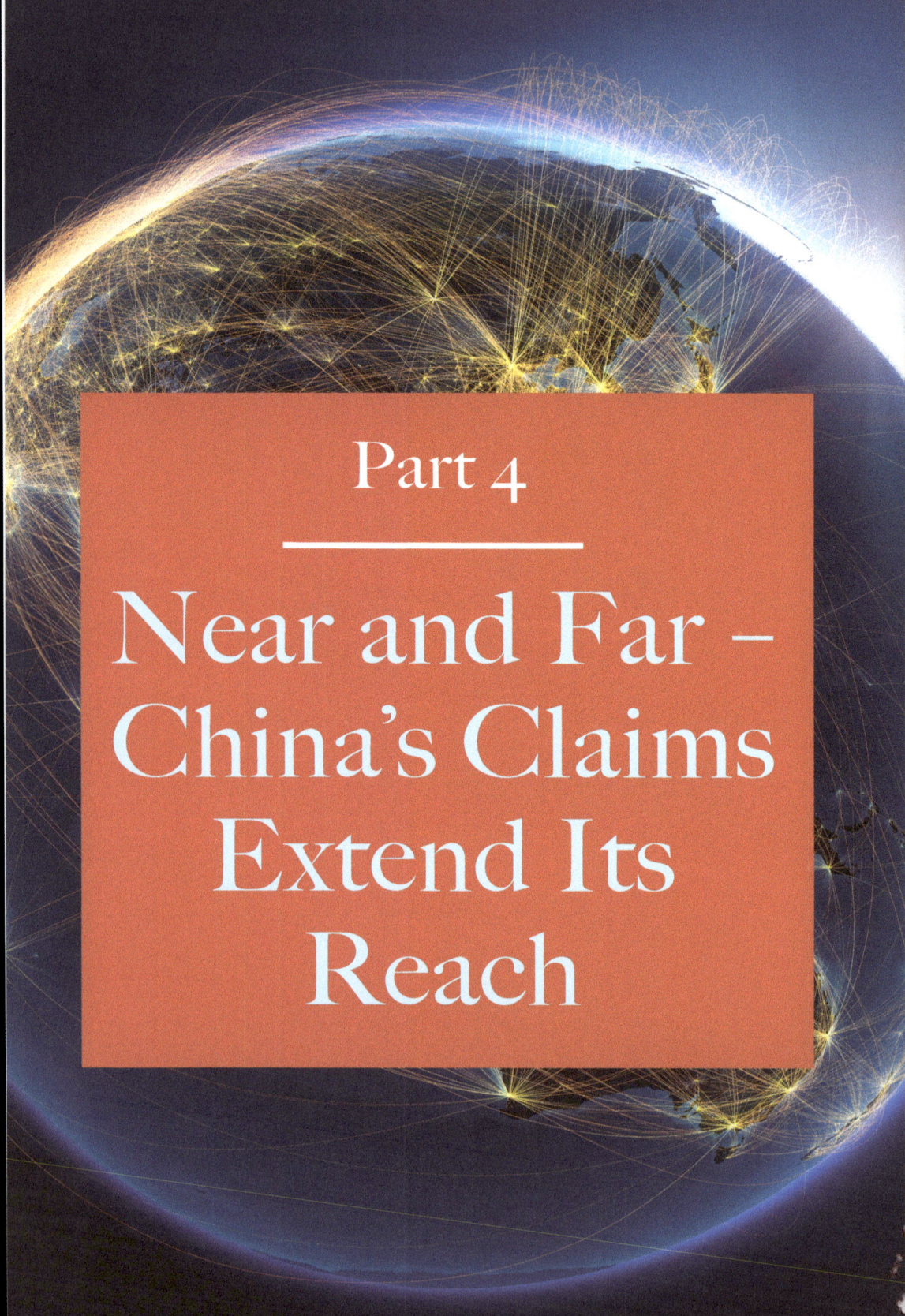

Part 4

Near and Far – China's Claims Extend Its Reach

Reaching Beyond the Asian Continent

Two thousand years ago, the Silk Road extended across Eurasia with exotic products packed on camels and wheeled behind horses. Stretching from China to Europe and back, long journeys transported silk, porcelain, tea, tobacco, spices, jade, and silver across the Central Asian countries, "the Stans", and down south toward India. The Roman Empire filled its treasure chests as did the Emperors of the Chinese dynasties. Over time, war, conquest, religion, and greed closed this thoroughfare. Thereafter maritime transit became predominant.

As World War II ended, countries from Southeast Asia to Africa gained independence, seeking money to rebuild. After the Cold War, global peace seemed increasingly likely, and investments helped economies grow. China began extending its reach to Africa and Southeast Asia, seeking avenues to prosper. Deng Xiaoping spearheaded a massive diplomacy effort that connected China to the world. For the next twenty years, while increasing its productivity and GDP in year-after-year growth, China regrouped as it worked to resolve internal problems. Hu Jintao, seeking to resolve China's poverty, expanded these efforts, and Xi Jinping took the baton, solidifying his paramount role for life as he expanded China's Belt and Road.

In 2021, Xi Jinping announced that China realized a "historic leap" to eliminate poverty, transforming his country with a "great rejuvenation". Extending olive branches around the world, China extended its reach to 140 countries, employing its citizens globally through its Belt and Road Initiative. With win-win diplomacy and a commitment to help countries thrive, the stage was set for China to step in with money, notably as America stepped out.

With great success, strongman coercion, and militaristic power also came mounting fear. The peaceful rhetoric elucidated at the World Economic Forum and other high-profile events failed to ameliorate the tensions of governments that could not pay and were being forced to give up land, rights, and natural resources. Thus, while China extended its reach globally, employing its citizens, and securing its stake in the world, the Chinese Community Party's global militarization introduced friction, anxiety, and distrust, leading global citizens to ask, "Does the world want to live under an authoritarian, Communist regime and relinquish liberty, freedom, and individualism?"

Chapter 1

Benevolent Development or Nefarious Goals

Will China Rise Peacefully or Change the Rules-Based Order?

Introduction

Prevailing international theory suggests that China will not rise peacefully. John Mearsheimer argues that the U.S. and China will engage in an intense security competition which will lead others who are fearful of Beijing to attempt to contain the CCP's power. China is aware of this attempt at containment and will work harder in asserting its economic, political, and military control. Mearsheimer explains in his book, *The Tragedy of Great Power Politics,* that China will seek to establish regional hegemony while ensuring that no other great power establishes a foothold.[1]

This security competition is why China will attempt to push the United States out of the South and East China Seas, past the first island chain to the second island chain as soon as it can. Thus, China will pursue both hard and soft power through the teaching of Socialist principles and Mandarin in schools while controlling the media and fusing economic power through the purchase of sectors with its products. China announced its "Made in China 2025",[2] which is designed to establish China's manufacturing, technical, and economic superiority.

Wolf Warrior Superiority and Aggression

Chinese propaganda relentlessly pumps out media content heralding China's successes and superiority. Other pomp and fanfare include its military drills, announcements of new military equipment, and successes in having virtually no deaths due to COVID-19. The internal promotion of China's power has led to a vast network of Wolf Warriors who take to their 'Twitter fingers' to blast social media threats and to level vicious chastisements on anyone who speaks against China.

Meanwhile, the more aggressive the Wolf Warriors get towards political and thought leaders, the more fearful states become, spiraling into an inevitable conflict. In a heightened state of possible conflict, particularly in the South or East China Seas, carefully crafted political and military signaling is essential to avoid a misinterpretation or an unintended consequence.

Internal and External Threats and Anxiety

China's Belt and Road Initiative, which has spread into 140 countries, is seen as Beijing's quest to bring countries into its web. However, the successes Beijing promised have not materialized and, with the pandemic, countries are in worse shape than before. Delays, overcharges, and setbacks have caused state leaders and their citizens to question the value of projects within their countries. Predatory lending practices, waste, fraud, and coercion have made leaders uneasy, not to mention corruption and illicit deals.[3]

---

1. John Mearsheimer, *The Tragedy of Great Power Politics* (W. W. Norton & Company, 2014).
2. The State Council of the People's Republic of China, "Homepage," *The State Council of the People's Republic of China,* May 25, 2021, http://english.www.gov.cn/2016special/madeinchina2025/
3. Elaine K. Dezenski, "Below the Belt and Road," *Foundation for Defense of Democracies,* May 6, 2020, https://www.fdd.org/analysis/2020/05/04/below-the-belt-and-road/

While China builds friendships in numerous states, conflict is rampant. Chinese manufacturing facilities have been threatened and Chinese workers and locals are being harassed in Italy, Myanmar, and Pakistan. Competition with Chinese workers in Kyrgyzstan led to anxiety and anger. In one incident, a hundred workers were involved in fist fighting at a local mine.[4]

The rules-based order has also been shaken by predatory practices, infrastructure transfer, and violation of laws. As China becomes more powerful and exerts more pressure on countries to pay on their debt, fear is likely to lead to defense mechanisms and conflict. China's goals may be benevolent, though as it threatens, particularly in the post-pandemic

environment, anxiety and action are likely.

Profile on Afghanistan

At the May 2021 "China + Central Asia" foreign ministers' meeting, Chinese Foreign Minister Wang Yi exclaimed that China was in "staunch support" and ready to play a role in Afghanistan's "stability and development".[5] The opportunity posed by the United States' withdrawal opened the door for Beijing to seize the moment to play a more pivotal role,

---

4   Xinhua, "18 Chinese Workers Injured in Kyrgyzstan Clash," *China Daily*, Updated January 10, 2013, http://www.chinadaily.com.cn/world/2013-01/10/content_16103803.htm

5   Ministry of Foreign Affairs of the People's Republic of China, "Wang Yi Talks About Eight-Point Consensus and Ten Outcomes of "China + Central Asia" Foreign Ministers' Meeting," *Ministry of Foreign Affairs of the People's Republic of China*, May 12, 2021, https://www.fmprc.gov.cn/mfa_eng/wjdt_665385/wshd_665389/t1875501.shtml

though cautious of the possibilities of war, chaos, and violent extremism.[6] Starting with China's military inroads into Afghanistan, Xi Jinping's Belt and Road Initiative cautiously moved into the region to traverse Afghanistan with trainloads of manufactured goods and raw materials for its factories. However, the Chinese Communist Party (CCP) is also concerned about Afghani extremist groups targeting China in the past.

China and Afghanistan share a very short border, which is a source of opportunity and concern. However, China is unlikely to leave its future to chance. Beijing may use this opportunity for greater military engagement in and around Afghanistan. If so, this effort would necessitate the diversion of forces from Beijing's other hotspots (Hong Kong, Taiwan, South China Sea, India, Myanmar, Vietnam, and Xinjiang). Consequently, it may take more work to protect against militants than to befriend its leadership. China's oppression of the Uyghur Muslims alone may require China to expend more political capital than a billion dollars in infrastructure support could offer.

Located in a strategically important location, Afghanistan is sandwiched between Pakistan and Iran, two close economic allies of Beijing. China's southern rail transportation route could provide another corridor through Afghanistan though the terrain is rugged. Meanwhile, mounting evidence suggests that Chinese ground troops have been operating inside Afghanistan, detailed by *Reuters*, *Wion News*, and the *Military Times*. They report that Beijing plans to play a significant role in Afghanistan's future. However, military officials in Washington and Kabul remain silent, possibly due to a geopolitical arrangement.[7]

China increased its involvement in Afghanistan providing investment capital of $240 million USD between 2001 and 2013, increasing this after the 2014 NATO troop withdrawal, and authorizing a $100 million MOU for BRI investment projects in 2016.[8] In preparation for a timely opportunity, China built a freight rail link to Afghanistan's border. The bounty in natural resources is the approximately $1 trillion USD of copper, coal, iron, gas, cobalt, mercury, gold, and lithium in the world's largest, unexploited reserves. Beijing seeks to acquire these while negotiating the exclusive right to extract copper from the Mes Aynak mine.

China is also working to strategically connect its interests with Kyrgyzstan, Tajikistan, Afghanistan, and Iran through the 2,100 km, $2 billion USD Five Nations Railway Corridor (FNRC).[9] The planning processes are complete, though China's fruitless record of on time project completion, implementation delays, and increased project costs stymie

---

6 James Griffiths and Nectar Gan, "As US Pulls Out of Afghanistan, China Sees Opportunities – and Potential for Chaos," *CNN*, Updated May 14, 2021, https://www.cnn.com/2021/05/14/china/china-afghanistan-central-asia-mic-intl-hnk/?hpt=ob_blogfooterold

7 Shawn Snow, "Chinese Troops Appear to be Operating in Afghanistan, and the Pentagon is OK With It," *Military Times*, March 5, 2017, https://www.militarytimes.com/news/pentagon-congress/2017/03/05/chinese-troops-appear-to-be-operating-in-afghanistan-and-the-pentagon-is-ok-with-it/

8 Federica Lai, "China's Economic Influence in Afghanistan in a Belt & Road Context," *Asia Power Watch*, December 1, 2020, https://asiapowerwatch.com/chinas-economic-influence-in-afghanistan-in-a-belt-road-context/

9 Regional Economic Cooperation Conference on Afghanistan, "Five Nations Railway Corridor," *Regional Economic Cooperation Conference on Afghanistan*, n.d., http://recca.af/?page_id=2086

completion.[10] Like with the 2018 launch of the China-Afghanistan Air Corridor, "non-delivery on economic commitments and investments have come to be understood as characteristic of Chinese projects…maybe motivated by China's desire to crowd out other stakeholders, rather than a genuine commitment to a mutually beneficial arrangement."[11]

Conclusion

An ancient Chinese poem reads, "To see a thousand miles, one should ascend another story."[12] One country after another in one continent after another, China climbs another story.

At a 2015 meeting in South Africa, Xi Jinping explained, "Nothing, not even mountains or oceans, can separate people with shared goals and vision."[13] "South Africa, the Rainbow Nation, is a shining pearl on the southern tip of the African continent…Over the past 17 years, our friendship and cooperation has grown from a small boat to a gigantic vessel, riding the wind and waves and forging ahead toward greater mutual benefit and common development. China-South Africa relationship is at its best in history."[14]

Beijing has made concerted effort to forge relationships with leaders worldwide. Cooperation is the mantra as China draws more countries into the Belt and Road Initiative. As Xi Jinping said in a speech he gave in Zimbabwe, the Chinese people have a saying that goes "when everybody adds firewood, the flames will rise high."[15] The question is whether adding more firewood would bring countries around the world together or ignite all of the Belt and Road countries in flames.

Anti-U.S. sentiments partly fuel China's push for land and resources, while seeking primacy in 5G connectivity and digital currencies like the e-RMB. Competition stokes the fire. With the pandemic starting in Wuhan, China, many countries are piling on the firewood.

What's at Stake?

First, at the crossroads of Asia, Afghanistan is in a strategically important location. Its interior contains valuable resources as Russia, the U.S., and China are well aware. The economic potential and the opportunity to create a viable thoroughfare, regional connectivity, and financial independence through the rugged terrain fits the goals of China's

---

10 Harsh V. Pant and Premesha Saha, "Mapping the Belt and Road Initiative," RF, n.d., https://www.orfonline.org/wp-content/uploads/2021/02/BRI-report-FINAL.pdf

11 Ibid.

12 Guangyu Huang, *Theory of Mountainurbanology* (Springer, 2021).

13 Xi Jinping, "A Rainbow of Friendship and Cooperation with Greater Splendor," *Ministry of Foreign Affairs of the People's Republic of China*, December 5, 2015, https://www.fmprc.gov.cn/mfa_eng/wjdt_665385/zyjh_665391/t1328502.shtml

14 Ibid.

15 H.E. Xi Jinping, "Let the Flower of China-Zimbabwe Friendship Bloom with New Splendor," *Ministry of Foreign Affairs of the People's Republic of China,* November 30, 2015, https://www.fmprc.gov.cn/mfa_eng/wjdt_665385/zyjh_665391/t1328506.shtml

Belt and Road Initiative. China is poised to capture the bounty, though surviving in Afghanistan has not worked well for Russia or the U.S. as history suggests.

Second, with $1 trillion in untapped resources on the line, China seeks to secure Afghanistan, especially since the U.S. is pulling out, though tensions, instability, and terrorism pose significant threats. Furthermore, China's lack of transparency, secretive decision-making, and coercive political influence pose problems for countries involved in BRI projects.

Third, John Mearsheimer explains that the United States will not tolerate China as a peer competitor, adding that the goal of actors in international politics is survival.[16] As China rises to great power status, other staes are likely to feel threatened, increasing the possibility of conflict.

---

16 Rodion Ebbighausen, "Mearsheimer: 'The US Won't Tolerate China as Peer Competitor," *DW*, September 23, 2020, https://www.dw.com/en/chinas-rise-and-conflict-with-us/a-55026173

Chapter 2
A Global Trading Network
Shipping Transport and Trade Breakdowns

Introduction

Trade between countries requires a mechanism for transport – air, land, or sea. Overland is time-consuming, and air is expensive in per-unit cost. Thus, the most cost-effective method is via the sea. According to the United Nations Conference on Trade and Development (UNCTAD) Review of Maritime Transport 2020, approximately 80 percent of global trade by volume and 70 percent of trade by value is transported by sea.[1]

More than one-third of all global shipping goes through the South China Sea. Dependent upon the Strait of Malacca, commercial centers in East Asia move products through to the Indian Ocean, Arabian Sea, and points north through the Suez Canal and west and south to Africa. China, Taiwan, Japan, and South Korea are heavily reliant on the South China Sea and the Strait of Malacca. More than 60 percent of China's trade flows travel by sea, most through the South China Sea.

Pandemic Impact

During the pandemic, lockdowns and quarantines changed the needs of global citizens to a greater dependence on home products, relying predominantly on online purchases. Immediate needs for health and sanitation products produced a high demand. This pressure set in motion increased production capacities along with quick delivery. Supply chains adapted to the increasing need and global consumption. One consequence of the magnitude of this demand on production and distribution is that the Maritime Silk Road grew in dimension and purpose as China ramped up its channels for manufacturing and delivery. However, this burgeoning need also brought to the fore the need to protect workers on ships and in distant harbors.

The pandemic posed challenging and volatile circumstances for trade. Disruptions to business and life required businesses to readjust their production and distribution models. Against the backdrop of illness and death, those companies able to rapidly adapt and respond were the clear winners. Some companies diversified their portfolio of products and services while also seeking the most efficient sales platforms and delivery mechanisms.

China used the period of the pandemic to grow economically, technologically, and militarily. Beijing ramped up its manufacturing and shipping sectors to sell PPE, supplies, food, and technology at a faster pace. According to the United Nations Industrial Development Organization, China's manufacturing picked up speed, accelerating to an even higher rate of growth.[2] Surging with the high demand, any loss China had at the beginning of the pandemic it has quickly regained.

---

1   United Nations Conference on Trade and Development (UNCTAD), "Review of Maritime Transport 2020," *United Nations Conference on Trade and Development (UNCTAD),* 2020, https://unctad.org/system/files/official-document/rmt2020_en.pdf

2   United Nations Industrial Development Organization, "World Manufacturing: One Year of COVID-19," *United Nations Industrial Development Organization*, June 21, 2021, https://www.unido.org/news/world-manufacturing-one-year-covid-19

The following table shows economic growth, along with the percent change in imports and exports for comparison.³

World Growth and Trade (Annual Percent Change)							
Region/Country	Economic Growth			Imports		Exports	
	2019	2020	2021	2019	2020	2019	2020
United States	2.3	-5.4	2.8	-0.3	-9.8	-0.5	-13.3
China	6.1	1.3	8.1	-0.4	-0.9	0.5	-4.5
Europe	1.5	-7.3	3.5	0	-12.1	-0.2	-13.3
Japan	0.6	-4.5	1.9	0.9	-4.9	-1.6	-11.3

Trade Wars and Imbalances

While maritime trade fell during 2020, demand remained high with certain products, though overall sales dropped. Along with decreased personal incomes globally, China's trade wars with Australia, Taiwan, and the United States weakened sectors of the maritime economy. Among trade balance losers was Australia, as China rejected Australian wine, barley, lobsters, meat, timber, coal, and cotton.⁴

---

3 CPB Netherlands Bureau for Economic Policy Analysis, "CPG World Trade Monitor August 2020, CPB *Netherlands Bureau for Economic Policy Analysis*, October 23, 2020, https://www.cpb.nl/en/cpb-world-trade-monitor-august-2020

4 BBC, "Australia Accuses China of Undermining Trade Agreement," *BBC*, December 9, 2020, https://www.bbc.com/news/world-australia-55240898

In March 2021, maritime trade hit another sticking point when China began rejecting Taiwanese pineapples leading Taiwan to promote a campaign for its citizens to buy pineapples and create new foods and drinks, calling them 'freedom pineapples'.[5] Using a chapter from China's trade aggression against Australia and their #FreedomWine, Taiwan created #pineapplesolidarity and #FreedomPineapple in response to China's bullying.[6] Accusing China of unfair trade practices, Taiwanese President Tsai Ing-wen kicked off a social media campaign called, "pineapple challenge" to purchase pineapples and counter China, while also urging "like-minded friends around the globe to stand with #Taiwan & rally behind the #FreedomPineapple".[7]

To deescalate U.S.-China tensions, the two countries signed an agreement in January 2020 that China would increase its merchandise imports from the U.S. while the U.S would cut its tariffs on imports from China by one-half. This agreement did not materialize. The net result was that trade decreased in 2020.[8]

With the decrease in U.S. trade with China, patterns of commerce changed as American manufacturers and raw material suppliers searched for new sources. The U.S. Census Bureau's May 2021 report highlights America's growing deficit of exports over imports of $27.7 billion from the same time in 2020. "Year-to-date, the goods and services deficit increased $83.2 billion, or 64.2 percent, from the same period in 2020. Exports decreased $21.0 billion or 3.5 percent. Imports increased $62.2 billion or 8.5 percent."[9]

To demonstrate the perils of putting national prosperity in the hands of a competitor, the global trading network realized its overwhelming dependence on semiconductor chips, which is heavily reliant on China's manufacturing sector for production. The resulting reduction of high demand items added a new rivalry with Beijing since microchips are needed in cars, cell phones, and houseware products.

Chinese manufacturers have been stockpiling chips, resulting in leaders calling China a "techno-autocracy", causing a surge in demand and exposing America's weakness in its supply chains.[10] In response to the inability to manufacture cutting-edge products, a new push among democratic states has rallied support to ramp up semiconductor fabrication.[11]

---

5   Helen Davidson, "Taiwanese Urged to Eat 'Freedom Pineapples' after China Import Ban," *The Guardian*, March 2, 2021, https://www.theguardian.com/world/2021/mar/02/taiwanese-urged-to-eat-freedom-pineapples-after-china-import-ban

6   Brian Hioe, "Freedom Pineapple Campaign Illustrates Identity Consolidation in Response to Chinese Bullying," *New Bloom*, n.d., https://newbloommag.net/2021/03/03/freedom-pineapple-campaign/

7   Explained Desk, "Explained: Why the Latest China-Taiwan Clash Kicked off the #FreedomPineapple Campaign," *The Indian Express*, Updated March 22, 2021, https://indianexpress.com/article/explained/china-taiwan-clash-freedom-pineapple-campaign-7238679/

8   Shannon Tiezzi, "China, US Sign 'Historic' Trade Deal," *The Diplomat*, January 16, 2020, https://thediplomat.com/2020/01/china-us-sign-historic-trade-deal/

9   U.S. Department of Commerce, "Monthly U.S. International Trade in Goods and Services, March 2021," *U.S. Census Bureau*, May 4, 2021, https://www.census.gov/foreign-trade/Press-Release/current_press_release/ft900.pdf

10   Nick Wadhams, "Biden Putting Tech, Not Troops, at Core of US-China Strategy," *Bloomberg*, March 1, 2021, https://www.bloomberg.com/news/articles/2021-03-01/biden-putting-tech-not-troops-at-center-of-u-s-china-strategy

11   Jenny Leonard, Keith Laing, Josh Wingrove, and Bloomberg, "In Call with CEOs, Biden Doubles Down on a $50 Billion Plan to Invest in Chips," *Fortune*, April 13, 2021, https://fortune.com/2021/04/13/in-call-with-ceos-biden-doubles-down-50-billion-plan-invest-chips/

In June 2021, a $250 billion infrastructure, research, and manufacturing bill was passed, aimed at countering China's technology control.[12]

Environmental Consciousness

The global trading network has also been influenced by an increased awareness and demand for environmentally sustainable practices. In the air, land, and sea, transportation routes and vehicle emissions have come under fire for their pollution, fuel use, and waste. Increased regulation, varying by country, added complexity to maritime trade. Additionally, corporate and citizen consciousness regarding the reduction of carbon emissions, greenhouse gases (GHGs), and refuse dumping presented challenges to the global waterways and their ecosystems. Renewable energy mechanisms continue to be developed for airplanes, land vehicles, and marine vessels. Green transition targets allow governments and businesses to work toward attainable goals in decreasing overall carbon footprints.

Conclusion

Trade is the lifeblood for any country. To grow an economy, governments need to sell more than they buy. Trade fuels economic growth while providing employment to domestic workers. High employment levels lift the standard of living, increase purchasing power, and

---

12   John D. McKinnon, "Senate Approves $250 Billion Bill to Boost Tech Research," *The Wall Street Journal*, June 8, 2021, https://www.wsj.com/articles/senate-approves-250-billion-bill-to-boost-tech-research-11623192584

offer families the chance to access technology, transportation, and services. Countries seek infrastructure, connectivity, and education to increase employability in higher-paying jobs.

Trade flows and sectors tell much about a country. Countries often have an abundance of agricultural, manufacturing, natural resources, or services that can be traded with other states. Yet, in 2020, much of this flow of goods and services halted. The pandemic crippled economies with people out of work, sectors closed to production, and imports outpacing exports. Thus, 2020 resulted in a contraction of trade worldwide. China capitalized on its production capacity and distribution networks, allowing it to become more prosperous as the rest of the world suffered. However, 2021 is expected to rebound many economies with an improved outlook and thereby support countries, companies, and families in taking their next steps in the recovery.

What's at Stake?

First, trade expansion is necessary for an economy. Moreover, countries must produce or have reliable access to basic components, as evidenced by China's stockpiling of chips, which resulted in shortages and the disruption of production lines. This wake-up call reminded the U.S. that it must keep abreast of items vital to manufacturing and production sectors of the economy.

Second, trade and employment keep the economy moving. An open, competitive, and flexible economy ensures growth by providing the conditions from which businesses can be developed and made profitable. Enhancements in trade expanded in the 21st century with hyper-globalization. The future will depend on open markets and free trade areas where emerging and developing economies can participate and compete on a more equal footing.

Third, the increase in deliveries of coal has risen steadily. In nearly twenty years, China increased its coal and iron ore imports from 121.7 million tons to 1.3 billion tons for more than a thousand percent increase, with a global market share of nearly 50 percent.[13] What is at stake is the increase in global carbon emissions from one country that dominates over all others in GHGs in the meantime, China has pledged to begin reduction starting in 2030.

---

13 Clarksons Research, "US-China Trade: Coming Back Into Focus," *Clarksons Research*, June 26, 2020, https://clarksonsresearch.wordpress.com/2020/06/26/us-china-trade-coming-back-into-focus/

Chapter 3

Financial Transactions

Renminbi or Chinese Digital Money as a Global Currency?

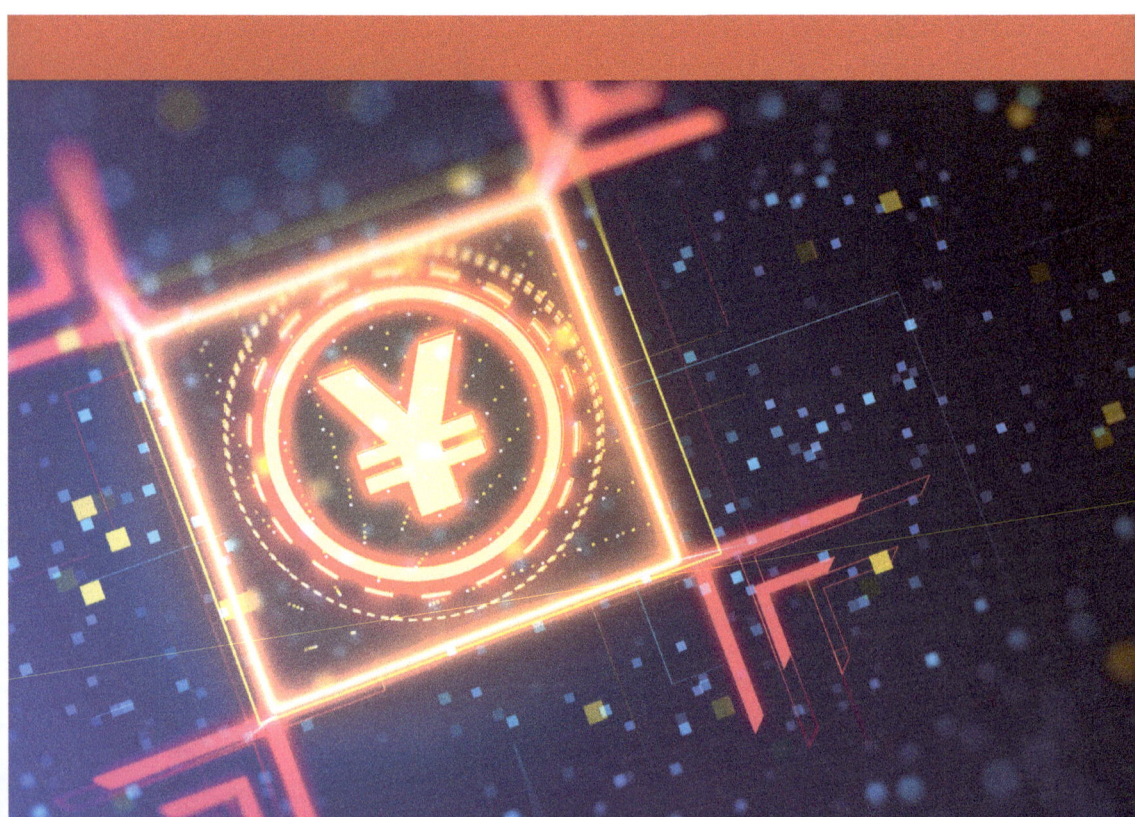

Introduction

Aspirationally, China's development of a global digital currency is well underway. In addition to building Alibaba's online hubs, mirroring those of Amazon, the foundation for the digital yuan has been constructed. Furthermore, while Amazon is an online giant and Alibaba has played 'follow the leader', the gap between the two is narrowing. The institution of the digital yuan, through Alipay, Alibaba's mobile payment service with ele.me, Tmall supermarket, and Hema on-demand, online grocery delivery is transforming the payment processing for its one billion person customer base.[1] Alibaba owns 30% of one of China's largest banks involved with the test development of the digital yuan. One reason for Alibaba's potential to overtake Amazon is China's digital currency.

Furthermore, with Beijing's worldwide construction and resource acquisition projects, greater circulation of the yuan, and the inroads China is developing in international bodies, the probability of the RMB replacing the USD is steadily increasing.[2] The flow of capital through Chinese banks is aiding in this development. In 2021, seven of China's private and state-owned banks have signed on to test the digital yuan.[3]

Xi Jinping began his quest to implement the Chinese yuan as soon as he begun his presidency. At a 2013 forum in Kazakhstan, President Xi announced the need to enhance local monetary circulation. Xi stated,[4]

> China and Russia have already had sound cooperation on settling trade in local currencies, and have gained gratifying results and rich experience. There is no reason not to share this good practice with others in the region. If our region can realize local currency convertibility and settlement under current and capital accounts, it will significantly lower circulation cost, increase our ability to fend off financial risks and make our region more competitive economically in the world.

A few goals of China's 13th Five-Year Plan are to benefit Chinese industries, expand export markets, increase investments abroad, drive China's role in the international economic agenda, set new international standards, and encourage the international use of the RMB.[5]

---

1   Hu Yue and Denise Jia, "China's Digital Yuan Gets Access to Alibaba's 1 Billion-Person User Base," *Caixin*, May 11, 2021, https://www.caixinglobal.com/2021-05-11/chinas-digital-yuan-gets-access-to-alibabas-1-billion-person-user-base-101709359.html

2   Kimberly Amadeo, "How the Yuan Could Become a Global Currency," *The Balance*, Updated November 30, 2020, https://www.thebalance.com/yuan-reserve-currency-to-global-currency-3970465

3   Chen Jia, "Digital RMB Trial Expands to Include First Private Bank," *China Daily*, Updated May 11, 2021, http://www.chinadaily.com.cn/a/202105/11/WS6099bb86a31024ad0babd0b1.html

4   H.E. Xi Jinping, "Promote Friendship Between Our People and Work Together to Build a Bright Future," *Ministry of Foreign Affairs of the People's Republic of China*, September 8, 2013, https://www.fmprc.gov.cn/mfa_eng/wjdt_665385/zyjh_665391/t1078088.shtml

5   Katherine Koleski, "The 13th Five-Year Plan," *U.S.-China Economic and Security Review Commission*, February 14, 2017, https://www.uscc.gov/research/13th-five-year-plan

The United States Efforts Toward a Digital Currency

In the summer of 2021, the United States Federal Reserve released a white paper exploring the potential move toward a centrally driven digital currency, which will lag behind the tested digital yuan. Efforts have been ongoing with the Fed observing and adapting to the interplay of AI, bitcoin, marketplaces, and consumer confidence. The goal is to ensure faith and confidence in the dollar while integrating the currency into banking, credit card, and other payment systems.[6]

Facebook famously announced its version, called Libra, which originally faced strong opposition from regulators; some who initially supported and financed the opportunity stepped back.[7] However, Facebook has come back with a new coin called Diem that is pegged to the dollar.[8]

Other countries have also attempted to create digital currencies like Ecuador with its dinero electrónico and Venezuela with its petro.

Cryptocurrency

These moves are on the heels of the volatility of bitcoin and other online monetary transactions. Yet, cryptocurrencies have a very different model, limited supply, and do not have a central bank.[9] The rise and fall have made huge winners and dramatic losers. This was partly due to significant sales from major players like Elon Musk and environmental consciousness of the energy required to mine the currency.

Concerns have been raised about the energy consumption required, increased carbon emissions, 11.5 kilotons of e-waste, and climate change issues, though some cryptocurrencies have no significant impact.[10] Some estimate that bitcoin uses as much energy per year as all of Argentina. Furthermore, since 65% of the miners are located in China, which uses coal-fired energy sources, the impact is environmentally damaging.[11]

Central Bank Digital Currency

Despite uncertainties surrounding the digitization of currency, approximately 80% of the world's central banks have begun research into developing alternatives, including

---

6   Jeff Cox, "The Fed This Summer Will Take Another Step in Developing a Digital Currency," *CNBC*, May 20, 2021, https://www.cnbc.com/2021/05/20/the-fed-this-summer-will-take-another-step-ahead-in-developing-a-digital-currency.html

7   Ryan Browne, "Here's Why Regulators Are So Worried about Facebook's Digital Currency," *CNBC*, September 19, 2019, https://www.cnbc.com/2019/09/19/heres-why-regulators-are-so-worried-about-facebooks-digital-currency.html

8   Ryan Browne, "Facebook-Backed Diem Aims to Launch Digital Currency Pilot Later This Year," *CNBC*, April 20, 2021, https://www.cnbc.com/2021/04/20/facebook-backed-diem-aims-to-launch-digital-currency-pilot-in-2021.html

9   MacKenzie Sigalos, "Bitcoin's Wild Price Moves Stem from its Design – You'll Need Strong Nerves to Trade It," *CNBC*, May 19, 2021, https://www.cnbc.com/2021/05/19/why-is-bitcoin-so-volatile.html

10 Nathan Reiff, "What's the Environmental Impact of Cryptocurrency?," *Investopedia*, Updated May 13, 2021, https://www.investopedia.com/tech/whats-environmental-impact-cryptocurrency/

11 Ibid.

a Central Bank Digital Currency (CBDC).[12] In this light, China will be the first major economy to launch a CBDC, called the Digital Currency Electronic Payment, alternatively called DCEP, digital yuan, e-RMB, or Chinese digital currency.

Concerns Raised Over China's Digital Currency

Concerns about decoupling the U.S. from the global financial system and fracturing the geopolitical, financial markets are valid, but not imminent. Nevertheless, there should be a pragmatic concern along with a strategy of observation, standards, and measured development that is trusted in the international system. There is no doubt that China's DCEP is a star that is rising fast. Furthermore, there is the risk of global digital authoritarianism that may hit like a tidal wave and inhibit freedom to speak, live, and participate on all levels. With China controlling the access to your money, if you do not obey its anti-religion, anti-human rights, and anti-freedom rules, you may not be able to make purchases. Thus, fintech experts and policymakers must be aware of the opportunities and challenges of the digital yuan as it flows into market spaces and across borders.[13]

The Chinese government has been accused of invading individual privacy, tracking, facial recognition, and surveillance. The CCP states that this tracking is to protect the country and prevent corruption, money laundering, and tax evasion. However, it can also

---

12 Benoît Cœuré, "CBDCs Mean Evolution, Not Revolution," *BIS*, October 20, 2020, https://www.bis.org/speeches/sp201021a.htm

13 Alex Capri, "How China's Digital Currency Could Fracture Global Finance," *Forbes*, April 29, 2021, https://www.forbes.com/sites/alexcapri/2021/04/29/how-chinas-digital-currency-could-fracture-global-finance/?sh=1fdbe51056da

stop individuals from purchasing items, travel, and food. Particularly for those who are targets for China's political attacks or danger perceived by the government, global citizens need to be cautious about using Beijing's digital currency.

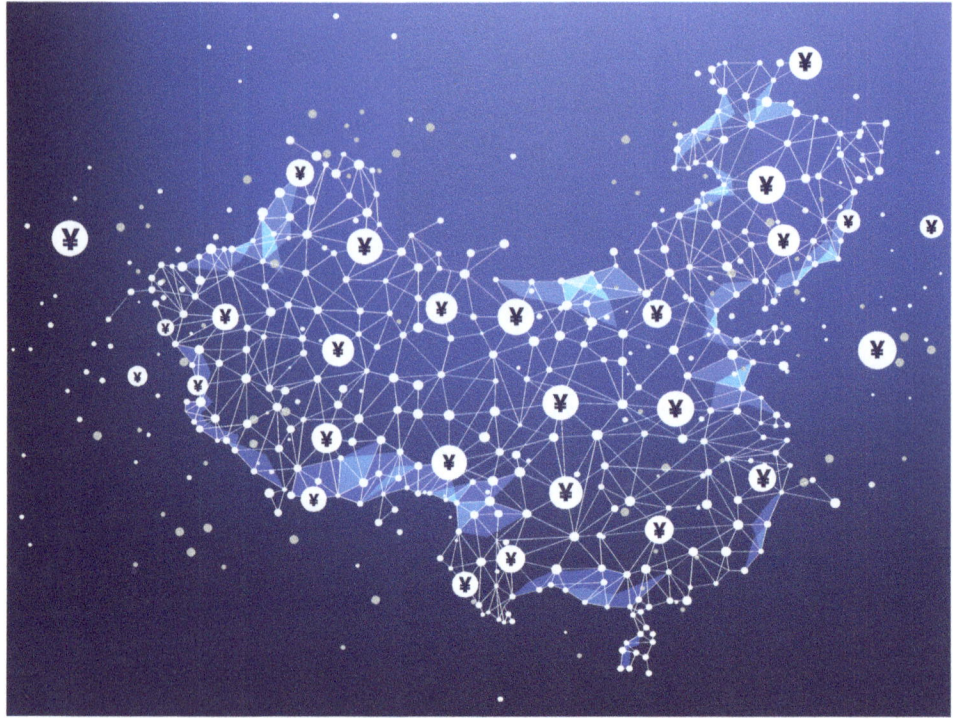

Conclusion

China has not been silent in its goal to supersede and circumvent the U.S. dollar. Currency domination is at the forefront of China's geopolitical objectives. The People's Bank of China (PBOC) officially announced its commitment to creating a digital currency in 2014 and presented its three-year plan in 2019 for its rollout.[14]

The 2021 use of digital currencies in Shenzhen, Suzhou, Xiong'an, and Chengdu was just a test, though also a significant move toward China's wider use both within the country and outside.[15] China continues to invest in technology, R&D, and infrastructure for its digital currency and will undoubtedly play a critical role in the CCP's domestic affairs and geopolitical pursuits.[16]

---

14 Arjun Kharpal and Evelyn Cheng, "Bitcoin Price Surge May Be Driving Up Interest in China's Digital Yuan, Central Bank Says," *CNBC*, April 2, 2021, https://www.cnbc.com/2021/04/02/chinas-digital-yuan-interest-could-be-due-to-bitcoin-surge-pboc-says.html

15 David Pan, "Just a Test: China Central Bank Confirms Digital Yuan Mobile App Trials," *Coindesk*, April 20, 2020, Just a Test: China Central Bank Confirms Digital Yuan Mobile App Trials - CoinDesk

16 Mercy A. Kuo, "China's Digital Currency: Implications for the US," *The Diplomat*, March 31, 2021, https://thediplomat.com/2021/03/chinas-digital-currency-implications-for-the-us/

What's at Stake?

First, China's digital currency offers the CCP access and control of its people by monitoring all expenditures, tracking locations, and the ability to giveth or taketh away. Giving the CCP considerable authority for surveillance and oversight, China's digital currency keeps track of inputs and outflows in real time for all individuals and corporations working in China through distribution channels and payment interfaces.[17]

Second, there is significant geopolitical risk of circumventing the U.S. dollar that is used in 90% of all transactions and 60% of foreign exchange reserves, though, in 2021, the renminbi (RMB) makes up only 2% of global payments.[18] In addition to raising the stakes on the global financial system, China's digital dominance would empower a country that lacks transparency, controls its people, violates human rights, and ravages the environment. Furthermore, Beijing sells arms to despot leaders and evades U.S. sanctions by accepting Iran's oil.[19]

Third, China has used this moment with the instability of cryptocurrencies to "seize the opportunity" and push out its digital currency Blockchain and Blockchain+ as soon as possible.[20] President Xi called for his top-down approach including regulation, investments, and innovation teams to lay the foundation for a China-led digital world, take advantage of the marketplace to become the global innovative leader, and improve China's financial standing.

Fourth, though there is a big difference between digital currencies and cryptocurrencies, like blockchain technology, centralized authority, and user identification, many have mentally linked the two and have raised concerns about freedom, privacy, and criminal activity. The centralization part is what worries individuals whose accounts could be seized and access to money refused.

---

17 Mercy A. Kuo, "China's Digital Currency: Implications for the US," *The Diplomat,* March 31, 2021, https://thediplomat.com/2021/03/chinas-digital-currency-implications-for-the-us/

18 Evan Freidin, "The E-RMB: China's Digital Currency in the COVID-19 Era," *Foreign Brief,* May 27, 2020, https://foreignbrief.com/asia-pacific/china/the-e-rmb-chinas-digital-currency-in-the-covid-19-era/

19 Ibid.

20 William Foxley, "President Xi Says China Should 'Seize Opportunity' to Adopt Blockchain," *Coindesk,* October 25, 2019, https://www.coindesk.com/president-xi-says-china-should-seize-opportunity-to-adopt-blockchain

Chapter 4

China's Largest Banks and State-Owned Enterprises

Understanding China's Socialist Businesses and Beijing's Control

Introduction

To understand China it is essential to understand their state-owned enterprises. Rather than individuals solely controlling companies in China, the Chinese government has the power to change, break up, or eliminate enterprises. China's banks are also powerful, not just in lending but controlling citizen and company cash flow. With Belt and Road Initiative projects, Chinese banks like the China Development Bank, China Construction Bank, Industrial & Commercial Bank of China, Export-Import (EXIM) Bank of China, People's Bank of China (PBOC), and Agricultural Bank of China provide loans that are secretive or lack transparency.

Belt and Road Initiative Loans

China's infrastructure project funding has undisclosed rules and requirements which are hidden from the people. These practices have outraged many country's internal leaders, particularly in Asia and Africa. Credit is extended with no apparent strings attached. China's credit allocations, often with an opaque debt, have grown, shrouded in secrecy, and hiding unreported debt levels that could grow significantly higher.[1] Beijing's lack of oversight is welcomed by leaders who do not want the encumbrance of Western regulatory, political, labor, and environmental protections.

On the other hand, the conditions under which the International Monetary Fund (IMF) and World Bank loans are granted often require years of feasibility studies and approvals that Beijing does not demand. There is no need for the project to be viable or financially successful either since China will take the assets or resources it desires if payments cannot be made. Delays and additional costs add to the loans, which sometimes balloon out of proportion. However, loan approvals are quick.

China's growth has far surpassed underdeveloped countries with initially similar economic circumstances.[2] Economic reforms paved the way, including liberalized foreign trade, growth in capital assets, relaxed state control, educating a broader population base, and the ability for citizens to create private businesses and form rural collective enterprises. China's engagement strategy included offering billions in loan guarantees to countries like Laos, Pakistan, Tajikistan, Kyrgyzstan, Mongolia, Djibouti, Ethiopia, Nigeria, and Zambia with a high probability of imperial debt servitude.

China's Involvement in Global Banking Systems

China has become increasingly involved in the World Bank's lending arm, the International Bank for Reconstruction and Development (IBRD). In 2021, China also had more than 6% of the voting power in the International Monetary Fund (IMF). The IBRD and IMF provide loans to developing countries, the IBRD for infrastructure development and the IMF for financial stability. As China seeks to take a greater stake in global power, it has increased its presence as a stakeholder in international financial leadership.

---

1 Weizhen Tan, "China's Loans to Other Countries are Causing 'Hidden' Debt. That May be a Problem," *CNBC*, June 11, 2019, https://www.cnbc.com/2019/06/12/chinas-loans-causing-hidden-debt-risk-to-economies.html

2 Jinghai Zheng, Arne Bigsten, and Angang Hu, "Can China's Growth Be Sustained? A Productivity Perspective," *World Development 37*, no. 4(2009), 874-888.

According to the *New York Times*, China created a World Bank of its own. With dozens of countries on board for support, the China-led Asian Infrastructure Investment Bank (AIIB) has taken a leadership position in the global economy and is poised to promote its global ambitions. Meanwhile, the World Bank continues to lend to China, the second leading economy, leading to questions about why U.S. taxpayers are subsidizing loans to China.[3] In 2021, China was second in taking loans from the World Bank, next only to India.[4]

China created new rules that place limits on foreign banks to control Chinese currency and give its banks a competitive edge in the international lending marketplace.[5] Beijing wants to ensure that its citizens do not take their personal money out of the country, which they can increasingly control with its digital yuan and authority over currency values.

Seeking greater autonomy in global lending and commerce, while breaking free from its dependence on the dollar, China has rapidly moved to take greater control of international markets and systems. For years, China has sought to develop alternatives to the Western-dominated SWIFT system, taken seats in prominent global governance institutions, and created avenues to access payments, buying decisions, and taxable wealth.[6]

Global Leadership and Investment

Investment is one of the core secrets of China's overwhelming success. China has loaned money to more than three-fourths of the countries on the planet.

4 of the top 5 largest banks belong to China

3 of the top 5 companies belong to China

4 of the top 5 largest ports belong to China

5 of the top 8 internet companies belong to China

6 of the top 10 social media sites are Chinese

Banks

The banking and financial institutions are laid out clearly in the Green Belt and Road Initiative document.[7]

- Chinese financial institutions, including the Silk Road Fund, China Development Bank, and China Exim Bank,

---

3   Yukon Huang, "Why is the World Bank Still Lending to China?," *Carnegie Endowment for International Peace*, January 15, 2020, https://carnegieendowment.org/2020/01/15/why-is-world-bank-still-lending-to-china-pub-80830

4   Jason Beaubien, "Flush with Cash, China Continues to Borrow Billions from the World Bank," *NPR*, January 31, 2019, https://www.npr.org/sections/goatsandsoda/2019/01/31/689960866/flush-with-cash-china-continues-to-borrow-billions-from-world-bank

5   Keith Bradsher, "China Puts Limits on Foreign Banks, Worrying Businesses," *New York Times*, April 2, 2021, https://www.nytimes.com/2021/04/02/business/china-foreign-banks.html

6   Sune Sorensen, "China is Opting Out of US-Run Financial System," *Coindesk*, April 30, 2021, https://www.coindesk.com/china-is-opting-out-of-us-run-financial-system

7   Green Belt and Road Initiative Center, "Belt and Road Initiative Quick Info," *Green Belt and Road Initiative Center*, n.d., https://green-bri.org/belt-and-road-initiative-quick-info/

- Multilateral financial institutions, such as the Asian Infrastructure and Investment Bank (AIIB) and the New Development Bank (NDB),
- Commercial banks, such as the Industrial and Commercial Bank of China (ICBC), China Construction Bank, or the Agricultural Bank of China,
- Chinese regulators, such as the State Council that oversees all ministries and special commissions in China and establishes the overall blueprint for overseas investments (ODI) from China, or the China Banking and Insurance Regulatory Commission (CBIRC) that approves ODI projects by Chinese banks and oversees China's insurance industry,
- Chinese central bank – the People's Bank of China (PBoC), which establishes monetary policy and manages foreign exchange reserves,
- Chinese ministries, such as the Ministry of Commerce (MOFCOM), which approves certain OFDI projects; the National Development and Reform Commission (NDRC), which develops OFDI goals and policies; the Ministry of Foreign Affairs (MFA) that administers China's diplomatic relations and policies; and the Ministry of Ecology and Environment (MEE) that co-issues environmental guidelines.

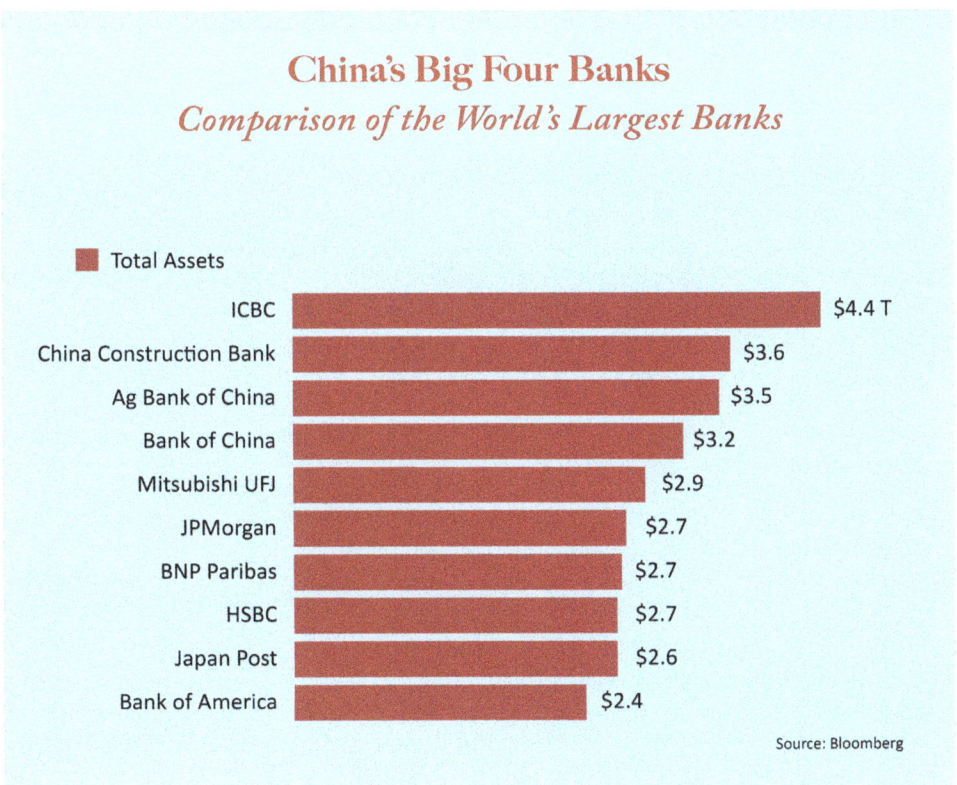

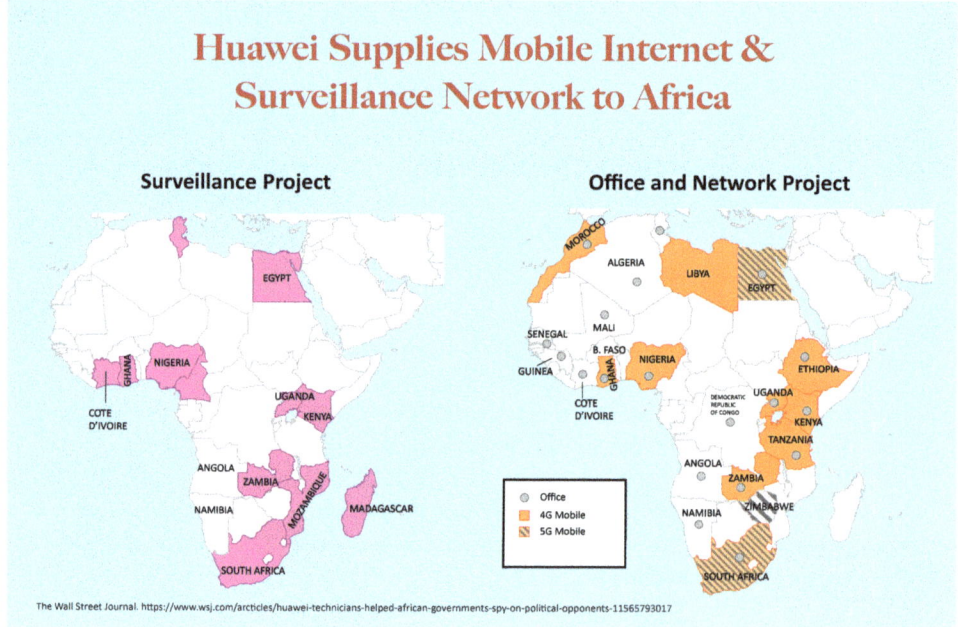

The Wall Street Journal. https://www.wsj.com/arcticles/huawei-technicians-helped-african-governments-spy-on-political-opponents-11565793017

Profile on Debt: Zambia

Although Zambia was in debt trouble before the coronavirus, with debts in excess of $23 billion, in 2020, the African state defaulted on its payments during the pandemic.[8] State leaders worry that Zambia's inability to pay will require the country to turn over its assets to China. Zambia started by turning over its media outlet, *ZNBC*, to Chinese authorities. Its national electricity company, ZESCO, is next, with power outages to consumers amounting to more than 80% of every day, and plans in place for the Chinese takeover.[9] Rate hikes introduced excessive fees that residents cannot afford.[10] Now, citizens worry that they will lose access and resources from Zambia's copper mines and international airport.[11] Zambia's sovereign debt is expected to rise to 96% of the country's

---

8   William Orr, "The Curse of the White Elephant: The Pitfalls of Zambia's Dependence on China," *Global Risk Insights,* December 1, 2020, https://globalriskinsights.com/2020/12/the-curse-of-the-white-elephant-the-pitfalls-of-zambias-dependence-on-china/

9   China Go Abroad, "China to Take Over ZESCO – Africa Confidential," *China Go Abroad,* n.d., http://www.chinagoabroad.com/en/article/china-to-take-over-zesco-africa-confidential

10 Kate Bayliss and Gabriel Pollen, "The Power Paradigm in Practice: A Critical Review of Developments in the Zambian Electricity Sector," *World Development 140,* (2021), retrieved from: https://www.sciencedirect.com/science/article/pii/S0305750X20304861

11 Ibrahim Anoba, "China is Taking Over Zambia's National Assets, but the Nightmare is Just Getting Started for Africa," *African Liberty,* September 10, 2018, https://www.africanliberty.org/2018/09/10/china-is-taking-over-zambia-national-assets-but-the-nightmare-is-just-starting-for-africa/

2020 GDP.[12] Simply serving its loan costs in interest, the country expends nearly 25% of its entire national budget.[13] Among causes for debt insolvency, Zambia signed agreements to construct massive 'white elephant' projects like a football stadium that it could not afford.

Three chapter titles in Kaytlin Ernske's Trinty College thesis on Zambia tell all.[14]

1. A Wolf in Sheep's Clothing: Contextualizing the Historic and Contemporary Sino-African Relationship
2. From "Win-Win" to No-Win: Sino-Zambian Relations, Underdevelopment, and African Agency
3. Investors or "Infesters"?: Social Fragmentation and the Rise of Anti-Chinese Sentiment in Lusaka

Zambia is not the only country with debt, but it exemplifies the growing problem among many African nations, particularly after the pandemic, with their economic heartbeat barely pumping. Concerns have arisen among its people. Outcries are muffled by authoritarian state surveillance and imprisonment for speaking out in numerous countries.

Using a term only Orwell could have perfected, China is rolling out its "Safe City" authoritarian camera and Huawei Internet surveillance to monitor populations and ensure compliance in obeying China and not speaking out against client governments' over-reach. Myanmar's military junta is now accessing this "Safe City" to force a crackdown with facial recognition, license plate recognition, and internet scanning to coerce or punish protestors or others who express views that oppose the military takeover. In the capital, Naypyidaw, 335 Huawei surveillance cameras have been added with artificial intelligence and tracking.[15] New clampdowns in Mandalay and Yangon will aid in military control of all residents.

Conclusion

Historically, China turned away from the World Bank as a capitalist funding mechanism. However, recently Beijing changed its position, now becoming the second-largest borrower. As a leading borrower and leading lender, China stands on both sides at a time when the amount of money lent to China is sorely needed in other parts of the world.

Albeit, some of the loans are for rural areas and climate change projects since China is the leading emitter of pollution in the world. However, China is not slowing down in emissions. Instead, they are building new coal plants in China and other parts of the world at a rapid rate. Scott Morris, who analyzed World Bank lending to China, explained that

---

12   Elliot Smith, "Zambia's Spiraling Debt Offers Glimpse into the Future of Chinese Loan Financing in Africa," *CNBC*, January 14, 2020, https://www.cnbc.com/2020/01/14/zambias-spiraling-debt-and-the-future-of-chinese-loan-financing-in-africa.html

13   CUTS International, "#DebtConcernsMe: Understanding the Impact of Zambia's Growing Debt on Different Stakeholders," *CUTS International*, January 2019.

14   Kaytlin Ernske, "The Dragon's Neocolonial White Elephant Development: China's Urban Infrastructure in Lusaka, Zambia," *Trinity College Digital Repository*, 2020, https://digitalrepository.trincoll.edu/theses/837

15   Human Rights Watch, "Myanmar: Facial Recognition System Threatens Rights," *Human Rights Watch*, March 12, 2021, https://www.hrw.org/news/2021/03/12/myanmar-facial-recognition-system-threatens-rights

the loans are also for agriculture, education, roads, and other infrastructure.[16] International leaders say that the loans give China an unfair economic advantage in the marketplace, including a port and logistics park for China's shipping containers.[17]

What's at Stake?

First, China's banks are the largest in the world and continue to grow within the anarchic international system where there are few controls and contracts lack transparency. Since few people can stop what they cannot see, Beijing can take greater control, undermining the increasingly volatile global financial system.

Second, according to an ancient Chinese proverb, "the man who moves a mountain begins by carrying away small stones." With small stones, China has infiltrated countries worldwide and introduced its loans, language, and now digital currency.

Third, while China builds its banking system, takes loans from international banks, and gives loans to other countries, it floods markets, often selling its goods at prices below the cost to manufacture, pushing out competitors and undercutting the competition.

---

16 Scott Morris and Gailyn Portelance, "Examining World Bank Lending to China: Graduation or Modulation?," *Center for Global Development*, January, 2019, https://www.cgdev.org/sites/default/files/examining-world-bank-lending-china-graduation-or-modulation.pdf

17 Jason Beaubien, "Flush with Cash, China Continues to Borrow Billions from the World Bank," *NPR*, January 31, 2019, https://www.npr.org/sections/goatsandsoda/2019/01/31/689960866/flush-with-cash-china-continues-to-borrow-billions-from-world-bank

Chapter 5
Fueling the Hungry Giant
China's Stake in Global Liquid Natural Gas, Oil Fields

Introduction

Control oil and you control nations; control food and you control the people.

- Henry Kissinger

With a growing population, China needs food, and with a burgeoning manufacturing sector, its industry is equally hungry for energy. Beijing's expanding manufacturing sector demands raw materials, natural resources, manpower, fuel, and power. Looking to the Middle East and Africa for resources, China extended its reach. Cash-rich, China invested in initiatives that would allow its money to grow. In December 2020, China signed a $6.3 billion asset purchase for a natural gas pipeline, known as PipeChina, as Kunlun Energy Company sold off part of its company to create this new state-owned firm.[1] As Xi Jinping consolidates his nation's pipelines under China Oil & Gas Pipeline Network Corp., he intends to secure China's national energy resources.

Energy Needs and Consumption

In addition to needing crude oil and liquefied natural gas (LNG) for its energy needs, China strives to solidify its standing as the world's largest manufacturer. As such, it produces significant amounts of plastics, food, and packaging, which require petrochemicals in the production, fabrication, and manufacturing processes.

As China's intake increased, its ability to process domestic and foreign energy grew as well. By 2025, China's Economics & Technology Research Institute advised the China National Petroleum Corp to expect crude processing capacity to reach 1 billion metric tons a year, increasing its capacity from 17.5 to 20 million barrels per day.[2]

According to the "Statistical Communiqué of the People's Republic of China on the 2020 National Economic and Social Development", more than half of China's total energy consumption is coal.[3] In 2021, China's National Energy Administration approved the construction of three times the amount of coal energy plants as in 2020 with new construction volume alone as much as the present capacity of all of Germany.[4] China, with its special status as an "underdeveloped country" in international bodies, is allowed greater freedom to have more emissions and build more coal plants.

Boosting domestic oil and gas reserves will allow China to respond to shifts in the presently precarious global political and economic climate. China's state-owned oil corporations, like PetroChina, Sinopec, and CNOOC, are also increasing domestic

---

1 Bloomberg, "China Pipeline Giant to Buy Kunlun Assets for $6.3 Billion," *Bloomberg*, December 22, 2020, https://www.bloomberg.com/news/articles/2020-12-22/china-s-pipeline-giant-buys-kunlun-energy-assets-for-6-billion

2 Ibid.

3 National Bureau of Statistics of China, "Statistical Communiqué of the People's Republic of China on the 2020 National Economic and Social Development," *National Bureau of Statistics of China,* February 28, 2021, http://www.stats.gov.cn/english/PressRelease/202102/t20210228_1814177.html

4 David Stanway, "China's New Coal Power Plant Capacity in 2020 More Than Three Times Rest of World's: Study," *Reuters*, February 2, 2021, https://www.reuters.com/article/us-china-coal/chinas-new-coal-power-plant-capacity-in-2020-more-than-three-times-rest-of-worlds-study-idUSKBN2A308U

production levels. In Q1, 2021, domestic gas production jumped 13.1% and, according to a Hong Kong-based analyst, "The growths are sustainable and likely to rise the rest of the year, especially for gas, as more new domestic projects come on stream, like CNOOC's flagship projects in Bohai and South China Sea."[5]

Foreign Oil and Gas

China's span of intercontinental pipelines is impressive. A pipedream of sorts, China has pipelines from its Western province of Xinjiang down to Gwadar, its port in Pakistan. Beijing is also tapping into Myanmar's diverse energy sources through the China-Myanmar oil and gas pipeline: from Kyaukpyu to Kunming through Ruili.[6]

As a consequence of global terrorism and China's demand, Beijing rushed to diversify its energy resource acquisition and ensure that its oil and natural gas pipelines were shored up with secure locations. China began investing in oil options in countries like Peru, Canada, Venezuela, Thailand, Kuwait, Central Asia, Russia, Sudan, Angola, Niger, Nigeria, SaoTome Principe, and Equatorial Guinea, led by visionary oil engineer Qin Anmin, president of the CNPC subsidiary China Petroleum Engineering Construction Enterprise Group (CPECEG), and Tan Zhuzhou, head of the China Petroleum Commerce and Industry Association (CPCIA) and honorary Chairman of Kunshan Dikun Fine Chemicals Ltd.[7]

Beijing has pipelines traveling across Eurasia. Many of China's pipelines across the continent travel through Central Asia and "the Stans" across or around the Caspian Sea. China also cooperated in a strategic partnership with Russia to diversify its sales, adding to those from Western countries. Despite Xi Jinping's insistence that China and Russia are best friends,[8] they are also competitors in a European and Asian marketplace that is slowly crowding out Russia. With China's investments worldwide, China does not need Russia, so their partnerships are fragile at best. China can use this as leverage over Russia. Nevertheless, Russia has vast oil areas that have not been tapped, and this positioning may change over time.

Other countries are clamoring for investment money and sales. In May 2021, Qatar shifted its reliance on Western powers for technology and global outreach to China for a new liquefied natural gas (LNG) expansion project, the world's largest to date.[9] Meanwhile, Belarus, which was highly dependent on Russia for oil used to export to other countries, has sought to diversify. As such, Belarus has joined hands with Chinese energy companies

---

5   Oceana Zhou and Cindy Liang, "China Set to Cap Coal Consumption, Boost Domestic Oil & Gas Output in 2021," *S&P Global*, April 26, 2021, https://www.spglobal.com/platts/en/market-insights/latest-news/coal/042621-china-set-to-cap-coal-consumption-boost-domestic-oil-amp-gas-output-in-2021

6   Neslihan Topcu, "A Relationship on a Pipeline: China and Myanmar," *China Center*, October 12, 2020, https://www.chinacenter.net/2020/china_currents/19-3/a-relationship-on-a-pipeline-china-and-myanmar/

7   Institute of Developing Economies Japan External Trade Organization (IDE-JETRO), "7. China's Energy Footprint in Africa," *IDE-JETRO*, n.d., https://www.ide.go.jp/English/Data/Africa_file/Manualreport/cia_07.html

8   Scott Neuman, "As Relations with U.S. Sour, Xi Describes Putin As 'Best Friend' At Moscow Meeting," *NPR*, June 6, 2019, https://www.npr.org/2019/06/06/730200317/as-relations-with-u-s-sour-xi-describes-putin-as-best-friend-at-moscow-meeting

9   Muyu Xu and Chen Aizhu, "Qatar Pivots to LNG-Hungry China in Strategy Shift," *Reuters*, May 11, 2021, https://www.reuters.com/business/energy/exclusive-qatar-pivots-lng-hungry-china-strategy-shift-2021-05-11/

and banking institutions. Power China and North China Power Engineering will collaborate with Belarus, including facilitating its energy sales and a $5 billion loan from China's EXIM bank to support its infrastructure.[10]

Across Africa, China has placed a stake in infrastructure development as well as oil and gas exploration. Originally, the China National Petroleum Corporation (CNPC) was the major player in Sudan and Egypt, where it was deeply involved. However, in 2021, China operated in twenty African countries, which has challenged smaller, local oil companies.

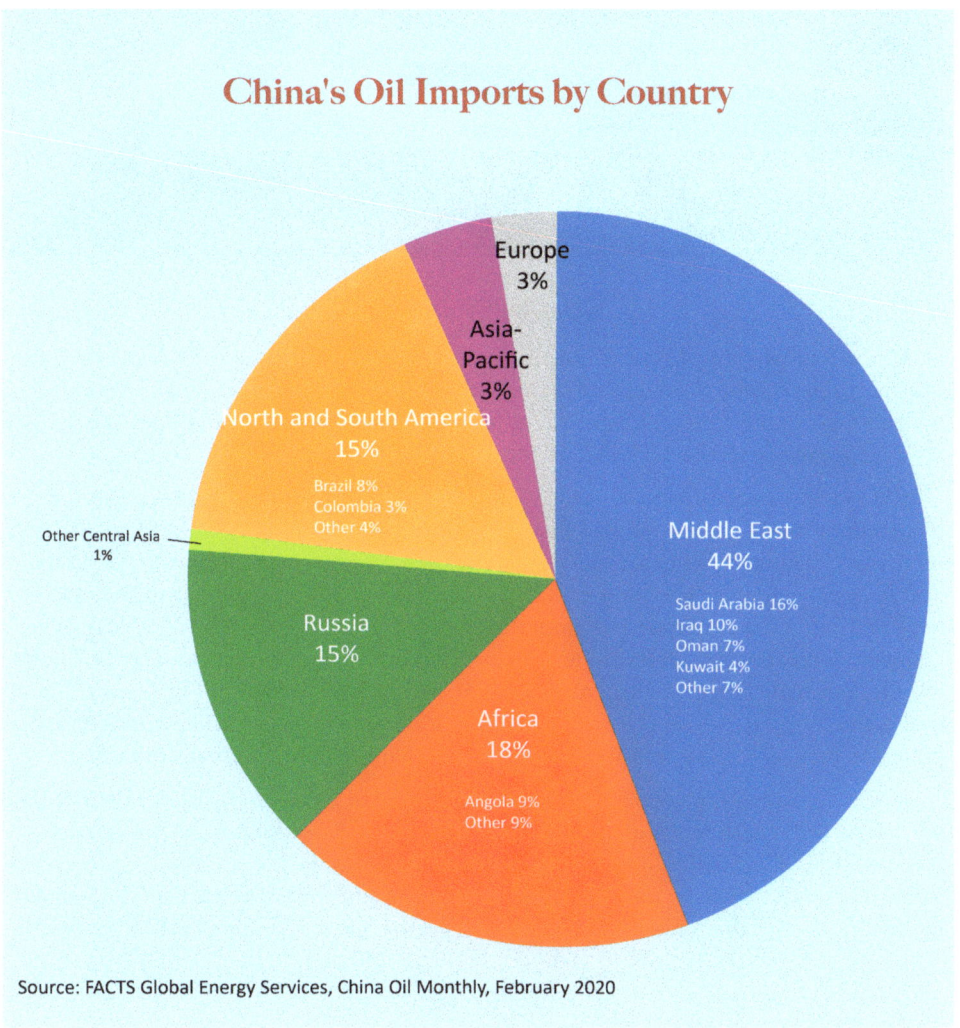

---

10 BNS/TBT Staff, "Chinese Companies Help Belarus to Sell Astravets Power," *Baltic Times*, December 12, 2019, https://www.baltictimes.com/chinese_companies_help_belarus_to_sell_astravyets_power/

Spotlight on Iran

China is moving in where the U.S. is moving out. With unrest in the Middle East, Joe Biden's goal of leaving the Middle East may take longer than he had planned. Nevertheless, China is wasting no time staking its claim to large swaths of territory, like Afghanistan, that are all too ready to see the United States leave. One of these is Iran.

China and Iran are inking a massive $400 billion deal.[11] Putting this into perspective, that amount would pay for railroad tracks and roads enough to crisscross the United States more than 100,000 times based on China's costs along with ten naval ships, ten military aircraft, and an airport. The amount is enormous. However, with the West's sanctions, Iran has had a hard time obtaining cash, and they desperately want infrastructure. Meanwhile, China wants geopolitical influence and the security of continued, unencumbered oil flows, which it can trade for money and manpower to pull off Iran's long list of projects.[12] The deal is also likely to include close defense cooperation, intelligence sharing, and access to ports, rail lines, and other transit thoroughfares for China's Belt and Road Initiative.[13]

While the China-Iran deal is nearing fruition, concern abounds regarding whether Iran will have to relinquish much of its oil to pay China back. According to the World Bank, Iran's 2021 GDP is $628 billion.[14] Thus, $400 billion is nearly two-thirds of its total value added to its economy in a year. As a result of the pandemic, international sanctions, and internal tensions, Tehran needs this money, and China knows it and can call its terms. By

---

11 Ariel Cohen, "China and Iran Approach Massive $400 Billion Deal," *Forbes*, July 17, 2020, https://www.forbes.com/sites/arielcohen/2020/07/17/china-and-iran-approach-massive-400-billion-deal/?sh=2991c79c2a16

12 Dave Lawler, "China-Iran Deal Envisions Massive Investments from Beijing," *Axios*, July 13, 2020, https://www.axios.com/china-iran-investment-deal-oil-infrastructure-c919646d-2ece-4ee5-bfd7-c8a16a7f53b0.html

13 Ariel Cohen, "China and Iran Approach Massive $400 Billion Deal," *Forbes*, July 17, 2020, https://www.forbes.com/sites/arielcohen/2020/07/17/china-and-iran-approach-massive-400-billion-deal/?sh=2991c79c2a16

14 The World Bank, "Islamic Republic of Iran," *The World Bank*, 2021, https://www.worldbank.org/en/country/iran/overview

agreeing to this investment transaction, Iran offers China unprecedented access to Iran's oil and stitches another port in the web woven around India.

Pundits abound, including those who question the imprisonment and torture of China's Muslim population, with a very real concern that Beijing may replicate its efforts against "Muslim terrorists" elsewhere. Former Iranian President Mahmud Ahmadinejad warned in a 2020 speech that this agreement was being conducted without consultation, effectively "handing Iran's purse to other countries without informing the nation," while former lawmaker Ali Motahari appeared to suggest on Twitter that Iran should raise the fate of Muslims who are persecuted in China, and Reza Pahlavi, eldest son of the last Shah, blasted the "shameful" treaty that "plunders our natural resources and places foreign soldiers on our soil."[15]

Conclusion

China's appetite is ravenous. China consumes nearly twice the energy as any other country in the world, including the U.S. However, oil and natural gas are finite commodities. With a limit, China seeks to reach peak oil in 2025 as it launches into a race for electric vehicle supremacy, committing to becoming carbon-neutral by 2060.[16] Meanwhile, it expects to reach peak energy consumption by 2035, according to China National Petroleum Company (CNPC).[17]

---

15 Golnaz Esfandiari, "Explainer: Why Are Iranians Angry Over A Long-Term Deal With China?," *Radio Free Europe*, July 13, 2020, https://www.rferl.org/a/explainer-iranian-china-deal-anger-among-iranians/30724344.html

16 Nathaniel Taplin, "China is Approaching its Own Peak Oil," *The Wall Street Journal*, February 12, 2021, https://www.wsj.com/articles/china-is-approaching-its-own-peak-oil-11613131201

17 Reuters, "China's Energy Use to Peak in 2035 Under Carbon-Neutral Goal – CNPC Research," *Reuters*, December 16, 2020, https://www.reuters.com/business/energy/chinas-energy-use-peak-2035-under-carbon-neutral-goal-cnpc-research-2020-12-17/

In 2020, during the pandemic, oil demand dropped, as did the price. This demand has remarkably increased, as have the prices, which has helped bolster production in oil-producing countries. The challenge is that long-term supply will not be available at this rate for much farther than the mid-2030s.

Middle Eastern oil prominence dominates markets, and South China Sea oil has great potential for the future. However, there is a significant amount of African oil. One of China's most strategic partners is Nigeria for its location on the Gulf of Guinea off the Atlantic and access to the African consumer base. However, whether China's focus will be on the Middle East, Russia, South China Sea, South America, or Africa depends on the global geopolitical climate through the rest of the 2020s.

What's at Stake?

First, with tense U.S.-China relations and terse words shared on the global stage, uncertainty regarding oil and gas looms. Furthermore, Beijing remains dependent on foreign oil for its production of manufactured goods.

Second, there are trillions of barrels of oil under the South China Sea, which China is attempting to access by force. This coercion is disrupting the geopolitical climate in Southeast Asia as China takes islands away from the Philippines and Vietnam to stake its claim.

Third, many countries offer opportunities for China, and the direction Beijing heads will depend largely on international pushback regarding the pandemic and China's assertion of its interests in countries around the world.

Chapter 6

Dark Fleets

China's Fishing and Shipping in Ecuador, the Arctic, and Elsewhere on the Planet

Introduction

From 2014 to 2017, waterway and ecosystem preservation commitments increased. In 2018, leaders on environmental action converged and subsequently donated a U.S. $10 billion to safeguard the oceans.[1] One primary objective of this mission was to halt illegal, unreported, and unregulated (IUU) fishing.

The alarming rate at which fish are being hauled from the seas and oceans raised concerns worldwide. The numbers are staggering and the take is significantly larger and faster than new marine life enters the system. Yet, evidence shows that they can be replenished. While overfishing and marine habitat destruction threatened seas and oceans, a recent research study published in *Nature* offers hope that these environments can recover as many did after destructive points in history, like World War II.[2]

Note in the following table, that the combined total of fish production in India, Indonesia, Japan, Philippines, Republic of Korea, Thailand, Vietnam, Africa, and the European Union is less than that of China. While China plans to increase its aquaculture development, China has aslo significantly increased its illegal, unreported, and unregulated fish catch in its "Dark Fleets".

Fish Production Data from "2020 The State of World Fisheries and Aquaculture"[3]			
Country/Continent	2018	2030	% Growth
China	62,207	73,720	18.5
India	12,386	15,610	26.0
Indonesia	12,642	14,940	18.2
Japan	3,774	3,520	-6.7
Philippines	2,876	3,220	12.0
Republic of Korea	1,905	1,850	-2.9
Thailand	2,598	2,790	7.4
Vietnam	7,481	9,590	28.2
Africa	12,268	13,820	12.7
European Union	5,879	6,025	2.5
World Total	178, 529	204, 421	14.5

---

1 Our Ocean, "Our Ocean Commitments," *Our Ocean*, 2018, https://ourocean2018.org/?l=our-ocean-commitments

2 Duarte et al., "Rebuilding Marine Life," *Nature* 580, no. 7801 (2020): 39-51, https://www.nature.com/articles/s41586-020-2146-7.epdf

3 Food and Agriculture Organization of the United Nations, "Part 3: Outlook and Emerging Issues – Fisheries and Aquaculture Projections," *Food and Agriculture Organization of the United Nations*, n.d., http://www.fao.org/3/ca9229en/online/ca9229en.html#chapter-3_1

"Dark Fleets"

China's "dark fleets", either illegal, undetectable, or unmarked, have been sighted off the coasts of every continent. These are termed 'shipping vessels' since they do not appear in traditional monitoring systems, and hence their activities (legal or illegal) are challenging to monitor.[4] Many of these dark fleet vessels operate legally and broadcast their positions on country-mandated, private monitoring systems. These data are heavily guarded and not readily available to third-parties making accurate operation monitoring difficult.[5] This begs the question of just how legal these activities are when they occur in foreign and often disputed waters.

South America

In the waters outside of Ecuador, massive fleets of militarized vessels swarm the coastline, arriving daily from China. Many of these ships have reportedly gone "dark". Hundreds of these vessels have been fishing near the Galapagos archipelago. The massive size of this fleet is referred to by some as a "floating city."[6] Chinese fishing vessels favor this location due to its vast patches of fish. Since the summer of 2017, Chinese large-scale militarized fishing vessels have come in droves searching for giant squids and hammerhead sharks (an endangered species).

---

4   Ramona Pelich et al., "Large-Scale Automatic Vessel Monitoring Based on Dual-Polarization Sentinel-1 and AIS Data," *Remote Sensing* 11, no. 9 (2019), https://www.mdpi.com/2072-4292/11/9/1078

5   Nicolas Longépé et al., "Completing Fishing Monitoring with Spaceborne Vessel Detection System (VDS) and Automatic Identification System (AIS) to Assess Illegal Fishing in Indonesia, *Marine Pollution Bulletin 131*, (2018): 33-39, https://pubmed.ncbi.nlm.nih.gov/29106935/

6   Gonzalo Solano and Christopher Torchia, "260 Chinese Boats Fish Near Galapagos; Ecuador on Alert," *Washington Post*, July 3, 2020, https://www.washingtonpost.com/world/the_americas/260-chinese-boats-fish-near-galapagos-ecuador-on-alert/2020/07/30/01b0d98e-d29f-11ea-826b-cc394d824e35_story.html?outputType=amp

According to Navy Commander Rear Admiral Darwin Jarrin, Chinese ships fail to broadcast their locations to local authorities who monitor such activities.[7] He also added that some have gone as far as changing the names of their vessels to prevent supervision. From July 13, 2020 – August 13, 2020, "Oceana documented the Chinese fleet, which was primarily fishing for squid, logged more than 73,000 total hours of apparent fishing. In fact, 99% of the visible fishing activity off the Galapagos Islands during this one month was by Chinese-flagged vessels."[8]

New data now reveals that the fleet intentionally fished within Ecuador's Exclusive Economic Zone (EEZ), which violates the nation's sovereignty. The vessels were reported to have turned off their Automatic Identification System (AIS) tracking periodically for about 12 to 24 hours at a time, enough time to make colossal catches under the radar.[9] These clearly and continuously breach international law.[10]

In the light of the current situation, Ecuador is proverbially between the devil and the deep blue sea. Government officials and civilians cry out for help to environmental organizations about the activities of these "dark fleets" while at the same time attempting to preserve diplomatic relations with China, its biggest financier and also a major market for its shrimp exports.

Despite the Chinese government's continued promises to temporarily ban all fishing activities in the area, the evidence clearly shows that these vessels continued fishing in 2021 in the area close to the Galapagos Islands. Earlier in June 2020, the United Nations Food and Agriculture Organization reported that about one-third of fish stock is being harvested at "biologically unstable levels."[11]

Distant-water fishing is not uncommon. China has the largest distant water fleet (DWF) in the world. Its vessels have been located off the coast of many South American countries, including Chile, Argentina, Peru, and Ecuador, alarming environmental authorities in the region.[12] To clarify the extent of China's DWF, in June 2020, the Overseas Development Institute submitted a report registering 16,966 distant-water vessels with 1,000 additional Chinese DWF vessels flagged in other countries, 518 of these in the waters of African nations.[13]

---

7   Reuters, "Ecuador Says Chinese Fishing Fleet off Galapagos Has Gone Dark," *Aljazeera*, August 19, 2020, https://www.aljazeera.com/amp/economy/2020/8/19/ecuador-says-chinese-fishing-fleet-off-galapogos-has-gone-dark

8   Oceana, "New Oceana Anlysis Finds 300 Chinese Vessels Pillaging the Galapagos for Squid," *Oceana*, September 16, 2020, https://usa.oceana.org/press-releases/new-oceana-analysis-finds-300-chinese-vessels-pillaging-galapagos-squid

9   Trey Yingst and Yonat Friling, "Chinese Fishing Fleets Caught in Galapagos Islands Violating Ecuadorian Sovereignty," *Fox News*, September 30, 2020, https://www.foxnews.com/world/chinese-fishing-fleets-caught-in-galapagos-islands-violating-ecuadorian-sovereignty.amp

10 UN General Assembly, *Convention on the Law of the Sea*, December 10, 1982, available at: www.un.org/depts/los/convention_agreements/texts/unclos/unclos_e.pdf

11 Food and Agriculture Organization of the United Nations, "IUU Fishing is a Great Threat to Sustainable Fisheries," *Food and Agriculture Organization of the United Nations*, June 7, 2020, http://www.fao.org/news/story/en/item/1279305/icode/

12 Álvaro Etchegaray, "China's Fishing in South American Waters Raises Questions, Fears," *SupChina*, February 21, 2021, https://supchina.com/2021/02/21/chinas-fishing-in-south-american-waters-raises-questions-fears/

13 Guy Jobbins Miren Gutierrez, "China's Distant Water Fishing Fleet is More than Five Times Larger than Estimated – New ODI Report," *DI*, May 26, 2020, https://odi.org/en/press/chinas-distant-water-fishing-fleet-is-more-than-five-times-larger-than-estimated-new-odi-report/

U.S. Secretary of State, Michael Pompeo, commented on this issue, stating that these Chinese vessels' activities are "deeply troubling." He also reaffirmed the U.S. position to stand behind Ecuador and the fight against illegal fishing and preserve the UNESCO World Heritage Site of the Galapagos Islands.[14] The loss of the marine habitats in the Galapagos Islands would be destructive to regional economies as well.

Northeast Asia

Moving a few thousand miles away to Northeast Asia, "dark fleets" have been observed in increasing numbers.[15] The predominantly Chinese fleet's principal target is the Pacific flying squid, *Todarodes pacificus*, which densely populates the area. The Sea of Japan is one of the most disputed bodies of water in the world, contested by China, Japan, North Korea, South Korea, and even Russia.[16] This disagreement makes it even harder, therefore, to monitor fish stocks within the area and also effectively combat illegal fishing activities.

In 2017, researchers discovered that about 900 foreign vessels caught massive numbers of fish in North Korean waters. The operations of these vessels have been estimated to have made catches of over 160,000 metric tons of Pacific flying squid worth about $440 million in 2017 and 2018 alone.[17] This discovery demonstrated the decimation of a single species. Approximately 70% of the squid have been removed.[18]

Illegal, unreported, and unregulated (IUU) fishing is rampant and unsanctioned along national borders. This occurrence is also devastating in terms of both environmental and socio-economic outcomes. The events also spell out the enormity of violations of both local and international laws.[19] In March 2020, two countries filed a complaint to the United Nations regarding China's violations, providing evidence of the crimes and including satellite imagery. "Chinese fishing boats are famously aggressive, often armed and known for ramming competitors or foreign patrol vessels, according to U.S. Navy officials and maritime security specialists."[20]

Pacific flying squid is a staple food in the region. As such, squid is a crucial source of both income and livelihood for many communities in Japan and the Korean Peninsula. The removal of literally tons of marine life is therefore inhibiting these people's ability to make a living within their hometowns. Therefore, many regional fishermen have sought fish in

---

14 Caitlin McFall, "Pompeo Calls out China for 'Illegal Fishing' after Vessels Spotted off Galapagos Islands," *Fox News*, August 27, 2020, https://www.foxnews.com/world/pompeo-china-illegal-fishing-galapagos

15 Jaeyoon Park et al., "Illuminating Dark Fishing Fleets in North Korea," *Science Advances* 6, no. 30 (2020).

16 Jeongwon Bourdais Park, *Regional Environmental Politics in Northeast Asia: Conflict and Cooperation* (Routledge, 2018).

17 Trey Yingst and Yonat Friling, "Chinese Fishing Fleets Caught in Galapagos Islands Violating Ecuadorian Sovereignty," *Fox News*, September 30, 2020, https://www.foxnews.com/world/chinese-fishing-fleets-caught-in-galapagos-islands-violating-ecuadorian-sovereignty.amp

18 Ian Urbina, "The Deadly Secret of China's Invisible Armada," *NBC News*, July 22, 2020, https://www.nbcnews.com/specials/china-illegal-fishing-fleet/

19 Ministry of Agriculture and Rural Affairs of the People's Republic of China, "Distant Water Fisheries Management Regulations," *Ministry of Agriculture and Rural Affairs of the People's Republic of China*, 2003, www.moa.gov.cn/gk/tzgg_1/bl/200305/t20030519_83829.htm

20 Ian Urbina, "The Deadly Secret of China's Invisible Armada," *NBC News*, July 22, 2020, https://www.nbcnews.com/specials/china-illegal-fishing-fleet/

other locations as far as Russian waters since they have been outwitted by the larger and more technologically advanced foreign vessels. Voyages on less sturdy ships are also dangerous. The study found that in 2018, over 3000 small North Korean vessels fished in the Russian EEZ.[21] This activity is also illegal fishing, set off by the effects of the "dark fleet" activities.

NBC News reported, "The deadly secret of China's invisible armada. North Korean vessels have been found washed ashore on Japanese beaches, some empty, some with dead men as crew members, some split in half, and only a few of them had living crewmen.[22] About 505 of these vessels were found washed ashore between 2014–2018, which has led to some North Korean villages being called "widow's villages."[23] The men who fish never return.

The Korean Coast Guard has reported spotting hundreds of fishing vessels entering Korean waters, and randomized inspections by the East Sea Fisheries Management Service found "dark" vessels to be of Chinese origin.[24] This realization comes even as Beijing has repeated claims that it has a "zero tolerance" policy for illegal fishing.[25] This supposed "zero tolerance" does not hold much water as illegal, unreported, and unregulated (IUU) fishing continues in the waters surrounding several sovereign states at the expense of their local economies.[26]

21 Trey Yingst and Yonat Friling, "Chinese Fishing Fleets Caught in Galapagos Islands Violating Ecuadorian Sovereignty," *Fox News*, September 30, 2020, https://www.foxnews.com/world/chinese-fishing-fleets-caught-in-galapagos-islands-violating-ecuadorian-sovereignty.amp

22 Ian Urbina, "The Deadly Secret of China's Invisible Armada," *NBC News*, July 22, 2020, https://www.nbcnews.com/specials/china-illegal-fishing-fleet/

23 Jaeyoon Park et al., "Illuminating Dark Fishing Fleets in North Korea -Supplementary Materials," *Science Advances*, retrieved from: https://advances.sciencemag.org/content/suppl/2020/07/20/6.30.eabb1197.DC1

24 Tim Stephens, "Report Exposes Rampant Illegal Fishing in North Korean Waters," *UC Santa Cruz News Center*, July 22, 2020, https://news.ucsc.edu/2020/07/illegal-fishing.html

25 Zhou Wei, "China Promises Reforms of Coastal Fisheries," *China Dialogue*, December 18, 2020, https://chinadialogue.net/en/food/10302-china-promises-reform-of-coastal-fisheries/

26 Federation of American Scientists, "Global Implications of Illegal, Unreported, and Unregulated (IUU) Fishing," *Federation of American Scientists,* September 19, 2016, https://fas.org/irp/nic/fishing.pdf

Conclusion

In the past, "dark fleet" activities could neither be tracked nor monitored effectively. However, the advent of new technology has allowed for satellite imaging and tracking. Thus, observation of fishing activities can occur via satellite, potentially anywhere in the world. China often turns off its tracking system so that it cannot be monitored, tracked, or controlled, though this attempt to evade the law may not be effective in the future.

The United Nations Department of Economic and Social Affairs sustainable development goal 14 says, "Conserve and sustainably use the oceans, seas and marine resources for sustainable development."[27] Areas of specific interest include maritime security, marine protected areas, sustainable fisheries, marine pollution, sustainable blue economy, and climate change. Human-caused ecosystem changes threaten the oceans with pollution, over-fishing, artificial island-building, and underwater resource development. The rise in ocean temperature, increase in acids, discharge of industrial sewage, and widespread plastic trash have damaged marine life and habitats.[28] Protection is necessary, or else there may be no more fish in Asia, South America, and elsewhere worldwide.

What's At Stake?

First, Chinese ships are in Ecuadorian waters hauling in squid that are necessary for the Galapagos Islands food chain. Disrupting this marine ecosystem will necessarily change the diet of the area's marine life and destroy the Galapagos Islands' natural habitat.

Second, China's illegal fishing in their "dark fleets" is a sign of disrespect for the rule of law. While China has aggressively violated international fishing laws in the South China Sea and the East China Sea, South America is far from China. It is hard to justify why China believes it can violate South Americans' rights.

Third, the advent of better monitoring systems will enable proper supervision and enhance greater fairness in opportunities for fishing. International monitoring will also provide the evidence necessary for prompt legal action against such activities that destroy regional environments, civilian livelihoods, and fishing areas worldwide.

Fourth, with no authority to physically stop IUU fishing, China may continue to violate the law. International law has not stopped China in the South China Sea, only emboldened them to draft and implement their own Chinese laws that they impose and enforce on other states.

---

27 United Nations, "Conserve and Sustainably Use the Oceans, Seas, and Marine Resources for Sustainable Development," *United Nations,* 2020, https://sdgs.un.org/goals/goal14

28 Lorraine Chow, "Global Fish Stocks Depleted to 'Alarming' Levels," *EcoWatch,* July 8, 2016, https://www.ecowatch.com/one-third-of-commercial-fish-stocks-fished-at-unsustainable-levels-1910593830.html

Near and Far – China's Claims Extend Its Reach | Part 4 | 179

Chapter 7
Three Poles Environment and Climate Change
China's Ministry of Science and Technology (MOST) Project

Introduction

The South Pole, North Pole, and the Tibetan Plateau together comprise territory for a body that is known as the Three Poles Environment Project (TPE). The TPE Project was designed to collect, organize, and analyze research on frozen 'polar' environments. Born out of the need to understand these regions, particularly how the warming of the planet may impact large frozen water landmasses, a big data platform has been constructed. The TPE Project considers polar data acquisition, curation, integration, sharing, and application to better understand the impact of climate change and support decision-making for sustainable development.[1]

Challenges in Data Collection

Over the years, the data collected have shown drastic climatic and environmental changes in the three poles. Despite the wealth of information, it is not sufficient to make actionable conclusions. The data collection has been, in some cases, halted by limiting factors such as harsh living conditions, inaccessibility, as well as high labor costs.[2]

One project designed to aid in this exploration is the CASEarth Poles, a subsidiary project of the Big Earth Data Scientific Engineering program, supported by the Chinese Academy of Sciences.[3] The project aims to harness enough data to better address the issues of drastic changes in the polar environment while understanding their effects on a much larger scale.[4]

The CASEarth project seeks to break the bottleneck of polar data curation, integration, and sharing by developing high-resolution remote sensing over the three poles. These sensors would generate atmospheric reanalysis datasets, explore synchronization and asynchronization, and create a teleconnection that alerts leaders to environmental changes in the three poles.[5] While investigating climate, water cycle, ecosystem dynamics, and their interactions, the sensing platform supports decision-making regarding sea-ice forecasting, infrastructure, and sustainable development in polar regions.[6] The CASEarth project has agreed to work with other international bodies and other organizational efforts to ensure

---

1   CASEarth, "Spatiotemporal Three-Pole Environment," *CASEarth*, n.d., http://english.casearth.com/index.php?option=com_content&view=article&id=74&Itemid=194

2   National Geographic, "Limiting Factors," *National Geographic*, n.d., https://www.nationalgeographic.org/topics/limiting-factors/

3   World Data System, "CASEarth: A Big Earth Data Project Launched by Chinese Academy of Sciences," *World Data System*, April 12, 2018, https://www.worlddatasystem.org/news/blog/casearth-a-big-earth-data-project-launched-by-cas

4   United Nations, "Achieving Sustainable Development and Promoting Development Cooperation," *United Nations*, 2008, https://www.un.org/en/ecosoc/docs/pdfs/fina_08-45773.pdf

5   Xin Li et al., "CASEarth Poles: Big Data For The Three Poles," *Bulletin of the American Meteorological Society 101*, no. 9 (2020), https://journals.ametsoc.org/bams/article/101/9/E1475/345605/CASEarth-Poles-Big-Data-for-the-Three-Poles#

6   Ibid.

that big data and artificial intelligence can offer a better system for monitoring, tracking, and decision-making.[7]

Aside from the CASEarth, other organizations have expressed an interest in collaborating on data accessibility, availability, and attainability. Global Cryosphere Watch, in collaboration with the World Meteorological Organization, has agreed to throw its resources behind the TPE Project.[8] According to Dr. Johannes Cullman, World Meteorological Organization Water and Cryosphere Coordinator, this union's vision is to build an integrated global cryosphere information system to harness already existing information, observations, and methodologies while exploring options to incorporate technological advancements and long-term continuous data recordkeeping.[9]

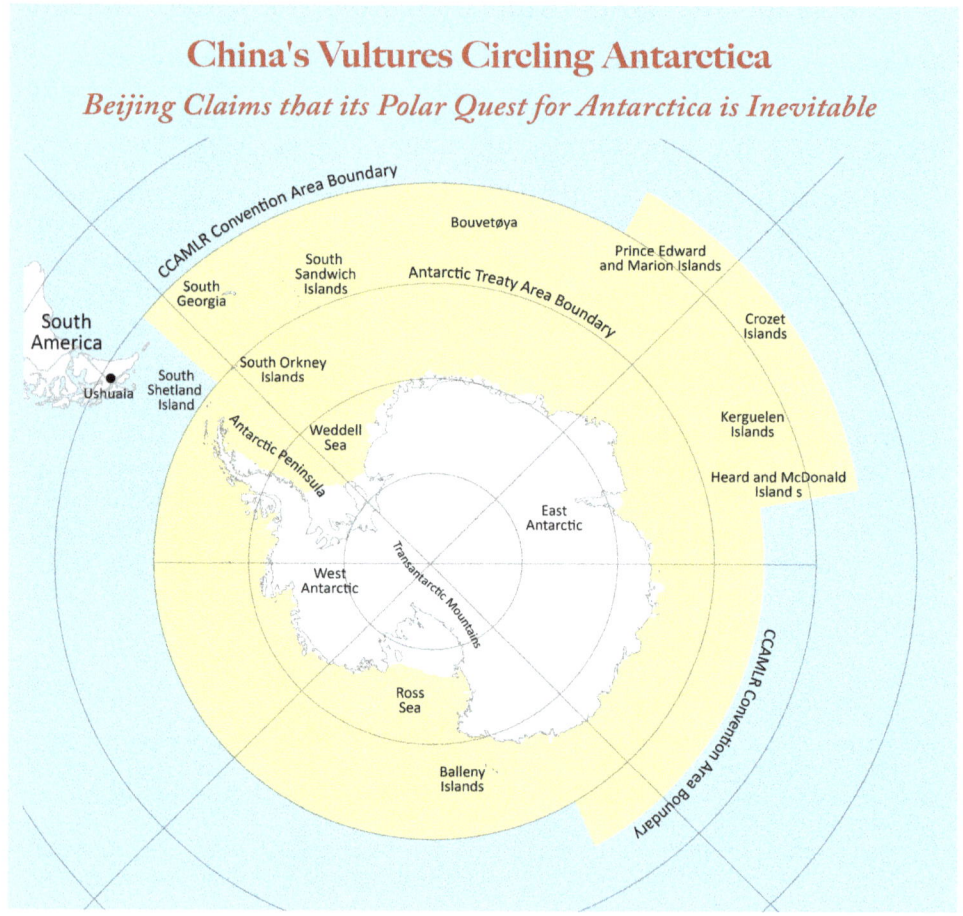

---

[7] Huadong Guo, "Big Earth Data: A New Frontier in Earth and Information," *Big Earth Data 1*, no. 1-2 (2017), https://www.researchgate.net/publication/321953344_Big_Earth_data_A_new_frontier_in_Earth_and_information_sciences

[8] World Meteorological Organization, "Global Cryosphere Watch: World Meteorological Organization," *World Meteorological Organization*, n.d., https://public.wmo.int/en/our-mandate/focus-areas/cryosphere/wmo-activities/global-cryosphere-watch

[9] World Meteorological Organization, "Third Pole: World Meteorological Organization," *World Meteorological Organization*, November 17-19, 2015. http://www.wmo.int/pages/prog/wcp/wcasp/meetings/linkedfiles/

China's Leadership

With efforts to collaborate, ensure better data outcomes and an improved communication system, China stepped up to the plate to assert itself as a leader in the Three Poles Project. China is seeking to spearhead a leading role in the ongoing development and affairs of the polar regions.[10] This leadership would be commendable and even possibly heralded, but Beijing's approach is questionable.

In November 2014, the Chinese media announced the words of Chinese President Xi Jinping. Xi gave a speech in Hobart, Australia, on China's polar agenda, with then Australian Prime Minister Tony Abbott standing beside him. Using political phraseology to describe China's Antarctic agenda, reported in English by the Chinese Foreign Ministry and in Chinese by *Xinhua* news service, Xi said, "The Chinese side stands ready to continuously work with Australia and the international community to better understand, protect, and exploit the Antarctic." However, the Chinese Communist Party's official English-language newspaper, *China Daily*, reported that Xi had expressed China's continued interest in cooperating with Australia and other nations to 'know, protect, and explore Antarctica'.[11]

Though this may appear as a nuance in rhetoric, upon further investigation, Chinese media outlets directed at Chinese nationals explained that the Chinese government's true aim was to know, protect, and exploit these polar areas. Meanwhile, in media outlets directed to foreigners, the word "exploit" was replaced with "explore".[12] Nevertheless, China sent its dozens of ships into the Antarctic and hundreds through the Arctic, while controlling much of the Tibetan plateau.

Trust, Leverage, and Coercion in the Tibetan Plateau

The challenge the world faces is trust, leverage, and coercion. China took the lead in its benevolent data-sharing with India regarding hydrological data-sharing in the Tibetan Plateau, the third pole. In this situation, China agreed to warn India of incoming floods from the Himalayas when the system detected dangerous levels. The collaboration and cooperation were appreciated from both sides as a win-win proposition to share information so that Indian villages did not get flooded.

In 2013, the agreements were signed. During the annual monsoon season, May 15 – October 15, China would send New Delhi information regarding the Brahmaputra and Sutlej Rivers, two major water sources that flow through South Asia to the Ganges

---

10 World Economic Forum, "China Aims to Play a Major Role in Arctic Affairs," *World Economic Forum,* July 27, 2018, https://www.weforum.org/agenda/2018/07/china-aims-to-play-a-major-role-in-arctic-affairs-here-are-its-5-key-policy-goals/

11 Anne-Marie Brady, "China Undeclared Foreign Policy at the Poles," *The Interpreter,* May 30, 2017, https://www.lowyinstitute.org/the-interpreter/china-undeclared-foreign-policy-poles

12 Ibid.

River,[13] alerting India to prepare for possible flooding.[14] Though this agreement began as a collaborative effort, China weaponized the treaty in a political battle.

In the 2017 Himalayan standoff between China and India, China began constructing a road along the China-India border.[15] Seeking to stop China's encroachment, Indian border troops crossed into Chinese territory, initiating a high-stakes standoff between the two nations that lasted for 73 days[16] and involved over 3,000 soldiers.[17] Though both country's militaries backed down, China's anger was still present. China retaliated by not providing the 2017 hydrological data report.[18] Meanwhile, according to the United Nations, 31 million people were adversely affected by flooding, including 12.33 million children, 15,455 schools, and 805,183 houses.

---

13 Ritesth K. Srivastava, "China Starts Sharing Hydrological Data for Brahmaputra River," *Zee News*, May 16, 2020, https://zeenews.india.com/india/china-starts-sharing-hydrological-data-for-brahmaputra-river-2283902.html

14 Navin Singh Khadka, "China and India Water 'Dispute' After Border Stand-Off," *BBC News*, September 18, 2017, https://www.bbc.com/news/world-asia-41303082

15 Christopher Woody, "Tensions are Still Simmering a Year After The World's 2 Biggest Countries Almost Clashed Over a Border At The Top Of The World," *Business Insider*, August 22, 2018, https://www.businessinsider.com/tensions-between-china-and-india-continue-year-after-doklam-standoff-2018-8

16 PTI, "Amid Border Tensions with India, China Starts Sharing Hydrological Data for Brahmaputra River," *The New Indian Express*, May 16, 2020, https://www.newindianexpress.com/nation/2020/may/16/amid-border-tensions-with-india-china-starts-sharing-hydrological-data-for-brahmaputra-river-2143909.html

17 Christopher Woody, "Tensions are Still Simmering a Year After The World's 2 Biggest Countries Almost Clashed Over a Border At The Top Of The World," *Business Insider*, August 22, 2018, https://www.businessinsider.com/tensions-between-china-and-india-continue-year-after-doklam-standoff-2018-8

18 PTI, "Can't Share Hydrological Data of Brahmaputra River With India For Now: China", *The Economic Times*, July 13, 2018, https://economictimes.indiatimes.com/news/defence/cant-share-hydrological-data-of-brahmaputra-river-with-india-for-now-china/articleshow/60478124.cms?from=mdr

Conclusion

If China can hold back a report of this consequence in the Tibetan Plateau using its leverage when millions of people's lives are at stake, what will it do if it controls the data for the Arctic, Antarctic, and the Tibetan Plateau? China wielded its power over India in a disagreement over a border dispute. The stakes may be considerably higher in an international conflict. Control of data may mean life and death next time to hundreds of millions of people, and that coercion is a serious risk based on China's previous actions. China's act of retaliation sent a message to the world that China will use its power to monopolize resources and information, as evidenced in its geopolitical leverage. While China's rhetoric declares that its efforts are win-win, it uses its control, deflects its actions, and denies culpability.

What's At Stake?

First, China used the hydrological data with India as a geopolitical weapon in 2017. There is no reason to doubt that it will use data from the Three Poles Project as a political weapon to force states into compliance with its demands. As long as states depend on China for information, Beijing can decide what, when, and how it delivers data other states need.

Second, the Chinese government has spent more on Three Poles Project efforts than other states.[19] This investment includes new equipment and infrastructure ranging from ice-breakers to base camps to specially designed planes.[20] The number of Chinese bases in Antarctica has doubled, including four research stations, three airfields, and support for its ships.[21] As China continues to move into the Arctic and Antarctic, Beijing increases its ability to make decisions using its economic might as a weapon.

Third, the Chinese government recognizes that strengthening its presence in Antarctica will give the Chinese Communist Party enough leverage to assert administrative rights and harness natural resources available in Antarctica.[22]

Fourth, the Chinese government's rhetoric, targeted to foreign audiences, expresses its good intentions and win-win support. Meanwhile, Beijing took unilateral steps forward with the TPE project thereby increasing its global stature as the leading environmentally proactive nation. What is at stake is trust, leverage, and coercion.

---

19   Anne-Marie Brady, "Evaluating China as a Polar Power," *Cambridge University Press*, 2017, https://www.cambridge.org/core/books/china-as-a-polar-great-power/evaluating-china-as-a-polar-power/F4F892A4A0DAFDAD5031DACBD135985D/core-reader

20   The Economist, "The Voyage of Two Icebreakers Have Been Creating Headlines in China," *The Economist*, November 28, 2019, https://www.economist.com/china/2019/11/28/the-voyage-of-two-icebreakers-have-been-creating-headlines-in-china

21   Anne-Marie Brady, "China's Rise in Antarctica?," *Asian Survey 50,* no. 4 (2010): 759-785, https://www.jstor.org/stable/10.1525/as.2010.50.4.759

22   Nengye Liu, "What Are China's Intentions in Antarctica?," *The Diplomat*, June 14, 2019, https://thediplomat.com/2019/06/what-are-chinas-intentions-in-antarctica/

Part 5
International Pushback

A Chinese Dream or Xi Jinping's Nightmare?

The international community tuned into Beijing's words while watching the CCP's actions. The interplay was seen clearly and heard loudly. Whether or not the COVID-19 virus emanated from a Wuhan lab, China's lack of transparency and continued secrecy did not engender trust. The international community pushed back socially, economically, and militarily.

China donated items only to make countries pay. China produced masks, ventilators, and antibody tests en masse that did not work. China distributed vaccines that were fifty percent effective, resulting in thousands of people getting the virus, even when they were vaccinated.

Meanwhile, the quarantines gave global citizens plenty of time to talk among themselves, pondering the world around them. What they saw was environmental damage from effluents polluting rivers, darkened skies from the exhaust of coal-fired plants, militarization in the mountains, islands, and seas, and military coups by despotic leaders. Meanwhile, China's Belt and Road coalition grew to 140, as new countries hopped onto Beijing's economic bandwagon.

Countries continued to take China's money, though corruption and graft whittled away at the monies until they were gone.

Some countries were drowning in a sea of debt as costs mounted, needs increased, and the poor were left behind. The Chinese view continued to be that the debts needed to be repaid no matter what. With their 'no-questions-asked' policy, the Chinese state-owned enterprises repeatedly said that it was not China's responsibility that the countries could not meet their obligations. Still, they would need to find money or collateral to pay back the loan.

When oil prices plummeted, countries like Angola needed to pay China double the amount of oil to pay back the loan. Other countries gave up port areas, railroads, and natural resources. Countries in the South China Sea faced an aggressive, formidable paramilitary circling other state's islands and natural resources like vultures waiting for the kill.

With China's string of pearls tightening around India, Africa, and Europe, maritime concerns sounded alarms. Simultaneously, the Arctic faced an increasingly aggressive China involved in Arctic Council activities, claiming that it was a "near-Arctic" state. Xi's speech at the World Economic Forum was another example of his grand showmanship with win-win cooperation and politically appealing narratives to offset the genocide the CCP was committing in Xinjiang Province. As China sought to be the planet's savior, professing that socialism was the right way forward for the world, international bodies like the G7 in June 2021 began to push back on the absence of transparency, disregard for rule of law, and insidious surveillance. The world is headed for a common destiny, but it has yet to be seen which path global citizens and their leaders will choose on the road to the future.

Chapter 1

Free and Open Indo-Pacific

Attempt to Prevent China from Taking Over a Non-Adjacent Waterway

Introduction

The seas and air should be freely traversable for commerce, transit, and tourism. In a perfect world, this would be the case when nations abide by the rule of law. However, China has taken control of the oceans and waterways outside of its jurisdiction, which has led to more than a 'conflict' but bullying, including capsizing boats, ramming vessels, taking other states' natural resources, and violating international rules governing the marine environment. The International Court of Justice ruled against China, but this has not stopped Beijing from inflicting economic, military, and political coercion, including killing fishermen and taking their catch.

Meanwhile, China's aggression and economic clout are growing. Even though governing bodies have ruled against China at the International Court of Justice, no governing body holds Beijing accountable. The seas are in a state of anarchy, witnessed prominently in the South and East China Seas. However, this lawlessness is surprisingly accepted. Unwilling to anger China after watching how its 'Wolf Warriors' aggressively attack brands and countries, international law is weakened to the point that there is no rule of law in some locations.

China insists on its wide-ranging territorial and maritime claims. Few countries have pushed back, and some have even turned to embrace China with its promises of economic, military, and political support, even when China's incursions into the country's territory and maritime areas have been fatal. A few countries, for reasons of regional stability, security, and peacekeeping, have stepped up to enforce the rule of law that China egregiously ignores.

UNCLOS and Rule of Law

The international law governing the seas is the United Nations Convention on the Law of the Sea (UNCLOS).[1] This agreement codifies the guidelines for individuals, businesses, and nations to follow. With 168 parties and 157 signatories, UNCLOS defines international waters, territorial waters, archipelagic waters, contiguous zone, exclusive economic zones, innocent passage, transit passage, environmental obligations, marine habitats, and the use of natural resources.

Along with describing nations' rights and responsibilities, UNCLOS explicitly discusses freedom of navigation and overflight subject to the regulation of coastal states. Additionally, coastal states are given jurisdiction to an Exclusive Economic Zone (EEZ) to explore and exploit marine resources in its adjacent continental shelf extending 200 nm from its shore. In this region, nations have sovereign rights to local fish, oil, natural gas, and sea formations, following the UNCLOS environmental protection and marine resource guidelines.[2]

---

1   UN General Assembly, *Convention on the Law of the Sea*, December 10, 1982, available at: www.un.org/depts/los/convention_agreements/texts/unclos/unclos_e.pdf

2   OECD, "Exclusive Economic Zone (EEZ)," *OECD*, Updated March 4, 2003, https://stats.oecd.org/glossary/detail.asp?ID=884

China participated in the process and was one of the first 119 UNCLOS signatories, ratifying the Convention on May 15, 1996.[3] Yet, China claims waters that are not in its Exclusive Economic Zone (EEZ). In doing so, it takes other state's territory and their marine and natural resources while destroying the environment at the same time. Despite complaints filed against China, Beijing uses its excess cash-for-sovereignty diplomacy to negotiate with individual countries using a divide and conquer strategy backed by its economic might.[4]

China-Vietnam Goodwill Waning

Any remaining goodwill between Beijing and Hanoi has been threatened by China's ultimatums regarding Vietnam's quest to access the natural resources in its EEZ. A 2019 Vietnamese Defense white paper discusses China's actions stating, "New developments in the East Sea [South China Sea], including unilateral actions, power-based coercion, violations of international law, militarization, change in the status quo, and infringement upon Viet Nam's sovereignty, sovereign rights, and jurisdiction as provided in international law, have undermined the interests of nations concerned and threatened peace, stability, security, safety, and freedom of navigation and overflight in the region."[5]

Vietnam lent its support to the Philippines in the April 2021 People's Liberation Army Navy (PLAN) menacing actions in the South China Sea.[6] Beijing's paramilitary has threatened to take another one of the Philippines' islands by sending hundreds of vessels to and around Whitsun Reef in the Philippines' EEZ.

Indian Ocean and Bay of Bengal

States in the Indo-Pacific have grown increasingly concerned outside of the South China Sea as well. In April 2021, the United States joined the Royal Australian Navy, French Navy, Indian Navy, and Japan Maritime Self-Defense Force for the third time in La Perouse.[7] In April 2021, joint navy war game exercises occurred at an Australian bay.

France, by sending its warships to the South China Sea, has demonstrated that Paris will confront Beijing's claims and work with Quad nations.[8] The Defense Minister of France,

---

3 Xinmin Ma, "China and the UNCLOS: Practices and Policies," *The Chinese Journal of Global Governance* 5, no. 1 (2019), https://doi.org/10.1163/23525207-12340036

4 Ralph Jennings, "China Uses Money, Diplomacy to Push Back Against US in Southeast Asia," *VOA News,* April 5, 2021, https://www.voanews.com/east-asia-pacific/voa-news-china/china-uses-money-diplomacy-push-back-against-us-southeast-asia

5 Socialist Republic of Viet Nam Ministry of National Defence, "2019 Viet Nam National Defence," *National Political Publishing House*, 2019, http://www.mod.gov.vn/wps/wcm/connect/08963129-c9cf-4c86-9b5c-81a9e2b14455/2019VietnamNationalDefence.pdf?MOD=AJPERES&CACHEID=08963129-c9cf-4c86-9b5c-81a9e2b14455

6 Ralph Jennings, "Vietnam Joins Opposition to Chinese Activity Near Disputed Sea Reef," *VOA News,* April 7, 2021, https://www.voanews.com/east-asia-pacific/voa-news-china/vietnam-joins-opposition-chinese-activity-near-disputed-sea-reef

7 Lt. Cmdr. Sherrie A. Flippin, "Multinational Naval Forces Conduct Exercise La Perouse," U.S. *Indo-Pacific Command,* April 6, 2021, https://www.pacom.mil/Media/News/News-Article-View/Article/2562895/multinational-naval-forces-conduct-exercise-la-perouse/

8 Rachel Zhang, "Explainer | South China Sea: Why France is Flexing Its Muscles in the Contested Waters," *South China Morning Post*, February 28, 2021, https://www.scmp.com/news/china/diplomacy/article/3123342/south-china-sea-why-france-flexing-its-muscles-contested?module=knowledge_LHS&pgtype=article&campaign=Asia%E2%80%99s_territorial_disputes

Economics, Trade, and Military
The Belt and Road Initiative Expands

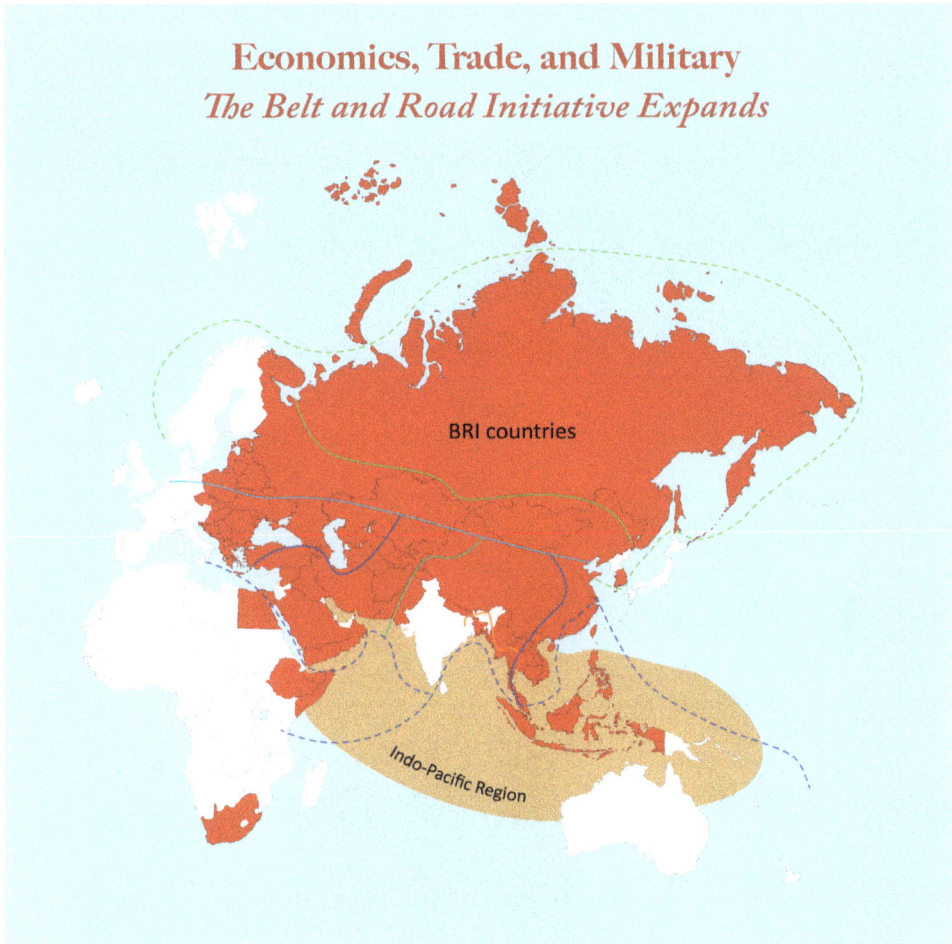

Florence Parly, affirmed "that international law is the only rule that is valid, whatever the sea where we sail."[9]

Britain has also committed itself to the Indo-Pacific, explaining that the region is fast becoming the world's geopolitical center, by sending an aircraft carrier to India in April 2021. Boris Johnson explained, "There is no question that China will pose a great challenge to an open society such as ours, but we will also work with China where that is consistent with our values and interests."[10]

---

9   Sarah Zheng, "France Says it Sent an Attack Submarine on an 'Extraordinary Patrol' Through the South China Sea," Insider, February 9, 2021, https://www.businessinsider.com/france-says-it-sent-attack-submarine-through-south-china-sea-2021-2

10 William James and Elizabeth Piper, "UK Seeks More Influence in Indo-Pacific as 'Moderating Impact' on China," Reuters, March 15, 2021, https://www.reuters.com/article/britain-politics-foreign/uk-seeks-more-influence-in-indo-pacific-as-moderating-impact-on-china-idUSKBN2B80AF

Germany plans to enter the Indo-Pacific region with its vessels amid China's ramped-up aggression against countries during the COVID-19 pandemic. Germany's increased naval activities in the area, included sending its frigate *Bayern* through international shipping routes to emphasize the need for a rules-based order.[11]

In 2021, France, Germany, and Britain issued a joint statement supporting the 2016 Hague tribunal ruling in the case, *Philippines v. China*, which ruled that Beijing did not have the right to claim the South China Sea. In a September 16, 2020 note verbal to the United Nations, "France, Germany and the United Kingdom underline the importance of the unhampered exercise of the freedom of the high seas, in particular the freedom of navigation and overflight, and the right of innocent passage enshrined in UNCLOS, including in the South China Sea."[12]

---

11 Arnaud Boehmann, "Why is Germany Sending a Frigate Through the South China Sea?," *South China Morning Post*, April 25, 2021, https://www.scmp.com/week-asia/opinion/article/3130854/why-germany-sending-frigate-through-south-china-sea

12 UN.org, "Note Verbale, UK NV No. 162/20," *UN.org*, September 16, 2020, https://www.un.org/Depts/los/clcs_new/submissions_files/mys_12_12_2019/2020_09_16_GBR_NV_UN_001.pdf

In a statement by the Netherlands, Amsterdam declared that the militarization of the South China Sea is troubling. "The EU should seek cooperation with countries in the region for free passage and guaranteed maritime safety," continuing, "In that context, the EU must express itself more often and more strongly on developments in the South China Sea that violate the United Nations Convention on the Law of the Sea."[13]

In June 2019, the Prime Minister of Thailand, Prayut Chan-o-cha, explained, "The Indo-Pacific region should be seen as a region of dialogue and cooperation instead of rivalry, and it should be seen as a region of development and prosperity for everyone."[14]

Japan's Pursuit of a Free and Open Indo-Pacific

To counter China, Japan has developed its open economic and transportation corridors through the Indo-Pacific region as a response to China's exclusive and secretive transit projects. The Japan International Cooperation Agency (JICA) has funded port projects like the Nacala in Mozambique, Mombasa in Kenya, the Taomasina in Madagascar, Duqm in Oman, Mumbai in India, Matarbari in Bangladesh, and Yangoon in Myanmar.[15] Japan's pursuit has been called the Bay of Bengal Industrial Growth Belt (BIGB), Asia-Africa Growth Corridor (AAGC), and the Free and Open Indo-Pacific (FOIP) strategies.

In November 2016, Prime Minister Narendra Modi and Prime Minister Shinzo Abe signed a joint declaration to create the Asia Africa Growth Corridor (AAGC). The goal was to collaborate on projects related to:

1. development and cooperation projects,
2. quality infrastructure and institutional connectivity,
3. capacity and skill enhancement, and
4. people-to-people partnerships.[16]

By deepening the relationship between India and Japan they can jointly implement the initiatives: "Digital India", "Skill India", "Smart City", "Swachh Bharat", and "Start-Up India".

Japanese efforts toward a free and open Indo-Pacific are not new. In "Asia's Democratic Security Diamond", December 27, 2012, a seed of 'The Quad', Prime Minister Shinzo Abe warned that the South China Sea was increasingly becoming "Lake Beijing" stating,[17]

---

13 Drake Long, "Netherlands Unveils Asia Strategy, Urges EU to Speak Out on South China Sea," *Radio Free Asia*, November 17, 2020, https://www.rfa.org/english/news/china/netherlands-southchina-sea-11172020161222.html

14 United States of America Department of State, "A Free and Open Indo-Pacific," *United States of America Department of State*, November 4, 2019, https://www.state.gov/wp-content/uploads/2019/11/Free-and-Open-Indo-Pacific-4Nov2019.pdf

15 Economic Research Institute for ASEAN and East Asia, "Asia Africa Growth Corridor," *Economic Research Institute for ASEAN and East Asia*, May 22-26, 2017, https://www.eria.org/Asia-Africa-Growth-Corridor-Document.pdf

16 Ibid.

17 Shinzo Abe, "Asia's Democratic Security Diamond," *Project Syndicate*, December 27, 2012, https://www.project-syndicate.org/onpoint/a-strategic-alliance-for-japan-and-india-by-shinzo-abe?barrier=accesspaylog

Peace, stability, and freedom of navigation in the Pacific Ocean are inseparable from peace, stability, and freedom of navigation in the Indian Ocean. Japan, as one of the oldest sea-faring democracies in Asia, should play a greater role—alongside Australia, India, and the US—in preserving the common good in both regions.

In an address at the Seventy-Third Session of the United Nations General Assembly, September 25, 2018, Prime Minister Shinzo Abe remarked,[18]

> What I call the 'Free and Open Indo-Pacific Strategy' derives from our desire to preserve the blessings of open seas, together with these very countries, as well as the United States, Australia, India, and others, and indeed, all countries and peoples who share the same intent.

He explained that Japan had centuries of naval explorations in the Indo-Pacific region and needs to be a part of a larger group of nations who are willing to secure international waters and air spaces while protecting the international rules-based order.

Australia and New Zealand's Vantage Point

Australia faced a fierce blizzard of competition with China in 2021. China stopped buying Australian lobster along with beef, wine, and barley to coerce Australia to agree to China's demands and punish Australia for adopting policies that do not fit China's agenda.[19] China's bullying has not been taken well in Australia.

Australia and New Zealand have economic ties with China but are increasingly threatened by China's assertive militaristic behavior, including interference in their political systems. Regional security is paramount for leaders and residents of both countries as Canberra and Wellington strategize how to intensify their engagement in the Indo-Pacific.[20]

Driven by concerns about security, development, and corruption, Australia seeks to play a critical political role in the Free and Open Indo-Pacific (FOIP) strategy as 'The Quad' diversifies its position from that of merely defense partners.[21] Despite a lack of significant funds to provide international policing, one way to support rule of law conduct is to coordinate connectivity, technology, and relationship building with potential regional partners like Myanmar, Bangladesh, Sri Lanka, and the Maldives. As China continues to push "white elephant" projects, Australia can take the lead in offering infrastructure projects to support regional government initiatives.

---

18   Ministry of Foreign Affairs of Japan, "Address by Prime Minister Abe at the Seventy-Third Session of the United Nations General Assembly," *Ministry of Foreign Affairs of Japan,* September 25, 2018, https://www.mofa.go.jp/fp/unp_a/page3e_000926.html

19   Stephen Long, Mary Fallon, and Naomi Selvaratnam, "Collateral Damage," *ABC News Australia,* Updated April 26, 2021, https://www.abc.net.au/news/2021-04-26/the-collateral-damage-of-australia-trade-war-with-china-/100071952

20   Michael S. Chase and Jennifer D.P. Moroney, "Regional Responses to U.S.-China Competition in the Indo-Pacific," *RAND Corporation,* 2020, https://www.rand.org/pubs/research_reports/RR4412z1.html

21   David Brewster, "A 'Free and Open Indo-Pacific' and What it Means for Australia," *The Interpreter,* March 7, 2018, https://www.lowyinstitute.org/the-interpreter/free-and-open-indo-pacific-and-what-it-means-australia

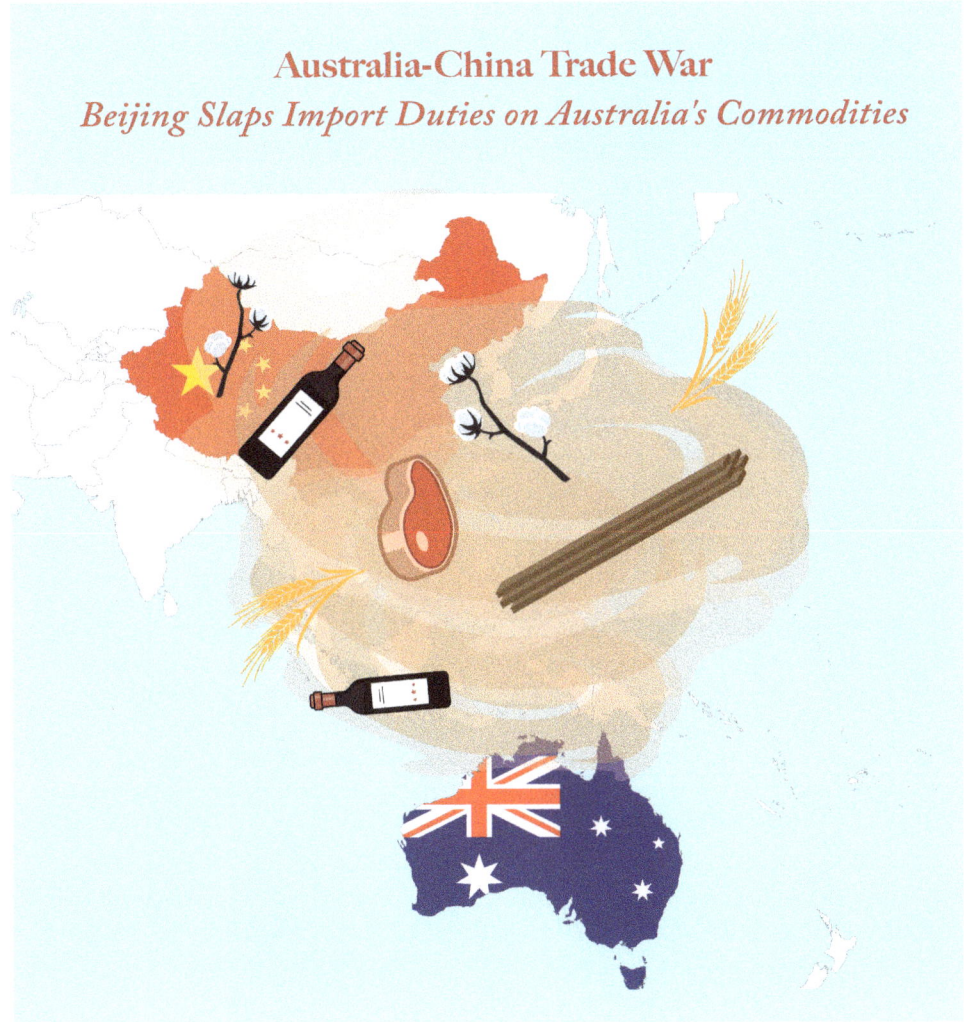

Australia-China Trade War
Beijing Slaps Import Duties on Australia's Commodities

Conclusion

Today, rule of law is eroded, weakened to the point of anarchy in the Indo-Pacific. This situation has led countries to step up and both advocate and support a Free and Open Indo-Pacific. There is no peacekeeping authority, though the United States and its allies have attempted to enforce the law, often at the detriment of their political reputations. The international media's mantra is that the 'containment' is being exerted by 'The Quad' (Australia, India, Japan, and the United States). However, other states are growing increasingly concerned by China's expanding claims in Asia and the Indo-Pacific and they too are not sitting idly by.

The conflicts in the Indo-Pacific region continue to be erroneously deemed a U.S.-China rivalry. However, the real problem is a China that is bullying states and then using 'carrot and stick' economic coercion with promises of money and political threats, both verbal and physical. China's rivalry is with other states too. Just ask Australia, Japan, India, Vietnam, the Philippines, and many more. The United States is not the only country involved in attempting to protect international rule of law.

India offers a strategic focal point with a vast population. Although China borders India, India has also been a critical partner in many projects. The country itself is the crucial pivot for any activity in the Indian Ocean, and its absence from China's BRI is a significant gap in that strategy. Furthermore, China is tightening its grip on the hardening string of pearls, with ports surrounding India and increasing control in Myanmar.

However, China continues to advance its expansive agenda despite instances of pushback. In February 2021, China unilaterally put into motion a Coast Guard Law whereby its coast guard, thousands of miles from the mainland, authorizes itself to commit militaristic acts against South China Sea states with impunity. "Using hand-held, ship-mounted, or airborne weapons, the law empowers the coast guard to demolish structures built by other countries on islands claimed by China and even to create 'exclusion zones', as required, where vessels of other nations will not be permitted to enter."[22]

What's at Stake?

First, the waters of the Indo-Pacific are heating up. U.S. officials say they sent Navy ships to the South China Sea ten times in 2020 adding B-52 bomber overflights at least once as a way of showing that the disputed waterway remains open to international use rather than exclusive Chinese control.[23] At different times, the U.S. has conducted drills alongside other navies in the Indo-Pacific inside and outside the South China Sea. Amid growing competition, the U.S. has taken the lead in ensuring that international waterways in the Indo-Pacific offer a safe thoroughfare.

Second, Australia is feeling China's heat. Australia's Home Affairs Department Secretary, Mike Pezzullo, warned of war on the horizon, stating, "Today, as free nations again hear the beating drums and watch worryingly the militarisation of issues that we had, until recent years, though unlikely to be catalysts for war, let us continue to search unceasingly for the chance for peace while bracing again...for the curse of war"[24]

Third, one of the strategic dilemmas faced by small states in Southeast Asia and other nations in the Indo-Pacific is called the Asian paradox, which occurs when states seek security from the United States while seeking financing from China.[25] As states align

---

22 Pratnashree Basu, "China's New Coast Guard Law: Will Recurrent Maritime Coercion Lead to a Denouement at Sea?," *Observer Research Foundation,* February 24, 2021, https://www.orfonline.org/expert-speak/chinas-new-coast-guard-law/

23 Ralph Jennings, "China Uses Money, Diplomacy to Push Back Against US in Southeast Asia," *VOA News,* April 5, 2021, https://www.voanews.com/east-asia-pacific/voa-news-china/china-uses-money-diplomacy-push-back-against-us-southeast-asia

24 Reuters, "Australian Official Warns Drums of War are Beating," *Reuters,* April 26, 2021, https://www.reuters.com/world/asia-pacific/australian-official-warns-drums-war-are-beating-2021-04-27/

25 Michael T. Rock and Heidi Bonnett, "The Comparative Politics of Corruption: Accounting for the East Asian Paradox in Empirical Studies of Corruption, Growth and Investment," *World Development* 32, no. 6 (2004): 999–1017.

with the United States, Japan, Australia, and India, they find themselves trapped by the existential reality of living in China's backyard, and feeling Beijing's influence.[26]

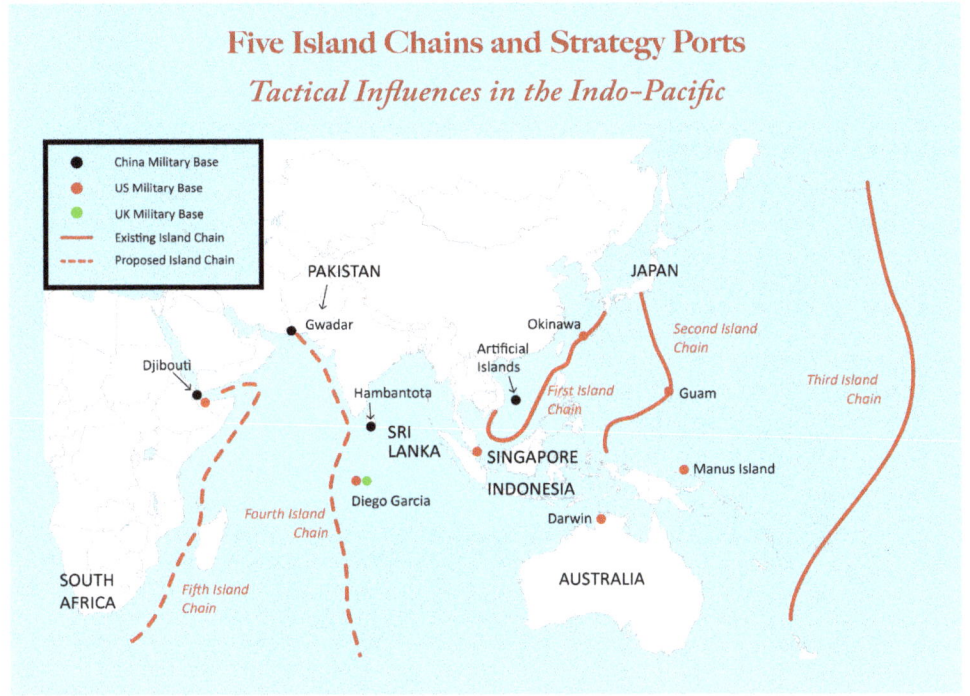

---

26   Mohd Aminul Karim and Faria Islam, "Bangladesh-China-India-Myanmar (BCIM) Economic Corridor: Challenges and Prosepcts," *The Korean Journal of Defense Analysis* 30, no. 2 (2018): 283-302.

Chapter 2

ASEAN, Code of Conduct, and the South China Sea

Unlawful Militarization and Relentless Aggression

Introduction

Stakeholders are watching China's militarization in the South China Sea. Chinese authorities state that they must safeguard their sovereignty and historic right to the South China Sea (SCS), even though international law states that China's claim is invalid. In the case, *Philippines v China*,[1] the International Court of Justice ruled that, by virtue of the United Nations Convention on the Law of the Sea (UNCLOS), China does not have a right to the SCS waters. UNCLOS, ratified by China and the other South China Sea claimant states, explains that each state has a lawful right to the 200 nm in the seas outside of their territory.

ASEAN, Code of Conduct, and Empty Promises

Since 1967, the Association of Southeast Asian Nations (ASEAN) has sought to maintain peace, security, and sovereignty among the nations of Southeast Asia without foreign interference. However, disputes between member nations concerning the South China Sea (SCS) constitute a significant obstacle. Furthermore, China claims 'undisputable sovereignty' over the SCS, which has led to significant tensions.[2]

ASEAN is an intergovernmental body that meets to discuss issues facing countries in their 'neighborhood' to find areas of mutual benefit and cooperation. ASEAN is made up of Brunei, Cambodia, Indonesia, Laos, Malaysia, Myanmar, the Philippines, Singapore, Thailand, and Vietnam. ASEAN has been successful in collaborating on economic development projects and cultivating relationships.

One of the most significant was the Regional Comprehensive Economic Partnership (RCEP), signed November 15, 2020, authorizing a free trade agreement covering a market of 2.2 billion people and 30% of the world's GDP.[3] The RCEP included ASEAN member states, Australia, China, Japan, the Republic of Korea, and New Zealand. Especially with the challenges of COVID-19 deficit spending, the multilateral RCEP boosted businesses with 65% of goods traded without tariffs and quotas and supply chains constructed to generate regional job growth.

Nevertheless, ASEAN faces challenges from China's economic, political, and military coercion. The ten-member body, influenced by China's flood of investment capital, has been unwilling to anger its financier. Thus, as Beijing expands its regional claims, a growing imbalance between Southeast Asian states and China has tilted the scale. ASEAN member states face difficult decisions in light of China's regional expansion and coercion.

Although Vietnam and the Philippines have been most vocal due to China's proximity and their loss of sovereignty, Brunei, Indonesia, Malaysia, Singapore, and Taiwan have

---

1   Permanent Court of Arbitration, "The South China Sea Arbitration (The Republic of Philippines v. The People's Republic of China," *Permanent Court of Arbitration*, n.d., https://pca-cpa.org/en/cases/7/

2   Sarah Lohschelder "Chinese Domestic Law in the South China Sea," *Center for Strategic & International Studies*, n.d., https://www.csis.org/npfp/chinese-domestic-law-south-china-sea

3   Association of Southeast Asian Nations, "ASEAN Hits Historic Milestone with Signing of RCEP," *Association of Southeast Asian Nations*, November 15, 2020, https://asean.org/asean-hits-historic-milestone-signing-rcep/

also experienced the People's Liberation Army Navy's provocative threats.[4] Brunei offered China access to its oil reserves. Indonesia's Natuna Islands were endangered by China's paramilitary. Malaysia attempted to deploy an oil exploration rig in the South China Sea, though China tailed and harassed Malaysian vessels in a month-long standoff. Singapore tried to remain neutral amid South China Sea conflicts, but a growing Chinese presence near their waters strain economic relations. Taiwan has islands in the South China Sea, including one in the Spratlys not far from China's militarized outposts.

ASEAN has sought to find common ground with China for decades but continues to find only empty promises. Ultimately, ASEAN aims to encourage China to agree to a Code of Conduct and uphold its commitment to cooperating with regional states and respecting their sovereignty. On the other hand, China would prefer negotiating diplomatic issues individually with states due to its asymmetric power imbalance and associated domination and coercion rather than abiding by multilateral, multinational agreements.[5] Nevertheless, China maintains that it is benevolent and willing to entertain the idea of a Code of Conduct. The 2020 Code of Conduct negotiations were the first attempt that genuinely appeared to be nearing an agreement. Even then, the meetings, held in China, occurred as Chinese boats rammed and sunk Vietnamese and Philippine vessels.

---

4   Rachel A. Winston and Ishika Sachdeva, *Raging Waters in the South China Sea* (Irvine: Lizard Publishing, 2020).
5   Ibid.

China's New Coast Guard Law

Despite this, China enacted a new law without agreement with the other claimant states, termed the Coast Guard Law. In February 2021, China unilaterally declared that this law went into effect. Since Beijing's one-sided law oversees territorial waters of Korea, Japan, Taiwan, Vietnam, the Philippines, Indonesia, Malaysia, and Brunei, in each of their Exclusive Economic Zones, the provisions have intensified and provoked conflict.

President Rodrigo Duterte said that with China's actions, to back the South China Sea, "the only way is by war…There is no way that we can get back the Philippine Sea without any bloodshed."[6] Philippine House of Representatives member, Manuel Cabochan III, exclaimed, "Friendship with China will lead nowhere. The harassment of our fishermen and our soldiers has intensified…The Philippines should not be silent to the abuse of China."[7]

Foreign Secretary Teodoro Locsin Jr. described the new Chinese law as "a verbal threat of war to any country that defies" its provisions.[8] In April 2021, Philippine Foreign Affairs Secretary Del Rosario said that Chinese officials should be held "criminally accountable for inflicting the most massive devastation" of the South China Sea and the Philippines should make "China pay monetarily for its crimes. China mercilessly destroyed the breeding grounds of fish and other marine life in the Spratlys."[9]

Passages of China's Coast Guard law include,[10]

> Article 17: For a foreign vessel that illegally enters the territorial sea of China or any waters within it, a coast guard agency shall have the power to order it to leave immediately or take measures such as detention, forcible expulsion, or forcible ejection by towing.

> Article 22: When the national sovereignty, sovereign rights, or jurisdiction is being illegally violated at sea by a foreign organization or individual, or is in imminent danger of illegal violation, a coast guard agency shall have the power to take all necessary measures including the use of weapons to stop the violation and eliminate the danger according to this Law and other applicable laws and regulations.

Fishermen's boats, ill-equipped to protect themselves against China's significantly larger armed paramilitary 'fishing vessels', are rammed and sunk. These fishermen spend their days as the Philippine and Vietnamese first line of defense while they reel in the catch for their coastal villages. Even then, Chinese vessels board their boats and confiscate their fish under the new 'law'. At the same time, the People's Liberation Army Navy (PLAN) constructed

---

6   Radio Free Asia, "Duterte: Philippines Prepared to Send Navy to Defend South China Sea Resources," *Radio Free Asia,* April 20, 2021, https://www.rfa.org/english/news/china/philippines-southchinasea-04202021155625.html

7   J.C. Gotinga, "Duterte: Philippines Prepared to Send Navy to Defend South China Sea Resources," *Benar News,* April 20, 2021, https://www.benarnews.org/english/news/philippine/ph-ch-scs-oil-04202021143200.html

8   Jim Gomez, "Philippines Protests New China Law as 'Verbal Threat of War'," *ABC News,* January 27, 2021, https://abcnews.go.com/International/wireStory/philippines-protests-china-law-verbal-threat-war-75511461

9   Tristan Nodalo, "Del Rosario to Duterte: Standing Up for Nation's Rights is Not War vs. China," *CNN Philippines,* April 23, 2021, https://cnnphilippines.com/news/2021/4/23/albert-del-rosario-duterte-stand-up-china-wps.html

10 Coast Guard Law of the People's Republic of China, "Order of the President of the People's Republic of China," *Peking University Center for Legal Information,* February 1, 2021, http://en.pkulaw.cn/display.aspx?id=09868c44d041e84ebdfb&lib=law

arsenals of weapons and manpower, militarizing islands that the United Nations Convention on the Law of the Sea states do not belong to them.

Drilling for Oil Threatened

China has prevented Malaysia and Vietnam from drilling for oil or natural gas on their UNCLOS-defined territorial waters. The People's Liberation Army Navy swarmed rigs with boats and stopped drilling operations. China then coerced countries into giving up their legal right to access their resources. Beijing drilled on Vietnam's Exclusive Economic Zone and built military posts in Vietnamese waters slowly, gradually, and incrementally just short of the pace that might have countries across the South China Sea call for war.

The oil companies are some of the many losers. China aggressively attacked those who worked on oil rigs. Xi Jinping threatened to strike if the Philippines drilled for oil.[11] While Duterte expressed his warm appreciation to President Xi on numerous occasions, after China threatened a war, he proclaimed, "We intend to drill oil there, if it's yours, well, that's your view, but my view is I can drill the oil, if there is some inside the bowels of the earth, because it is ours.[12] *Reuters* quoted President Xi as saying, "Do not touch it".[13]

Vietnam's oil drilling experience was not much different. The *BBC* reported that Repsol of Spain, helping Vietnam drill for oil, was ordered to leave or else China would attack Vietnam.[14] China uses its might to strongarm states into submitting to its wishes while preventing them from accessing their land and resources. Oil and natural gas resources are valuable in this region and critical to these states' economies, but they are not the only focus of China's attack and threaten strategy.

Nibbling Away at Other Country's Territory

In 2020, China sank vessels, confiscated fishing catch, stopped oil drilling, harassed other country's ships, threatened planes with lasers, prevented repairs on an island runway, held large-scale military exercises, flew over other country's airspace, established districts to 'administer' the South China Sea, installed high-tech surveillance, and threatened to create an ADIZ. Few people in the media focused on these threats because there were 'more pressing' stories, and China took advantage of this vacuum.

Conclusion

Beijing is playing a waiting game. China's long history, despite numerous challenges, demonstrates a "super" resilience that galvanizes the nation. The Chinese Communist Party

---

11 Manuel Mogato, "Duterte Says China's Xi Threatened War if Philippines Drills For Oil," *Reuters*, May 19, 2017, https://www.reuters.com/article/us-southchinasea-philippines-china/duterte-says-chinas-xi-threatened-war-if-philippines-drills-for-oil-idUSKCN18F1DJ

12 Felipe Villamor, "Duterte Says Xi Warned Philippines of War Over South China Sea," *The New York times*, May 19, 2017, https://www.nytimes.com/2017/05/19/world/asia/philippines-south-china-sea-duterte-war.html

13 Manuel Mogato, "Duterte Says China's Xi Threatened War if Philippines Drills For Oil," *Reuters*, May 19, 2017, https://www.reuters.com/article/us-southchinasea-philippines-china/duterte-says-chinas-xi-threatened-war-if-philippines-drills-for-oil-idUSKCN18F1DJ

14 Bill Hayton, "South China Sea: Vietnam Halts Drilling After 'China Threats,'" *BBC News*, July 24, 2017, https://www.bbc.com/news/world-asia-40701121

(CCP) believes they can take one nibble of territory at a time, under the radar, without repercussions. The People's Liberation Army Navy (PLAN) has demonstrated numerous times that it is willing to use force. Chinese President Xi Jinping patiently waits, building his military and expanding his economy in ways his predecessors embraced.[15] Beijing believes that time is on its side.

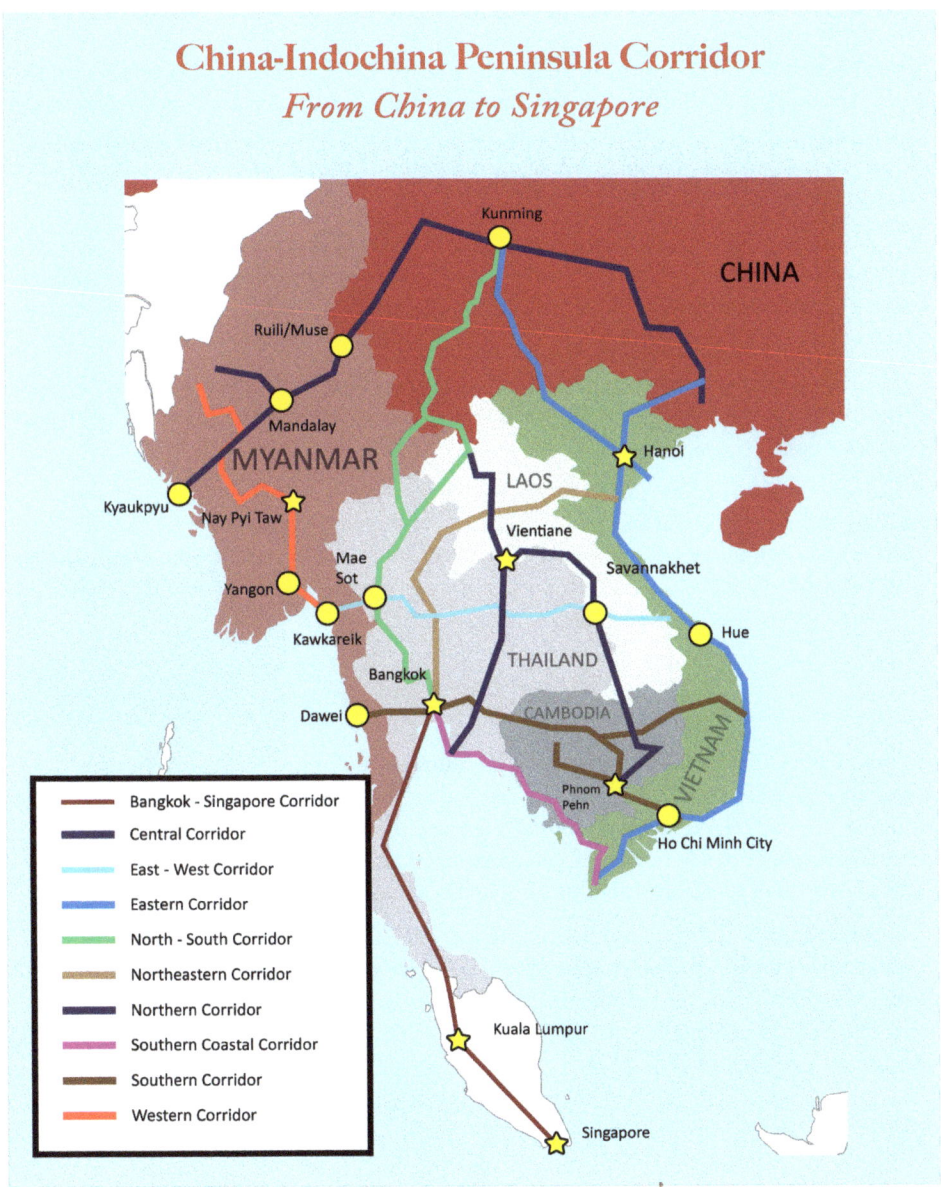

---

15 Rachel A. Winston and Ishika Sachdeva, *Raging Waters in the South China Sea* (Irvine: Lizard Publishing, 2020).

China has emerged as a dominant world force. China believes it has the sole right to the South China Sea, which disavows credence to other states' claims. Thus, China's expansive nine-dash line reach causes great consternation for claimant states who see China's encroachment, militarization, and rule-making as unfair and illegal. For example, China instituted a fishing ban in May 2020, angering Vietnamese fishermen. Yet, with each country's hesitancy to intervene and anger China, fishermen have taken action into their own hands.

As the Association of Southeast Asian Nations (ASEAN) pursued a Code of Conduct (CoC), attempting to establish rules and norms, little has been accomplished regardless of rhetoric about progress. Moreover, during the COVID-19 pandemic, China's assertion of its claims grew particularly egregious, alarming states with theft, takeovers, coercion, and military action.

A Declaration on the Conduct of Parties in the South China Sea (DoC) allowed states to move closer to adopt a CoC for the entire South China Sea. However, questions regarding monitoring, settling disputes, and arbitrating binding claims remain unanswered. China seeks to be the dominant force and therefore does not want the United States involved.

Even if a CoC were created, there is no evidence China would abide by the agreement or whether Beijing would ignore the provisions just as it did with the International Court of Justice ruling.

China's nibbling process, often called 'salami slicing', sounded faint alarms, barely heard around the world during the COVID-19 pandemic, though they grew louder as China's aggression increased. Meanwhile, since ASEAN made progress with the Regional Comprehensive Economic Partnership (RCEP), there is hope that this first step may improve relations enough to simmer the tensions.

What's at Stake?

First, China's preference for bilateral talks allows it to dominate in the asymmetric power play. As ASEAN member states make concessions with China, preferring Beijing's promises of money, agreements regarding a Code of Conduct will push a balanced resolution further off. Meanwhile, China seeks to draft a Code of Conduct that favors Beijing. As a result, a peaceful resolution remains elusive.

Second, China's ability to dominate is reduced if ASEAN remains strong as a multilateral governing body that rejects bullying. However, if ASEAN submits to Chinese demands for bilateral negotiations, ASEAN loses its legitimacy. As China asserts its economic, military, and political might over ASEAN states, there are valid fears that China will take over the South China Sea.[16]

---

16   Rachel A. Winston and Ishika Sachdeva, *Raging Waters in the South China Sea* (Irvine: Lizard Publishing, 2020).

Third, without a rules-based order, commerce can be stolen, any product can be replicated, and anyone can be imprisoned for any reason.[17] Rules and laws impede China's ambitious quest for the 'Chinese Dream' of a communist world with 'Chinese characteristics'. Although the International Court of Justice ruled in *Philippines v. China* that Beijing had 'no basis' for its claim to the South China Sea, China ignored the ruling, even though it signed and agreed to the United Nations Convention on the Law of the Sea. With China's coercive force, Beijing remains in control.

Fourth, Vietnam's neighbor to the north has superior firepower and has proven that it will use force, like when it took the Paracel Islands. Disputes over fish, oil, and natural gas, have raised questions about Vietnamese sovereignty. Yet, China and Vietnam will undoubtedly defend their claims, prolonging the seemingly unresolvable conflict.

17   Wade Shepard, "China's Copycat Manufacturers Are Now Pushing the Boundaries of Innovation," *South China Morning Post,* n.d. https://www.scmp.com/native/business/topics/invest-china/article/1802238/chinas-copycat-manufacturers-are-now-pushing

Chapter 3
Five Eyes Alliance
Australia, Canada, New Zealand, U.K., & U.S.

Introduction

Alliances closely tie states together for national security and defense. Without this vital information, countries will fall throught the cracks, possibly resulting in a catastrophic event. For example, information was available that could have prevented 9/11, but the lack of coordination resulted in the loss of thousands of lives and the destruction of New York's iconic landmarks. The lofty goal is for information to be collected and used to protect against geopolitical rivals, like China, Iran, North Korea, and Russia. However, the vast amount of information collected could be used for nefarious purposes if used to block or defame rivals, thwart elections, or expose political groups.

Secret information is intended to be guarded by those entrusted with it. However, as Edward Snowden demonstrated when he used his position to steal information from the government, sharing personal details about individuals, it is clear that stored information anywhere is not safe. He fled to China afterward and then to Russia, where he was given permanent residency in October 2020.[1] After his leak, along with the leaks of Julian Assange and others, questions emerged regarding safety, secrets, power, and privacy. Nonetheless, countries are rendered defenseless against foreign powers without secure information. It was for this reason that Five Eyes was created - to protect against severely critical external threats.

Five Eyes, Six Eyes, Ten Eyes, Fifteen Eyes

The Five Eyes Alliance, also referred to as FVEY, is an intelligence alliance, composed of five nations - Australia, Canada, New Zealand, the United Kingdom, and the United States.[2] Although Japan has closely cooperated with the Five Eyes, in 2020, Japan announced that it is interested in becoming a 'sixth eye', an idea strengthened by China's aggression in the East China Sea, increasing military production, and cyber capabilities along with the uncertainty of North Korean decision-making.[3]

For intelligence-sharing, the Five Eyes and Japan are joined by four additional states, Denmark, France, the Netherlands, and Norway to form the 'Ten Eyes'. The Fifteen Eyes add Germany, Belgium, Italy, Sweden, and Spain. Third party contributors include: Israel, Japan, Singapore, and South Korea.[4]

Origin of the Five Eyes

The origins of the FVEY can be traced back to the post–World War II period, when the Atlantic Charter was issued by the Allies on August 14, 1941 to lay out their goals. In

---

1. Anton Troianovski, "Edward Snowden, in Russia Since 2013, Is Granted Permanent Residency," *The New York Times*, Updated November 2, 2020, https://www.nytimes.com/2020/10/23/world/europe/russia-putin-snowden-resident.html

2. Office of the Director of National Intelligence, "Five Eyes Intelligence Oversight and Review Council (FIORC)," *Office of the Director of National Intelligence*, n.d., https://www.dni.gov/index.php/ncsc-how-we-work/217-about/organization/icig-pages/2660-icig-fiorc

3. Jagannath Panda and Ankit Panda, "RESOLVED: Japan Is Ready to Become a Formal Member of Five Eyes," *CSIS*, December 8, 2020, https://www.csis.org/analysis/resolved-japan-ready-become-formal-member-five-eyes

4. Barney Cotton, "Five Eyes Alliance: Everything You Need to Know," *Business Leader*, September 20, 2019, https://www.businessleader.co.uk/five-eyes-alliance-everything-you-need-to-know/73523/

a recently disclosed 'Top Secret' document, "Historical Note on the UKUSA COMINT Agreement", signed by President Truman September 12, 1945, post-World War II intelligence sharing began.[5] During the Cold War, the ECHELON surveillance system was initially developed by the FVEY to monitor the communications of the former Soviet Union and the Eastern Bloc, although it is now used to monitor private communications worldwide.[6]

These five countries have come together to form an alliance, under the UKUSA Agreement, for joint cooperation in signals intelligence.[7] Despite its global reach and close collaboration, the Five Eyes Alliance is constrained by its small membership and overburdened by current and developing global issues that need constant, up-to-date intelligence to address them. Therefore, it could be advantageous for the Five Eyes Alliance to consider expanding its membership.[8]

Five Eyes is not a centrally organized entity but rather a coalition of independent intelligence agencies. It is the most enduring and comprehensive intelligence alliance in the world, and is uniquely situated to handle the challenges brought by globalization. Primarily a signals intelligence (SIGINT) organization, Five Eyes does not conduct covert operations, but complements each nation's respective national intelligence capability with extensive coverage on a global scale.[9] The countries under the Five Eyes Alliance are not bound or subservient to any government or laws, and so, has the power, to spy on the citizens of its member states.[10]

Signals intelligence (SIGINT) is the backbone of the Five Eyes intelligence framework, including two components:[11]

> Communications intelligence (COMINT) – interception of voice communications, such as telephone calls, as well as text comms (emails, text messages, etc.)
>
> Electronic intelligence (ELINT) – use of electronic sensors to signals unrelated to communication, e.g. signals from radars or surface-to-air missile systems

Given the importance of SIGINT, Japan's savvy electronic data collections would make

---

5   Privacy International, "Historical Note on the UKUSA COMINT Agreement," *Privacy International*, October 31, 1972, https://www.documentcloud.org/documents/5759136-1-Historical-Note-on-the-UKUSA-COMINT-Agreement.html

6   Robert Siciliano, "How the Government (and Bad Guys) Intercept Electronic Data," *Huffington Post*, Updated October 8, 2013, https://www.huffpost.com/entry/how-the-government-and-ba_b_3725676

7   United States Department of Navy, "PKI Interoperability with FVEY Partner Nations on the NIPRNet," *United States Department of the Navy*, Archived from the original on 1 February 2014.

8   Dailey J., "The Intelligence Club: A Comparative Look at Five Eyes," *Journal of Political Sciences & Public Affairs 5*, no. 2 (2017), Retrieved from: https://www.longdom.org/open-access/the-intelligence-club-a-comparative-look-at-five-eyes-2332-0761-1000261.pdf

9   Martin Asser, "Echelon: Big Brother Without a Cause?," *BBC News*, July 6, 2000, http://news.bbc.co.uk/2/hi/europe/820758.stm

10 The Mainichi, "Five Eyes Intel Group Ties Up with Japan, Germany, France to Counter China in Cyberspace," *The Mainichi*, February 4, 2019, https://mainichi.jp/english/articles/20190204/p2a/00m/0na/001000c

11 Tadas Švenčionis, "5-Eyes, 9-Eyes, and 14-Eyes Agreement Explained," *Cyber News*, December 18, 2020, https://cybernews.com/resources/5-eyes-9-eyes-14-eyes-countries/

Japan a good partner. Inviting Japan to share on a more holistic level as a 'sixth eye' for ready-alert to security threats could prove to be valuable in containing China, Iran, North Korea, and Russia.[12]

Born out of necessity during the Cold War, the Five Eyes Alliance was created to monitor communications, and pass on information regarding the Soviet Union, along with Eastern Bloc communications and activities, with the intent to prevent another war. The Five Eyes alliance allows its member nations to share and support both the collection and analysis of global threats. While specific dissemination and coordination is not officially known, research indicates that Australia monitors South and East Asia and New Zealand covers the South Pacific and Southeast Asia.[13] The United Kingdom devotes its attention to Europe and Western Russia, while the United States monitors the Caribbean, China, Russia, the Middle East, and Africa.[14]

12 Jagannath Panda and Ankit Panda, "RESOLVED: Japan Is Ready to Become a Formal Member of Five Eyes," *CSIS*, December 8, 2020, https://www.csis.org/analysis/resolved-japan-ready-become-formal-member-five-eyes

13 James Cox, "Canada and the Five Eyes Intelligence Community," *Canadian Defence & Foreign Affairs Institute*, (2013) 6.

14 Ibid.

Since 2018, the Five Eyes Alliance countries have come together to help fight the threats arising from the foreign activities of, primarily Russia and China. Along with other interested and like-minded countries such as France and Japan, the union of members have formed a structure for sharing information amongst themselves, to help them combat geopolitical threats.[15]

The Safety and Secrets

The outbreak of the coronavirus and the resulting pandemic has opened the eyes of Western countries, making them painfully aware of their almost total dependence on China for essential products.[16] Though poor and underdeveloped just four decades ago, China is now an essential part of today's global industrial machine. China's development, manufacturing, and finance accounts for roughly one-sixth of global economic output, and is the world's largest manufacturer.[17]

Before the pandemic, China produced half the world's medical masks and was a major source of pharmaceuticals and protective equipment. Thus, at the time when countries around the globe are experiencing shortages, China had already prepared stocks of supplies to sell. "The world is dependent on China for manufacturing," explained Willy Shih, Harvard Business School professor and expert on U.S.-China supply-chain issues. China's manufacturing and distribution system provides more than just medical supplies, but electronics, clothing, furniture, toys, and daily use products.

To reduce this dependency, the countries under the Five Eyes Alliance pooled their resources and boosted the production of rare and semi-rare metals in Australia, Canada, and the United States.[18] This increased production intends to ensure the drastic reduction of the West's reliance on China for these precious commodities.[19]

Proposals have been raised by the Five Eyes Alliance to form a force that is formidable, both economically and politically, to compete with China. These proposals give ample room and opportunities to expand the trading reaches of these countries to countries outside of China and to the European Union as a whole.[20] The strategic interest of these democracies is to provide security for development and manufacturing for its industries and the world as China chooses its path, 'crosses the river by feeling the stones', and acts without aggression moderately and lawfully. This measured and law-abiding approach is supported by the ever-

---

15 Noah Barkin, "Five Eyes Intelligence Alliance Builds Coalition to Counter China," *Reuters*, October 11, 2018, https://www.reuters.com/article/us-china-fiveeyes-idUSKCN1MM0GH

16 Yasmeen Serhan and Kathy Gilsinan, "Can the West Actually Ditch China?," *The Atlantic*, April 24, 2020, https://www.theatlantic.com/politics/archive/2020/04/us-britain-dependence-china-trade/610615/

17 Alexandra Stevenson, "Coronavirus Outbreak Tests World's Dependence On China," *The New York Times*, January 29, 2020, https://www.nytimes.com/2020/01/29/business/china-coronavirus-economy.html

18 Patrick Wintour, "Five Eyes Alliance Could Expand in Scope to Counteract China," *The Guardian*, July 29, 2020, https://www.theguardian.com/uk-news/2020/jul/29/five-eyes-alliance-could-expand-in-scope-to-counteract-china

19 Ibid.

20 Melanie Hart and Kelly Magsamen, "Limit, Leverage, and Compete: A New Strategy on China," Center for American Progress, April 3, 2019, https://www.americanprogress.org/issues/security/reports/2019/04/03/468136/limit-leverage-compete-new-strategy-china/

more watchful ring of "eyes" to match and expose Chinese subterfuge, and to check China's rhetoric as it says one thing and ruthlessly and coercively does another.[21]

Xi Jinping and Joe Biden
Will America Stand by its Allies Or Let China Take Away Sovereignty?

Conclusion

While national security is of paramount importance to countries, individuals consider privacy and personal security a safeguarded right. Edward Snowden's cautionary note is valuable whether you think he is a hero or a villain. He explained,

> ...even if you're not doing anything wrong you're being watched and recorded. And the storage capability of these systems increases every year consistently by orders of magnitude to where it's getting to the point where you don't have to have done

---

21 David Howell, "Why Five Eyes Should Become Six," *The Japan Times*, June 30, 2020, https://www.japantimes.co.jp/opinion/2020/06/30/commentary/japan-commentary/five-eyes-now-become-six/

anything wrong. You simply have to eventually fall under suspicion from somebody even by a wrong call. And then they can use this system to go back in time and scrutinize every decision you've ever made, every friend you've ever discussed something with. And attack you on that basis to sort to derive suspicion from an innocent life and paint anyone in the context of a wrongdoer.[22]

However, Google, Facebook, and Twitter also have long memories and vast information databases that can access, cancel, and threaten with the same veracity. It is hard to imagine that, with the tremendous number of employees at these companies, that one or many could not use this information against others for social, political, or economic reasons.

Finally, and probably equally important, China has amassed field offices globally of extraordinary breath as it captures every detail of a human's movement. First, China has more cameras with facial recognition technology than any other country on the planet. In August 2020, according to *U.S. News & World Report*, of the top ten cities in the world with the greatest number of security cameras, nine out of the ten are in China.[23] China is on the forefront of the most ambitious artificial intelligence and DNA tracing collection of data on individuals worldwide.[24] China's successful ability to control its people is further enhanced by its social credit system and national digital currency so that every purchase or transaction can be monitored, controlled, and turned off.[25]

What's at Stake?

First, the Five Eyes, Six Eyes, Ten Eyes, and Fifteen Eyes are alliances to protect countries in a world where information control, abusive intrusion, and millions of surveillance cameras watch every move and keystroke.

Second, social media companies are equally corrupted by the righteousness of their moral high ground as they determine who can share information and who cannot.

Third, China's version of the National Security Agency in Guizhou Province is a massive artificial intelligence infused effort set to control its citizens as well as citizenry around the world as it collects DNA and personal information from individuals worldwide.

---

22 Robert Romano, "Why Americans Should Thank Edward Snowden," *Fox News Opinion*, Updated May 8, 2015, https://www.foxnews.com/opinion/why-americans-should-thank-edward-snowden

23 Matthew Keegan, "The Most Surveilled Cities in the World," U.S. *News & World Report*, August 14, 2020, https://www.usnews.com/news/cities/articles/2020-08-14/the-top-10-most-surveilled-cities-in-the-world

24 Paul Mozur, "One Month, 500,000 Face Scans: How China is Using A.I. to Profile a Minority," *The New York Times*, April 14, 2019, https://www.nytimes.com/2019/04/14/technology/china-surveillance-artificial-intelligence-racial-profiling.html

25 Nathaniel Popper and Cao Li, "China Charges Ahead with a National Digital Currency," *The New York Times*, March 1, 2021, https://www.nytimes.com/2021/03/01/technology/china-national-digital-currency.html

Chapter 4
The Quad
United Countries to Oppose China's Coercion and Aggression

Introduction

The Quad is a diplomatic security group comprised of Australia, India, Japan, and the United States. Each of these states seeks to provide a secure environment for trade, travel, and communication. With China's aggressive flashpoints in the South China Sea and East China Sea, the seas and skies have flared up. The prospects of war are nearer than they have been in many decades. In particular, China has entered Indian territory and killed Indian soldiers. China has threatened Japanese fishermen and has challenged its sovereignty over the Senkaku Islands.

Indo-Pacific security is essential to all parties as China's territorial expansion is a win-lose aggressive tactic. The Quad's development was not a fait accompli given India's reluctance to ruffle China's feathers. However, with China's aggression in the Himalayas and its threat to redirect water, India has a real problem with Beijing, pushing New Delhi farther away from China's orbit. Thus, New Delhi must hedge between China and the United States. However, China does not want to affiliate with a group that may stoke China's ire.

India is not the only nation shoved away from the Sinocentric orbit. Australia has received the brunt of Chinese bullying with both verbal and economic aggression. Chinese threats have been constant with Beijing's repulsion of Australian wine, barley, meat, and cotton. In November 2020, members of the defense forces of The Quad met in the Bay of Bengal to participate in Exercise MALABAR 2020 to enhance cooperation in Indo-Pacific maritime security and protect common interests.[1] This naval exercise seemed provocative to China, particularly as Australia tore apart the agreed-upon Belt and Road Initiative project with Australia in April 2021. This act was seen as more threatening, resulting in a stern warning from Beijing.[2]

Japan, though, is closer to China's most significant firepower. The East China Sea borders on the Taiwan Strait, where China has made its military presence known in daily bullying acts to threaten and warn Taiwan. However, Japan's Senkaku Islands are close to Taiwan, and the People's Liberation Army Navy (PLAN) and Beijing's paramilitary fleet patrol Japanese waters assertively pronouncing their claim to Japan's islands. If China declares war on Taiwan, Japan is almost inevitably involved. If Japan goes to war, the U.S. will be at war too via the Mutual Defense Treaty. Furthermore, Japan's State Minister of Defense Yasuhide Nakayama relayed that in the face of China's aggression, attacking Taiwan would be Japan's "red line".[3]

Thus, the deepening military association between the four members of The Quad is being propelled by China's aggressive military actions. In November 2020, Japan and

---

1   Senator the Hon Marise Payne, "Australia to Participate in Exercise Malabar 2020," *Australian Government Department of Defence Ministers*, October 19, 2020, https://www.minister.defence.gov.au/minister/lreynolds/media-releases/australia-participate-exercise-malabar-2020

2   Kirsty Needham, "Australia Cancels Belt and Road Deals; China Warns of Further Damage to Ties," *Reuters*, April 21, 2021, https://www.reuters.com/world/china/australia-cancels-victoria-states-belt-road-deals-with-china-2021-04-21/

3   Ju-min Park, "Japan Official, Calling Taiwan 'Red Line,' Urges Biden to 'Be Strong,'" *Yahoo Money*, December 25, 2020, https://money.yahoo.com/japan-official-calling-taiwan-red-103218677.html

Australia agreed to a pivotal military information-sharing agreement.[4] Air, land, sea, and submarine coordination were avenues discussed to deter PLA activities. In March 2021, The Quad met again to discuss mutual health challenges and security in the Indo-Pacific region. Australian Prime Minister, Scott Morrison, called the meeting "a historic moment" to "create a new anchor for peace and stability in the Indo-Pacific."[5]

While The Quad's ties are laudable, deeper economic cooperation is necessary since each country needs Beijing as a pipeline for trade. One effort put forth is to provide regional states with vaccines. Diplomatic and peacekeeping action in Myanmar may offer some solace to simmer the military coup and reassure surrounding nations. However, merely an anti-China stance offers little except the knowledge that they will stand together if China provokes war. The Quad alliance would also provide Taiwan some relief that it may not be alone in its fight for sovereignty and freedom.

China Uses its Economic Might to Stop Trades and Shipments on Wine, Beef, and Barley

China's Wolf Warrior Zhao Lijian Ignites a Fight with Digitally-Altered Image and Inflammatory Rhetoric in Unrestrained Attacks Against Australia

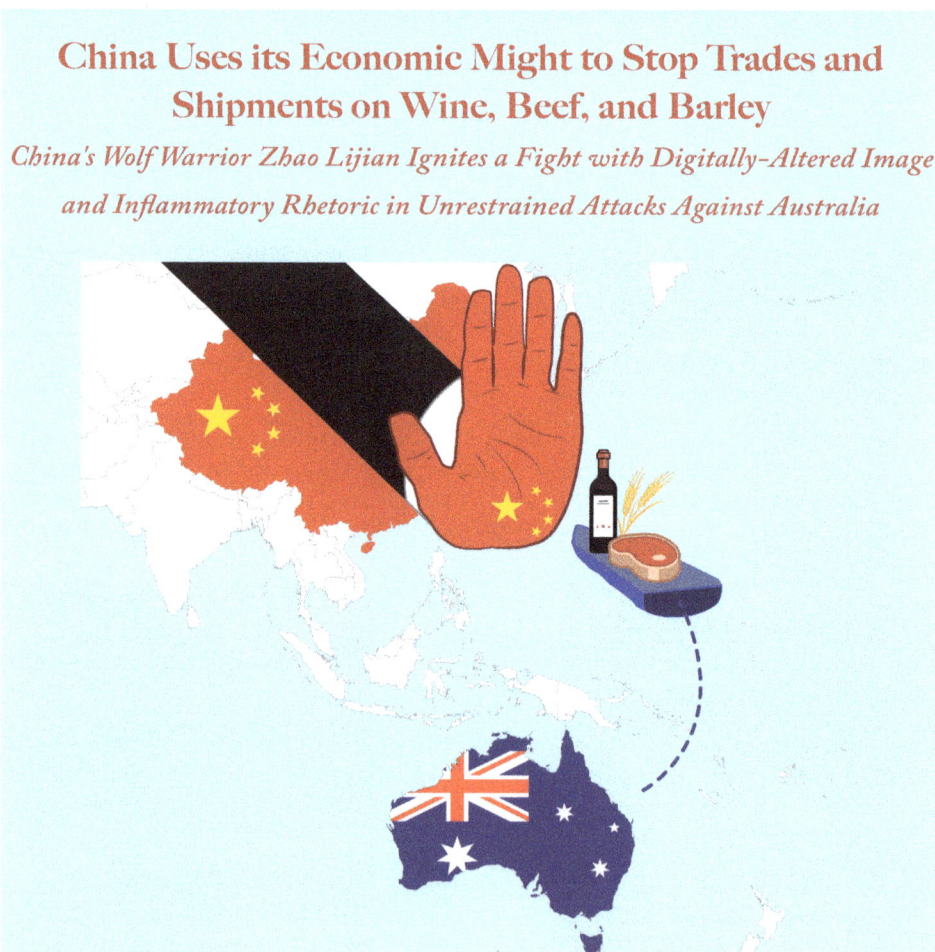

---

4 Prime Minister of Australia, "Reciprocal Access Agreement," *Prime Minister of Australia*, November 17, 2020, https://www.pm.gov.au/media/reciprocal-access-agreement

5 Wang Kao-cheng, "Quad Meeting a Key Turning Point," *Taipei Times*, March 21, 2021, https://www.taipeitimes.com/News/editorials/archives/2021/03/21/2003754195

Conclusion

Just as Xi Jinping began his speech at the April 2021 Boao Forum, The Quad can also say, "True friendship brings people close however far apart they may be."[6] While the four countries in The Quad may not have always been close friends, this is a time when they certainly need each other. Xi spoke in 2021 a few days after President Biden and Prime Minister Suga met in Washington, D.C. to discuss areas for cooperation, peace, Xinjiang, Hong Kong, and Taiwan.

From Beijing's perspective, The Quad may appear to be a coordinated force to contain China. However, they each remain trading partners with Beijing, and none want to jab at the dragon in their region, which has already viciously hurled flames at Australia. They may not even want to rail against China in any meaningful way.

---

6   Xinhua, "Full Text: Keynote Speech by Chinese President Xi Jinping at the Opening Ceremony of the Boao Forum for Asia Annual Conference 2021," *Xinhua*, April 20, 2021, http://www.xinhuanet.com/english/2021-04/20/c_139893137.htm

What's at Stake?

First, China's aggressive actions in the South China Sea, East China Sea, and the Indian Ocean have alarmed all of the nations bordering on or transiting these waters. However, those with smaller economies that rely on China for trade fear Beijing's reprisals, meaning that any effort to counter China's offensive measures must face larger forces united against threats of attack. As Beijing attempts to take over other country's sovereignty, clear signals should be sent.

Second, while The Quad is not an Asian NATO, it can be a clear warning that states will defend themselves and support one another. China has expanded its worldwide port and military base arsenal with no single country having capacity or will to limit Beijing's country-by-country dominating force. Instead, each country has chosen to take China's money, ignore Beijing's human rights abuses, and disregard the People's Liberation Army's expanded military presence.

Third, China is attempting to control the sea and sky around Taiwan. Beijing's aggressive actions pose a growing threat to Japan. Australia's tensions from China's bullying tactics have been no less concerning. India's military has met China's firepower face-to-face with the deaths of its soldiers and encirclement of Chinese ports. At stake is whether China will take its bullying and threats to the point of war and if its rabid paramilitary will ram or sink one too many boats.

Chapter 5

Beijing Warns about Boycotting Its 2022 Winter Olympics

180 Human Rights Groups Voice Opposition

Introduction

Beijing's grand celebration of the athletic spirit and disciplined training is within sight. This pinnacle of excellence offers skiers, skaters, bobsledders, and other individual and team competitors to demonstrate their talent. Since the first recorded Olympic Games in 776 B.C., athletes have united to compete head-to-head with the most disciplined and well-trained. Given the COVID-19 pandemic, challenges existed for athletes, trainers, and spectators. Regional, national, and international competitions leading up to the Olympics, if they took place, took on a different tone, including unplanned schedule diversions, travel restrictions, vaccine requirements, and ever-changing country-by-country regulations. The word resilience was never more apropos.

Nevertheless, around the corner, a spectacle of dramatic proportions will, once again, put Beijing in the international spotlight, and Xi Jinping will, undoubtedly, want to ensure that there are no snags. Beijing put on a spectacular show for the 2008 Summer Olympics, in which 3.5 billion people worldwide watched the remarkable, mesmerizing, and uniquely intriguing opening and closing ceremonies.

In December 2019, China's state-of-the-art high-speed railway went into operation, linking Beijing with its new winter Olympic venues in Zhangjiakou 100 miles away.[1] Hebei Province will be the host of 51 events. Yanqing, on the edge of the Gobi Desert, 55 miles away will host alpine skiing, bobsledding, and skeleton racing.[2] Neither of these cities has significant snowfall, with averages of eight inches per year and two inches per year, respectively.[3] Both venues will be covered in 100% artificial snow, a first in Winter Olympics history. One apparent snag for the Winter Olympics is the challenge of climate change. Temperatures in February 2021 rose to 78 degrees,[4] which is atypical for a winter Olympics and may cause problems for the events. In March 2021, China experienced a widespread sandstorm unseen in a decade that shrouded Beijing with sand so thick few people went outside.[5]

Calls for a Boycott

The calls for a boycott grew increasingly louder throughout the pandemic due to China's genocide of the Uyghur Muslims and the hundreds of concentration camps the Chinese Communist Party constructed in Xinjiang Province. China's 're-education and torture of its citizens in its western province alarmed people worldwide. However, China's actions in Hong Kong have been equally horrifying. And all of this stands in the

---

1   CGTN, "High-Speed Railway Opens Between Beijing and Zhangjiakou for 2022 Winter Olympics," *CGTN*, Updated December 31, 2019, https://newsus.cgtn.com/news/2019-12-30/China-s-Winter-Olympic-high-speed-railway-to-open-on-Monday--MO5HfJim9q/index.html

2   Sun Xiaochen, "Brick by Brick, Olympic Excitement Builds," *China Daily*, Updated January 11, 2021, https://global.chinadaily.com.cn/a/202101/11/WS5ffb85c7a31024ad0baa1993.html

3   James Gheerbrant, "Beijing 2022: A Winter Olympics without Snow?," *BBC Sport*, August 1, 2015, https://www.bbc.com/sport/winter-sports/33747313

4   Matthew Cappucci, "Beijing Soars to 78 Degrees, its Warmest Winter Temperature on Record," *The Washington Post*, February 22, 2021, https://www.washingtonpost.com/weather/2021/02/22/beijing-record-china-warmth/

5   Ibid.

foreground without mention of the traditional prisons, many, if not all of which are prison factories.

In previously free Hong Kong, Beijing stripped citizens of their rights through its National Security Law,[6] its courts thereafter convicting freedom activists for illegal congregation and for assembling during the 2019 pro-democracy rallies.[7] It should be clear, the world is on notice that they will not have rights that are protected in their home country if they come to the Olympics. In February 2021, a coalition of 180 human rights groups called for a boycott of the 2022 Beijing Olympics, according to the South China Morning Post.[8] The Hong Kong Free Press labeled Beijing's Winter Olympics the first "Genocide Olympics",[9] though many were aware of Germany's atrocities before the 1936 Summer Olympics in Berlin.

In 2020, freedom of speech activists and forty-seven journalists were imprisoned in China.[10] News organizations have pulled all of their reporters from China, and China has threatened to expel any remaining journalists.[11] Thus, there is grave concern about covering the Olympic games.

Berlin Olympics

The 1936 Berlin Olympics presented the first live public broadcast of Olympic events, beamed in black and white across screens worldwide.[12] Hitler showcased the unity and cooperation of the Nazi's Third Reich. Nazi propaganda fabricated during the early days of television portrayed Germany as open and accommodating. Television screenings showed Berlin as emerging from under the Treaty of Versailles and focused heavily on the hardships endured by the German people during the Great Depression. By manipulating the recordings and by filming and rerecording German athleticism, Nazi media displayed Aryan exceptionalism, drawing links between Nazi Germany and Ancient Greece.[13]

---

6   Rachel Winston and Ishika Sachdeva, *Raging Waters in the South China Sea: What the Battle for Supremacy Means for Southeast Asia* (Irvine: Lizard Publishing, 2020).

7   Zen Soo Associated Press, "7 Hong Kong Democracy Leaders Convicted as China Clamps Down," *ABC News*, April 1, 2021, https://abcnews.go.com/International/wireStory/hong-kong-activists-convicted-2019-illegal-assembly-76802866

8   Reuters, "Beijing 2022 Olympics: Activists Call for Boycott over China's Record on Human Rights," *South China Morning Post*, February 4, 2021, https://www.scmp.com/news/china/diplomacy/article/3120531/beijing-2022-olympics-activists-call-boycott-over-chinas

9   Peter Irwin and Zumretay Arkin, "In a Year, China Will Host the First Genocide Olympics," *Hong Kong Free Press*, February 6, 2021.

10   Helen Davidson, "China Worst Offender in Record-Breaking Year for Jailing of Journalists," *The Guardian*, December 15, 2020, https://www.theguardian.com/media/2020/dec/15/china-jails-the-most-journalists-for-second-year-running

11   Marc Tracy, Edward Wong, and Lara Jakes, "China Announces that it will Expel American Journalists," *The New York Times*, March 17, 2020, https://www.nytimes.com/2020/03/17/business/media/china-expels-american-journalists.html

12   Guinness World Records, "First Televised Olympics," *Guiness World Records*, n.d., https://www.guinnessworldrecords.com/world-records/first-televised-olympics

13   United States Holocaust Memorial Museum, "Nazi Propaganda," *United States Holocaust Memorial Museum*, n.d., https://www.ushmm.org/exhibition/olympics/?content=nazi_propaganda&lang=en

In 1936, there was also a call for a boycott, since the Nazi Party paper, the *Volkischer Beobachter*, stated that Jews and Blacks were not allowed to participate,[14] though this decree was lifted when countries threatened to boycott. Still, only a few athletes refused to come. However, as in 2021, there were movements in that earlier time from human rights groups that were actively seeking to withdraw. As a result, debates intensified in Great Britain, France, Sweden, Czechoslovakia, the Netherlands, the United States, and other countries.[15]

However, some athletes wanted to compete anyway, explaining that the best way to defeat Nazi power was to win athletically. Yet, those in support of the boycott adamantly protested the endorsement and tacit approval of Hitler and the Nazi Party. "The black athletes rationalized their decision by pointing to domestic prejudice and, like the Jewish athletes, by suggesting that their own victories in Berlin would embarrass the Third Reich and repudiate its claims of racial superiority."[16] This same argument will likely be used again for the 2022 Beijing Olympic games.

There is no doubt that with the pushback on human rights, President Xi will similarly highlight the remarkable talent of the Chinese, who are expected to make China appear extraordinary on the world stage. There is already an undercurrent that what the U.S. majority, privileged population does to its African-American population in America is just as bad as the Chinese Communist Party cutting people open to remove their organs, raping people, getting compliance using electric shock therapy, and hanging them from prison cells. Moreover, in the same way that "many contemporaries were dazzled by the splendor of the 1936 Olympics,"[17] President Xi is expected to attempt to similarly impress onlookers with the Beijing Olympics of 2022. It is ironic that Hitler's 1936 Games were the XI Olympics.

Caution When Speaking Out

Attending the Olympics may not be safe for foreigners. Furthermore, speaking out against forced organ removal, torture, genocide, and forced labor may land foreign nationals in jail. Mentioning Hong Kong, Taiwan, Tibet, or Xinjiang Province may put spectators in jail. The past President of the International Olympic Committee (IOC), Jacques Rogge, explained that it was "absolutely legitimate" for individuals to speak out against human rights and bring attention to the causes they passionately advocate.[18]

---

14 David Clay Large, *Nazi Games: The Olympics of 1936* (W.W. Norton & Company, 2007), 58.

15 United States Holocaust Memorial Museum, "The Nazi Olympics Berline 1936," *United States Holocaust Memorial Museum*, n.d., https://encyclopedia.ushmm.org/content/en/article/the-nazi-olympics-berlin-1936

16 Jeremy Schaap, "An Olympic Boycott that Almost Worked," *ESPN*, August 13, 2009, https://www.espn.com/olympics/news/story?id=4396362

17 Encyclopaedia Britannica, "Learn about the 1936 Berlin Olympics Games a Showcase for Hitler's Reich with its Technological Prowess," *Encyclopaedia Britannica*, n.d., https://www.britannica.com/video/180222/Overview-propaganda-Nazi-Berlin-Olympic-Games-performance-1936

18 Nick Mulvenney, "Interview – Games a Force for Good but No Panacea – Rogge," *Reuters*, August 6, 2007, https://www.reuters.com/article/idINIndia-28847320070806

However, in 2021, current IOC President, Thomas Bach, did not comment.[19]

Chinese CCP mouthpiece and state-run media Global Times writer Hu Xijin tweeted, "Boycotting 2022 Beijing Winter Games, an unpopular idea, won't receive wide support. IOC and athletes will both oppose it, and China will seriously sanction any country that follows such a call."[20] This threat to countries globally provides uncertainty about what 'seriously sanction' means, but the threat will undoubtedly be considered highly given Beijing's economic, political, and military might. The Wolf Warriors who defend China's nationalist propaganda are likely to be out in force attacking countries, athletes, and journalists who speak out for freedom, all the while loudly promoting China's "open, transparent, win-win commitment."

U.S. Secretary of State, Anthony Blinken, spoke with Yang Jiechi, CCP's Director of the Central Foreign Affairs Commission in February 2021. Yang explained that "no one can stop the great rejuvenation of the Chinese nation."[21] The human rights issues of torture, rape, sterilizations, human experimentation, and forced labor in Xinjiang Province are China's internal issues. Meanwhile, Blinken stated that he is in favor of cooperating with China.[22] Although the U.S. is unlikely to boycott the 2022 Olympic Games, no matter how much pressure is applied, the Chinese athletic committee will deliver stern warnings to team representatives. These team leaders will, in turn, tell athletes not to speak up for their beliefs given that (1) they are representing their country and (2) may be imprisoned.

Nonetheless, Chinese state-run media, *Xinhua*, ran an article on January 22, 2021, entitled "Beijing 2022 Preparation Receives a Vote of Confidence," citing President Xi as saying, "Not only will we host a successful Winter Olympic extravaganza, but also a spectacular Games with unique characteristics."[23] This propaganda served as a stamp of approval for the organizers while heralding Beijing's accomplishments, despite the pandemic, to ensure success.

Meanwhile, the People's Republic of China's (PRC) successful Olympics demonstrated to the world that the Chinese Communist Party could put on a fantastic show. Beijing's Games of the XXIX Olympiad (Beijing 2008) hosted 10,942 athletes from 204 National Olympics Committees in 28 sports and 302 events.[24] That event was the first time the PRC hosted the Olympic Games, and the result was astonishingly successful. No backlash happened at that time, and there was little fear.

---

19 Associated Press, "Beijing 2022: Human Rights Groups Urge IOC to Move Winter Olympics from China" *South China Morning Post*, September 10, 2020, https://www.scmp.com/sport/other-sport/article/3100944/beijing-2022-human-rights-groups-urge-ioc-move-winter-olympics

20 Xijin Hu, "Exposing the Hysterical, Insane British politician trying to thwart the Beijing Winter Olympics." *Global Times*, February 15, 2021 https://www.globaltimes.cn/page/202102/1215658.shtml

21 Naomi Xu Elegant, "What Biden and China President Xi Jinping Talked about in their First Phone Call," *Fortune*, February 10, 2021, https://fortune.com/2021/02/10/biden-china-president-xi-jinping-first-phone-call/

22 Humeyra Pamuk and David Brunnstrom, "New U.S. Secretary of State Favors Cooperation with China Despite Genocide of Uighurs," *Reuters*, January 27, 2021, https://www.reuters.com/article/us-usa-china-blinken/new-u-s-secretary-of-state-favors-cooperation-with-china-despite-genocide-of-uighurs-idUSKBN29W2RC

23 Xinhua, "Beijing 2022 Preparation Receives a Vote of Confidence," *China.org.cn*, January 22, 2021, http://www.china.org.cn/sports/2021-01/22/content_77142092.htm

24 Olympic.org, "Beijing 2008," *Olympic.org*, n.d., https://www.olympic.org/beijing-2008

Moreover, the IOC said that the 2008 Olympics would allow China to 'open up'. However, this did not happen. Particularly in Hong Kong and Xinjiang Province, "The Chinese government is heading in a much more repressive direction, not only violating the rights of its own people, but also targeting critics abroad and seeking to bully democratic nations into holding their tongue about crimes that shock the conscience," according to Real Clear Politics.[25]

Conclusion

It remains to be seen which celebrities appear and which companies continue to sponsor and promote the 2022 event. Freedom advocates suggest that "There should be no business as usual with a government that sends its citizens to "re-education camps," forces women to undergo involuntary sterilization, and imposes grotesquely long prison sentences on those who raise their voices on behalf of freedom."[26]

A distinct warning should echo across the planet. When China can lock up or detain, even famous journalists,[27] some from foreign countries,[28] and when activists can be rounded up, even in foreign countries,[29] the people of the world should sound a blaring alarm. Concerns will continue to be expressed regarding media access to players, national groups, and organizers. There may be some warnings emanating from Beijing itself. There is no doubt that China will take great care to protect against terrorist groups or protesters so that there are no problems.

What's at Stake?

First, the outcome of the entire 2022 Beijing Olympics is at stake.

Second, freedom of speech, as well as freedom itself, is at stake - the ability to speak freely without backlash or imprisonment from the Chinese Communist Party (CCP). One very real possible outcome is that of a spate of "hostage diplomacy", being caught in the crosshairs of a political firefight like Canadians Michael Spavor and Michael Kovrig, who have had to endure, as Canadians, imprisonment on trumped-up charges since December 2018.

Third, the CCP has warned of "serious sanctions" against any country that boycotts the Olympics and challenges China's internal affairs.

---

25 Michael Abramowitz and Arch Puddington, "China's Olympian Atrocity," *Real Clear Politics*, February 16, 2021, https://www.realclearpolitics.com/articles/2021/02/16/chinas_olympian_atrocity_145253.html

26 Ibid.

27 Reuters Staff, "Hong Kong Tycoon Jimmy Lai Arrested Again While in Jail, Papers Say," *Reuters*, February 17, 2021, https://www.reuters.com/article/us-hongkong-security/hong-kong-tycoon-jimmy-lai-arrested-again-while-in-jail-papers-say-idUSKBN2AH0RP

28 Stephen Dziedzic, "Australian Journalist Cheng Lei Formally Arrested in China, Says Foreign Minister Marise Payne," *ABC News*, February 7, 2021, https://www.abc.net.au/news/2021-02-08/australian-journalist-cheng-lei-arrested-in-china,-says-payne/13132192

29 Eli Pacheco, "US, EU Urge China to Release Missing Rights Activist 'Disappeared While Boarding Flight to Visit Sick Wife," *The Toys Matrix*, February 9, 2021, https://toysmatrix.com/us-eu-urge-china-to-release-missing-rights-activist-disappeared-while-boarding-flight-to-visit-sick-wife/

International Pushback | Part 5

Chapter 6

Questions and Quarantine

Power and Benevolence

Introduction

When countries make an agreement with an empire determined to change the world order, their leaders also tacitly agree to the consequences. From China's proclamations and expressed global ambitions, we know what that world order could look like. China has imprisoned more than a million of its own people in forced labor camps; some people believe it is two million. How much money is a country's sovereignty worth? How much is a life worth? How much is freedom worth? How much is a state's silence or tacit agreement worth?

States want to be on the 'right' side of the looming tidal wave that appears to be predicting the world's destiny. As countries deepen their dependence on China, they become trapped in Beijing's web. Stuck, they give up their assets, like Tajikistan's land transfer, give up ports, like in Sri Lanka and Greece, give up sovereignty, like the Philippines and Vietnam, give up gold mines, like in Tajikistan and Pakistan, give up energy, like in Laos and Myanmar, and give up oil, like in Iran, U.A.E., and Saudi Arabia.

These are not isolated incidents. China is taking over the world, piece by piece. Furthermore, while some will point out that anti-Chinese sentiment is rising globally, the anger is solely for the CCP and its coercive policies, though sadly and unfortunately, the Chinese people have been caught in the crosshairs. China is pushing back with an immense propaganda force called "Stop Anti-China Hate". Propaganda influencers have flooded social media with disinformation by employing Western' influencers' on Reddit, YouTube, TikTok, and Instagram. In one instance, there was an offer of significant money to tell the world the Pfizer vaccine had a high death rate.[1]

With 'colossal' budgets, Beijing and Moscow sowed "state-sponsored disinformation" campaigns casting doubt on Western COVID-19 vaccines while promoting their own. The April 2021 European Union report described China and Russia's "vaccine diplomacy" as "zero-sum game logic" to "undermine trust in Western-made vaccines, EU institutions, and Western/European vaccination strategies."[2]

China's Increasing Global Power

China's multitrillion-dollar initiative, paid by trade surpluses, firmly establishes Beijing's economic supremacy. With six economic corridors in Eurasia and additional transcontinental routes begun across Africa, China is well on its way to reaching its Made in China 2025 manufacturing dominance and 100th-anniversary goal of global, political, economic, and military dominance by 2049. With 140 countries signed on to the Belt and Road Initiative (BRI), two added in 2021, China has firmly planted its roots on planet Earth as an economic powerhouse.

---

1   Jon Henley, "Influencers Say Russia-Linked PR Agency Asked Them to Disparage Pfizer Vaccine," *The Guardian*, May 25, 2021, https://www.theguardian.com/media/2021/may/25/influencers-say-russia-linked-pr-agency-asked-them-to-disparage-pfizer-vaccine?mod=djemCMOToday

2   EU vs. Disinfo, "EEAS Special Report Update: Short Assessment of Narratives and Disinformation Around the COVID-19 Pandemic (Update December 2020-April 2021), *EU vs. Disinfo*, April 28, 2021, https://euvsdisinfo.eu/uploads/2021/04/EEAS-Special-Report-Covid-19-vaccine-related-disinformation-6.pdf

The BRI completed train routes from China to London and on to Spain. China has installed gas pipelines from the Caspian Sea through Kazakhstan and the Bay of Bengal through Myanmar. More are planned for Mongolia, Russia, Uzbekistan, and Iran. Oil flowing to China from Pakistan, Iran, and the Middle East is supported by rail, highways, and sea lanes. The Maritime Silk Road creates a chain of seaports from China through the South China Sea to the Middle East, Africa, and Europe.

China's trade flows stream across the planet. South American and Latin American countries are part of this master plan, too, though these are not covered in this book. However, China's increased interest in the Arctic is seen in its investment in nuclear-powered ice cutters. A Northern Sea Route (NSR) past Russia is another area China seeks to dominate. The NSR is shorter than the transit through the South China Sea, Strait of Malacca, and Suez Canal. However, China's massive effort with ports and trains in Greece provides an excellent Mediterranean gateway into the European market.

Initially, China sought countries with authoritarian dictators. Projects and locations were unpopular and not viable since the investment projects were incapable of making money. However, China promoted them as opportunities for the government to achieve financial success. Particularly in emerging economies, the idea of breaking out and becoming an integral part of the 21st-century global economy was too tantalizing to refuse.

However, China needed initial success stories to promote its future projects and thereby ensure the flexibility and completion of these untenable projects. Beijing's early effort with the China-Pakistan-Economic Corridor (CPEC) turned a small fishing town, Gwadar, into a thriving area with a new infrastructure network. Pakistan's GDP grew while other countries suffered, proving the power of China's investments, though Pakistan did have to relinquish sovereignty in areas of the country along with land and minerals.

China benefited from CPEC, offering Beijing an alternative route for its manufactured goods. China gained a pipeline route for oil traveling from the Middle East that previously needed to go through the Strait of Malacca to get to points north. With the CPEC, new mines were transferred to China as well as more direct oil flows. China's economy grew. Chinese citizens were employed throughout the world, though their working conditions were often remarkably draconian, with some living in baraccaded compounds with few comforts and no benefits if hurt.

Mandarin was required on projects as in-country citizens needed to master the language to either be employed or take higher-level positions. As soft power was sprinkled through the media, language study, Confucius Institutes, and Chinese cultural studies, China's goal was to build comradeship, trust, and cultural appreciation. Underpriced Chinese phones, internet services, video games, and films added to the increase in Eurasia and Africa's access to Chinese technology and ideology. Meanwhile, the installation of Chinese surveillance networks eliminated privacy and stifled individuality as access to information remained local while being shared with Beijing's AI networks on its mainland.

Conclusion

With a high debt to GDP ratio in some countries, ownerships in infrastructure is a more significant problem. Particularly during the pandemic, numerous countries were at risk of default and are unable to pay China back. Yet, China continued to lend countries

money. Why? China has strategically allocated its loans in countries where it can access essential rare earth minerals, oil, gas, and land for its domestic, commercial, political and military ambitions. Leveraging its economic power, China is on course to achieve its Five-Year Plan, Made in China 2025, and 100-year anniversary quest for global dominance set for 2049.

In the Western order of democratic states, rules are followed, the environment is protected, employees have rights, and projects need to be viable. Not with China. BRI contracts avoid the 'red tape' of ethics, laws, environment, and human rights. Thus, Chinese contracts often take off years to implement. With China's no-questions-asked policies, projects can begin quickly. The catch is that Chinese people must be employed, loans must be repaid one way or another, and political coercion is used to keep leaders and project managers in line.

Most of the countries in the world have bought into the BRI, and almost all have taken money from China. China owns some parts of most countries, even the United States, where it has 49% ownership in Houston's Terminal Link and Miami's container terminal and 13% ownership in the Port of Seattle.

1.44 bn
Population of China

747.45 m
Population of Europe

20 %
of European firms feel compelled to hand over their technology when working with Chinese partners

What's at Stake?

First, countries want to side with the winner. Getting on China's bad side will either put you in prison-like Jimmy Lai, 'missing' like Jack Ma, or property confiscated like Jackie Chan. Others are put in forced labor camps. Some are killed for their body parts like Falun Gong members whose hearts, livers, and kidneys were sold on the open market. China has installed cameras in many countries for 'security', but also to watch out for any dissension or expression of anti-Chinese sentiment.

Second, agreeing to collaborate with a country that commits genocide and legitimates egregious violations of human rights means accepting that organ harvesting, torture, rape, and murder are acceptable consequences of taking loan money.

Third, China is playing its cards patiently. It has time on its side and only needs to take small bits of land every month to gobble up the planet. During the pandemic, with other countries on lock down, China was fast at work, speedily sending out its manufactured goods and working on projects to develop its BRI network. In the shadows of a usually-vocal media, now more concerned with following stories of health and politics, China lost no time in creating its neocolonial, global empire through the Belt and Road Initiative.

Part 6

Conclusion

China's Fireworks Against a Darkened Sky

With thousands of years of history culminating in a "Century of Humiliation" which included imperial conquests, a brutal World War II, and a civil war, China embarked on a new course of resurgence. Worldly and multilingual, Deng Xiaoping opened China while "biding its time" and "crossing the river by feeling the stones". Picking up from early Chinese leaders, Xi Jinping ushered in a new era of diplomacy when he assumed the position as General Secretary of the Central Committee of the Chinese Communist Party. Xi advanced the idea of a "Chinese Dream" of national renewal and rejuvenation by expanding China's core interests while centralizing power and instilling a fervent sense of nationalism.

Using bilateral diplomacy, he and his spokespeople produced agreements with state leaders, promising large loans for infrastructure projects and leveraging in-state assets in case states were unable to pay. By appealing to leaders' egos and weaknesses while espousing the grand potential of projects that international banks and agencies believed were not viable, China expanded its reach, asserted its diplomacy, and raised questions as to China's true intentions.

While China has now onboarded 140 countries to its Belt and Road Initiative, Beijing is seeking greater influence on the world stage. Xi's Diplomacy with Chinese Characteristics is also assertive and aggressive, with Wolf Warrior tactics, intrusion into state politics, propaganda infiltration into media, and an unparalleled form of social control.

Meanwhile, outside of China, Beijing's assertive military and paramilitary behaviors have put the world on notice. This is no ordinary rising power, but one seeking global domination with uniquely Chinese Characteristics. Under the guise of U.S.-China antipathy, China took over islands and territories belonging to other countries, imposed new Chinese laws on Southeast Asian states, and trapped states under mounds of debt.

To get a sense of Diplomacy with Chinese Characteristics, the world can view the microcosm of Hong Kong with its swift, iron-fisted governance, complete removal of liberty, and silencing of both free speech and alternative media. China's leadership is moving like a swift river without the possibility of Xi or the world feeling the slippery stones underneath.

Chapter 1
Uncertain Future for China and the World
Achieving Xi Jinping's Chinese Dream and Global Ambitions

China's diplomacy in the 2020s reflects Beijing's vision in the long view of global history. The Chinese Communist Party exudes its confidence and consciousness through its rhetoric, social media communication, internal propaganda, and distinctive flair for personal style, work ethic, win-win negotiations, and skyline opulence. China's rise in power and central prominence on the world stage of manufacturing, technology, and infrastructure is coupled with its communist beliefs and socialist framework.

In June 2013, Wang Yi, China's Foreign Minister offered a vision for the future in his speech at Tsinghua University entitled, "Major Country Diplomacy with Chinese Characteristics".[1] This more action-oriented movement departs from the low profile recommended by Deng Xiaoping and into a more aspirational great power projection that captured and highlighted Xi Jinping's priorities as he leaned forward into his presidency. Xi began embarked on this quest by doubling his Foreign Ministry's budget, centralizing control, and increasing China's stake in the global sphere of influence. Xi propelled the country's notion that China would be a major player in building a harmonious world where progress was made in the developing world and the overarching goal of peaceful coexistence in the South China Sea and Indo-Pacific would provide a doctrine of hope.

In October 2017, "Xi Jinping Thought on Socialism with Chinese Characteristics for a New Era" emerged at the 19th National Congress of the Chinese Communist Party as a way of putting in motion a series of advances, mechanisms, and controls. In March 2018, China changed its Constitution, adding what was then called "Xi Jinping Thought" to the preamble and including Xi Jinping's "Socialism with Chinese Characteristics." Not only did this addition include President Xi's accomplishments and vision, but it underscored the importance of pointing China and the world forward with policies, plans, and leadership.

Xi Jinping is set on embedding his stamp on China's future, creating a persona of a great leader in the image of Mao Zedong whose leadership created the People's Republic of China and Deng Xiaoping who opened China to the world increasing its foreign direct investment, productivity, and GDP. With year over year economic successes from Deng's outward push and a growing fervent nationalism Xi Thought on diplomacy required a show of strength. Coalescing power inside and outside of China, Xi incorporated Mao Zedong's military strategy, famously articulated in the statement, "Where the enemy advances, we retreat. Where the enemy retreats, we pursue."

As Xi accelerated China economically, politically, and militarily, Beijing's power projection grew. Furthermore, Diplomacy with Chinese Characteristics took center stage. In July 2020, Xi Jinping Thought on Diplomacy Studies Centre opened to codify China's global efforts for national rejuvenation. China's Minister of Foreign Affairs, Wang Yi, speaking at the center's inauguration explained, "With the foresight of a great strategic thinker and a keen appreciation of the laws of human society, General Secretary Xi Jinping has made a comprehensive assessment of the trajectory of the international situation and the historical juncture in which China finds itself, and put forward a series of new ideas,

---

1   Wang Yi, "Exploring the Path of Major Country Diplomacy with Chinese Characteristics," *Ministry of Foreign Affairs of the People's Republic of China*, June 27, 2013, http://www.fmprc.gov.cn/eng/zxxx/t1053908.shtml

new propositions and new initiatives with distinctive Chinese features, which reflect the call of our times and lead the trend of human progress."[2] Wang continued,

- First, Xi Jinping Thought on Diplomacy is an integral component of Xi Jinping Thought on Socialism with Chinese Characteristics for a New Era.
- Second, Xi Jinping Thought on Diplomacy encapsulates the latest achievement of Marxism on the diplomatic front in the 21st century.
- Third, Xi Jinping Thought on Diplomacy carries forward and elevates the fine tradition of the Chinese culture.
- Fourth, Xi Jinping Thought on Diplomacy carries forward and further develops the diplomatic theories of New China.
- Fifth, Xi Jinping Thought on Diplomacy improves on and transcends traditional theories of international relations.
- We need to step up research and gain a deep and solid understanding of the tenets and essence of Xi Jinping Thought on Diplomacy.
- We need to conduct active international exchanges to better inform other countries and peoples of the world of the scientific and advanced nature of Xi Jinping Thought on Diplomacy.
- We need to fully apply and follow the guidance of Xi Jinping Thought on Diplomacy in conducting major-country diplomacy with Chinese characteristics. Actions and practice must be guided by ideas and theories.

Xi Jinping is determined to make his mark as changing world dynamics propels China into global leadership with a global network of partnerships through its Belt and Road Initiative. Meanwhile, prevailing international relations theory suggests that China will not rise peacefully. Security competition will lead states to contain the CCP's power as China seeks to push the United States out of the South and East China Seas. When countries make an agreement with an empire determined to change the world order, their leaders tacitly agree to the consequences.

China has not hidden its global ambitions with its loans, diplomacy, and dream of national renewal. As a new China emerges, uncertainty follows. Chinese propaganda relentlessly pumps out media content heralding its economic rise, financial success, and global superiority. China's blatant abrogation of laws, coercion of governments, and disregard of agreements are compounded by the takeover of South China Sea islands in inland territories.

No longer is freedom of speech allowed in Hong Kong where journalists are silenced and newspapers are shut down. China has subjugated, restricted, and arrested anyone seeking freedom. China's carrot-and-stick diplomacy coerces and controls with no-strings-

---

2   Ministry of Foreign Affairs of the People's Republic of China, "Study and Implement Xi Jinping Thought on Diplomacy Conscientiously and Break New Ground in Major-Country Diplomacy with Chinese Characteristics," *Ministry of Foreign Affairs of the People's Republic of China*, July 20, 2020, https://www.fmprc.gov.cn/mfa_eng/zxxx_662805/t1799305.shtml

attached loans becoming increasingly worrisome. Replacing the dollar with the digital yuan is the latest in a series of moves to dominate world currency and trade.

Even domestically, the "Chinese Dream", once heralded as a grand opportunity for national renewal has emerged with cracks in its pavement as state-owned enterprises, once allowed to explore business opportunities, now are broken apart, stymied by government control, and their leaders threatened with imprisonment. Paranoid about companies and their leaders gaining too much power, Xi Jinping has used his firm grip, complemented by social control mechanisms to ensure compliance to China's big goals of Made in China 2025 and the 100th anniversary of the People's Republic of China.

Diplomacy with Chinese Characteristics also includes China's ever-increasing immersion into global institutions. Since Xi Jinping began his presidency, he has navigated channels to have representatives on many of the United Nations committees, developed large banking institutions, and created some of the largest interstate partnerships. China's goal is to take greater responsibility, increase its leadership, and have a more profound influence to spread its brand of socialism.

Yet, evading rule of law, changing the international order, and replacing the global currency exemplify the means to which China will achieve its vision. Aggressively pursuing its geostrategic goals, China used the fog of the pandemic to encroach on territories, taking advantage of the overarching fears that consumed nations worldwide. With Chinese workers constructing roads, railways, bridges, and tunnels on Belt and Road projects while also building a massive artificial intelligence center, China is addressing stark challenges on the one hand and spreading its benevolent seeds of soft power on the other. Militarily, China is now a global powerhouse with an uncounted armed paramilitary larger than its advertised PLA forces.

Meanwhile, as China imprisons more than a million of its own people in forced labor camps and engages in hostage diplomacy, imprisoning foreigners without counsel, tourists are afraid to go where they may be put in prison without being charged with a crime. All the while, China engages in Win-Win Diplomacy, Facemask Diplomacy, Vaccine Diplomacy, Hostage Diplomacy, Wolf Warrior Diplomacy and a host of other entrapment strategies in its practice of *Diplomacy with Chinese Characteristics*.

Conclusion | Part 6

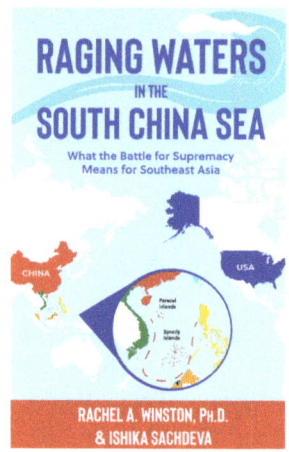

Chinese leaders navigate the raging waters slowly and carefully. Beijing's long view of world history serves as a source of national pride fueling its vessel. As China's 'Century of Humiliation' ended, China redrew maps, renamed islands, and crisscrossed the South China Sea to assert its claim and coerce states to comply with its wishes.

While China turned rocks into dangerous fortresses, militarized artificial islands, and destroyed marine ecosystems, Beijing stealthily doubled down during COVID-19 on nationalist policies, catching weaker states in the crosshairs of intensifying U.S.-China tensions.

In a waterway where one-third of global trade and half the world's fishing vessels traverse, the South China Sea is a flashpoint of conflict as China's military and paramilitary scour the waters, threaten fishermen, hinder oil exploration, and harass states. The authors provide 'What's at Stake' as regional disputes escalate, marine ecosystems risk destruction, and militarized islands demand global attention before it is too late.

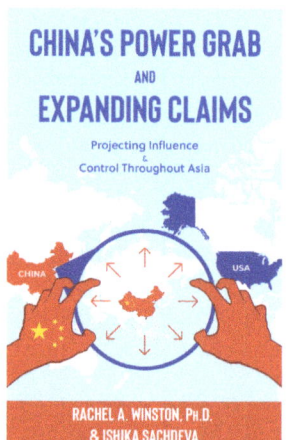

This book introduces readers to China's alarming concentration camps, persecution, social credit, and dominance. With the takeover of Hong Kong, threat to Taiwan, and expansion of power across all regional states, China has emerged with a vengeance. Beijing's alarming propaganda, military actions, and surveillance demand global attention before it is too late.

China is reimagining its borders as it rewrites history. Beijing's global impact and ambition cannot be underestimated as it nudges into, influences, and dismantles international institutions. This book is a primer for anyone wanting to understand the profound issues, aggressive tactics, cultural genocide, inhumane torture, and social control occurring both within China and in its periphery as the CCP broadens its reach throughout Asia.

As the world's manufacturer of cheap products, complicit companies fuel China's enterprises. Millions of imprisoned workers are forced into submission to supply labor for corporations that kowtow to Beijing's wishes. The threat to democracy cannot be understated. Global citizens will soon realize that their once-sacred freedom, liberty, rule of law, and human rights, cherished by the liberal order, will no longer exist. This book provides a powerful warning.

Contact

Email: drwinston@mylizard.org
Instagram: @greatpowerpolitics
Twitter: @grpowerpolitics

More Information

Raging Waters: southchinaseabook.com
Awakened Now: awakenednow.com

The books are available on Amazon, Barnes & Noble, and Lizard-publishing.com. Order from Lizard Publishing for a discount.

Conclusion | Part 6

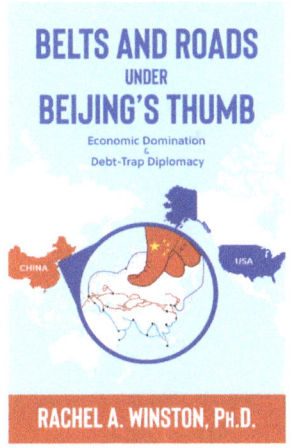

China's "Might Makes Right" maritime, arctic/polar, and digital silk roads have transformed a string of pearls into an alarming wake of global loans and traps.

The free world is facing the most significant geopolitical challenge of our time. Subversively, we are facing an undercurrent of economic, cybersecurity, satellite, political and military forces. A tectonic shift is changing society. Insidiously, through social media, Internet surveillance, and financial payouts, the way we live is being transformed from liberty and freedom to one of coercion and compliance. Democracy is under attack, infused by forces thrusting our relationships and communications under the authoritarian thought control of an empire that has spread its arms into most countries on the planet through no-questions-asked loans with dangerously costly back-end conditions. Debt traps define agreements wherein China offers countries the opportunity to pay back their loans with votes, geography, military bases, minerals, rights, and exclusive access. Money mismanagement, inefficiencies, greed, and pandemic-related problems have led to debt that cannot be repaid, and China will not forgive. Companies and whole countries are under Beijing's thumb. Some states will be forced to give up their land to China, and others will give up resources and infrastructure to Beijing's growing hunger for control. *Belts and Roads* provides a revealing primer to understand China's global hegemony with its alarming consequences.

The Raging Waters Series

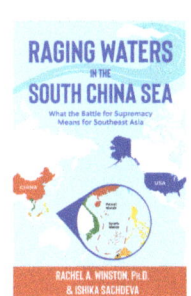 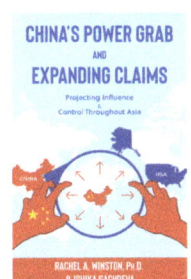 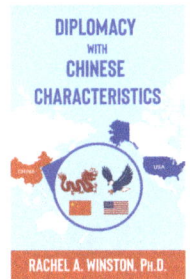 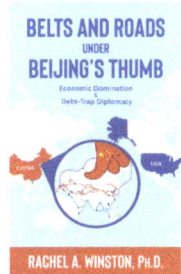

The Awakened Now Series

This captivating series highlights genocide and human rights abuses throughout history as well as China's violation of human rights in the 2020s.

Index

Symbols

5G xii, 142

99-Year Lease xii, 77, 78

A

Access Now 100

Afghanistan 140, 141, 142, 143, 168

Africa ix, xiii, xv, xviii, 14, 57, 59, 63, 64, 65, 66, 67, 69, 70, 71, 73, 100, 117, 122, 123, 124, 125, 126, 127, 128, 137, 142, 145, 157, 160, 161, 165, 166, 167, 170, 173, 187, 193, 209, 227, 228, 229

African American Human Rights Policy Act 115

Agricultural Bank of China 59, 157, 159

Mahmud Ahmadinejad 169

Air Defense Identification Zone (ADIZ) 50

Alibaba 151

Alipay 151

Amnesty International 132

Hans Christian Andersen 43

Angang Hu 31, 50, 157

Antarctic xiii, xiv, xv, xviii, 183, 185

Benigno Aquino III 94

Arabian Sea 145

Arctic Silk Road 47

ASEAN ix, xii, xiii, xix, 9, 59, 193, 198, 199, 200, 204

Asian Infrastructure and Investment Bank (AIIB) 59, 60, 159

Atlantic Council 114

Australia x, xiii, xv, 9, 50, 51, 108, 115, 116, 120, 121, 132, 146, 147, 183, 194, 195, 196, 197, 199, 206, 207, 209, 210, 215, 216, 217, 218

Austria 109

Automatic Identification System (AIS) 174, 175

Azerbaijan 109

B

Bangladesh xiii, 193, 194, 197

Bank of China xiii, xv, 59, 79, 154, 157, 159

Barry R. Weingast 25, 26

Fodei Batty 66

Belarus 166, 167–166, 167–170

Belgium 207

Belt and Road Initiative (BRI) 41, 57, 60, 85, 86, 87, 89, 227

Bhutan 50, 51

Bitcoin 152, 154

Bitter Winter 42, 43

Anthony Blinken 224

Blockchain 155

Boao Forum 93, 95, 96, 217

Brahmaputra River 184

Brazil 53, 109

Britain xii, 106, 191, 192, 223

Brunei xiii, 199, 200, 201

Burkina Faso 127

C

Cai Xia 43

Cambodia xiii, 199

Canada x, xv, 51, 116, 120, 166, 206, 207, 209, 210

CASEarth 181, 182

CCTV 126

Centers for Disease Control (CDC) 100

Central Bank Digital Currency (CBDC) 153

Century of Humiliation viii, xiii, 6, 7, 8, 9, 51, 235, 240

Jackie Chan 231

Anton Chekhov 43

Cheng Lei 120, 225

Chiang Ching-kuo 17, 18

Chiang Kai-shek 17

China Africa Research Initiative 65
China Banking and Insurance Regulatory Commission (CBIRC) 159
China Construction Bank Corp 59
China National Petroleum Company (CNPC) 169
China-Pakistan-Economic Corridor (CPEC) 228
Chinese Dream x, 39, 45, 93, 97, 187, 205, 235, 236, 239
Ivy Choi 117
Chung Chen 32, 35
Church 100
Cold War vi, 137, 208, 209
Communications intelligence (COMINT) 208
Confucius Institutes 127, 228
Corruption 79, 80, 82, 196
COVID-19 xiv, xv, 3, 7, 73, 89, 99, 100, 102, 105, 106, 108, 109, 110, 113, 114, 115, 117, 127, 128, 139, 145, 155, 187, 192, 199, 204, 221, 227, 240
Ted Cruz 116
Cryptocurrency 152
Cultural Revolution 12, 13, 14, 15, 18, 20, 23, 39, 45, 57
Customs and Border Protection xiii
Czech Republic vi, 106, 108

D

Dark Fleets ix, 172, 173, 174
Death Metal Diplomacy ix, 91, 130, 131, 132, 134
Debt Trap 71, 72, 74, 77, 79
Declaration on the Conduct 204
Daniel Defoe 43
John Demers 121
Democratic Progressive Party xiv
Deng Xiaoping viii, 11, 16, 17, 18, 19, 20, 23, 25, 28, 36, 41, 51, 53, 54, 113, 137, 235, 237
Digital Currency Electronic Payment 153

E

East China Sea 7, 50, 51, 178, 207, 215, 218

Ecuador ix, 152, 172, 174, 175, 176
Electronic intelligence (ELINT) 208
Ethiopia 127, 157
European Council on Foreign Relations 86, 87
European Parliament 49
European Union xv, 49, 87, 173, 210, 227
Export-Import Bank (EXIM) 59
Extradition Treaties ix, 118

F

Facebook 29, 101, 114, 152, 212
Facemask diplomacy 91, 105
Facemasks xv, 69, 105, 106, 108, 109, 110
Falun Gong vii, 231
Financial Assistance and Debt Service Relief 73
First island chain 139
Fisheries 173, 175, 176, 177
Five Eyes Alliance x, xv, 206, 207, 208, 209, 210
Bhavani Fonseka 79
Food & Drug Administration (FDA) 105
Foreign direct investment (FDI) 17, 32, 35
Formosa 131
Forum on China-Africa Cooperation (FOCAC) 64
France 17, 20, 190, 191, 192, 207, 208, 210, 223
Free and Open Indo-Pacific (FOIP) 193, 194
Thomas Friedman 26

G

G-20 69
Galapagos 174, 175, 176, 177, 178
GameStop 4
Ganges River 183
Genocide Olympics 222
Georgia 106, 107

Germany vi, 49, 57, 94, 165, 192, 207, 208, 222

Global Times 54, 115, 224

Gobi Desert 221

Google vi, 29, 37, 116, 117, 212

GoToMeeting 105

Great Britain xii, 223

Great Leap Forward 11, 12, 18, 20

Great Proletarian Cultural Revolution 12, 13, 18

Greenhouse gases (GHGs) 148

Guangzhou 127

Guoqiang Long 33, 34

H

Hambantota viii, xii, 76, 77, 79, 80, 81, 82, 83

Health diplomacy 91

Health Silk Road 99, 105

Himalayas 7, 183, 215

Hong Kong vi, vii, xii, 9, 15, 41, 51, 52, 96, 102, 114, 115, 116, 121, 131, 132, 133, 141, 166, 217, 221, 222, 223, 225, 235, 238, 240

Jeffrey W. Hornung 99

Hostage Diplomacy 91, 119, 120, 121, 225, 239

Hua Chunying 114, 115

Huawei 67, 119, 160, 161

Human rights vi, 43, 45, 49, 63, 64, 66, 67, 87, 89, 102, 120, 153, 155, 218, 222, 223, 224, 229, 231, 240, 241

Human Rights Watch 40, 161

Hungary 109

Hydrological Data 184

I

Illegal, unreported, and unregulated (IUU) 173, 177

India xiii, 7, 9, 51, 82, 86, 96, 97, 106, 107, 108, 117, 137, 141, 158, 169, 173, 183, 184, 185, 187, 191, 193, 194, 195, 196, 197, 215, 218

Indian Council of Medical Research (ICRM) 108

Indonesia xiii, 58, 59, 85, 109, 173, 174, 199, 200, 201

Industrial & Commercial Bank of China 59, 157

Instagram 227, 240

Intellectual property ii, 9, 20, 37, 49, 121

International Bank for Reconstruction and Development (IBRD) 157

International Court of Justice (ICJ) 94

International Debt Statistics 71

International Monetary Fund (IMF) 157

International Olympic Committee (IOC) 223

Iran 141, 155, 168, 169, 207, 209, 227, 228

Islam 197

Italy 109, 140, 207

Nobu Iwatani 121

J

Japan xiii, xiv, xv, xvi, 3, 86, 96, 109, 121, 131, 145, 146, 166, 173, 176, 190, 193, 194, 195, 196, 197, 199, 201, 207, 208, 209, 210, 211, 215, 218

Japanese xvi, 177, 193, 215

Darwin Jarrin 175

Johns Hopkins 64

K

Kai Li 121

Kazakhstan 57, 58, 85, 93, 151, 228

Kenya 126

Henry Kissinger 165

Michael Kovrig 119, 120, 225

Kowtow 240

Paul Krugman 25, 32

Kuomintang (KMT) 131

Kyrgyzstan 93, 140, 141, 157

L

Ladakh 97

Jimmy Lai 225, 231

Laos xiii, 73, 157, 199, 227

Laotian railway 73
Liberalism 32
Libra 152
Li Keqiang 66
Line of Actual Control xvi, 96
Liquefied natural gas (LNG) 165, 166
Little Red Book 12, 45
Teodoro Locsin Jr. 201
Palmer Luckey 116

M

Made in China 2025 xvii, 1, 9, 23, 50, 139, 227, 229, 239
Maglev xvi
Jack Ma 39, 231
MALABAR 2020 215
Malaysia xiii, 94, 106, 107, 199, 200, 201, 202
Maldives 194
Mandarin 59, 63, 126, 127, 139, 228
Mao Zedong 11, 12, 17, 18, 40, 41, 51, 124, 237
Maritime xvi, xvii, 47, 50, 58, 85, 88, 94, 145, 190, 196, 228
Maritime Silk Road (MSR) 58
McDonald's 128
John Mearsheimer 3, 139, 143
Memorandum of Understanding xvii
Meng Wanzhou 119
Mexico 109
Middle Kingdom 8, 18
Ministry of Commerce (MOFCOM) 159
Ministry of Foreign Affairs xvi, 58, 87, 89, 93, 99, 140, 142, 151, 159, 194, 237, 238
Narendra Modi 193
Mongolia xiv, 51, 157, 228
Scott Morrison 216
Ali Motahari 169
Elon Musk 152

Muslim 43, 44, 169

Mutual Defense Treaty 215

Myanmar xiii, 140, 141, 161, 166, 193, 194, 196, 197, 199, 216, 227, 228

N

Yasuhide Nakayama 215

National People's Congress 41, 49

National security law 116

NATO xvii, 116, 141, 218

Nazi Germany vi, 94, 222

NBA xvii

Netherlands 108, 146, 193, 207, 223

New Development Bank (NDB) 159

New Power Party (NPP) 132

Gavin Newsom 110

New Zealand x, xiii, xv, 116, 194, 199, 206, 207, 209

Northern Ireland 109

Northern Sea Route (NSR) 228

North Korea 119, 176, 177, 207, 209

Norway 207

Joseph Nye 102

Julius Nyerere 123

O

Richard O'Halloran 121

Olympics x, 220, 221, 222, 223, 224, 225

One Belt, One Road (OBOR) 57, 85, 89

P

Reza Pahlavi 169

Pakistan xiv, 59, 140, 141, 157, 166, 227, 228

pandemic xiv, 3, 7, 8, 33, 39, 47, 69, 70, 74, 86, 89, 99, 100, 101, 102, 106, 107, 108, 110, 113, 114, 115, 117, 127, 128, 139, 140, 142, 145, 149, 160, 161, 168, 170, 192, 204, 210, 221, 224, 228, 231, 239, 241

Paracel Islands xvii, 50, 205

Marise Payne 120, 215, 225

People's Bank of China (PBOC) 154, 157

People's Daily 14, 94

People's Liberation Army Air Force xviii

People's Liberation Army Navy Air Force xviii

People's Liberation Army Navy (PLAN) 51, 94, 96, 190, 201, 203, 215

People's Liberation Army (PLA) 9, 121, 134

People's Republic of China (PRC) 23, 39, 51, 113, 123

Pfizer 227

Sandy Phan-Gillis 121

Philippines xii, xiii, xiv, xv, xvi, xvii, xviii, 3, 7, 50, 52, 94, 109, 170, 173, 190, 192, 196, 199, 201, 202, 205, 227

Philippines v. China xvii, 7, 52, 192, 205

Michael Pompeo 176

J.B. Pritzker 110

Productivity 11, 17, 24, 25, 26, 27, 28, 29, 31, 32, 33, 34, 35, 36, 37, 69, 123, 137, 237

Propaganda 41, 45, 52, 63, 78, 89, 99, 102, 114, 115, 121, 139, 222, 223, 224, 227, 235, 237, 238, 240

Protestants 14

Mark Purdy 33–37, 34–37, 35–37, 36–37

Q

Qatar 109, 166

Qing dynasty 51

Quad x, 190, 193, 194, 195, 214, 215, 216, 217, 218

R

Radio Free Asia 193, 201

Raging Waters vi, vii, 50, 52, 200, 203, 204, 222, 240, 241

Mahinda Rajapaksa 77, 79

RAND Corporation 73, 99, 194

Ravi Ratnasabapathy 77

Reddit 227

Red Guards 12, 13, 14, 15, 39, 124

Regional Comprehensive Economic Partnership (RCEP) 199, 204

Renminbi (RMB) xix, 155

Republic of China xiii, xviii, 17, 23, 39, 41, 49, 51, 58, 78, 85, 87, 91, 93, 99, 113, 120, 123, 126, 139, 140, 142, 151, 165, 176, 199, 201, 224, 237, 238, 239

Robinson Crusoe 43

Rule of law 7, 32, 100, 117, 121, 178, 187, 189, 194, 195, 196, 239, 240

Russia xiv, 3, 93, 142, 143, 151, 166, 170, 176, 207, 209, 210, 227, 228

S

Salami slicing 204

Scarborough Shoal 51, 94, 96

Security and Exchange Commission 4

Senkaku Islands 215

Serbia 109

Shaanxi Province 39

Signals intelligence (SIGINT) 208

Silk Road Economic Belt xviii, 47, 57, 58

Singapore xiii, xvii, 199, 200, 203, 207

Skype 105

Slovakia 106

Social credit 212, 240

South China Sea vi, vii, ix, xiv, xvii, xviii, 7, 41, 50, 51, 52, 94, 95, 96, 132, 141, 145, 166, 170, 178, 187, 190, 191, 192, 193, 196, 198, 199, 200, 201, 202, 203, 204, 205, 215, 218, 222, 228, 237, 238, 240

South Korea xiii, 3, 106, 107, 145, 176, 207

Spain 106, 109, 202, 207, 228

Michael Spavor 119, 120, 225

Special Administrative Region xviii

Sri Lanka viii, xii, 51, 59, 60, 61, 76, 77, 78, 79, 80, 81, 82, 83, 194, 227

State-Owned Enterprises (SOEs) 66

Strait of Malacca 145, 228

Suga 217

Surveillance 9, 33, 35, 39, 45, 89, 153, 155, 161, 187, 202, 208, 212, 228, 240, 241

Susanne Weigelin-Schwiedrzik 42

Sweden 207, 223

T

Taiwan ix, xvii, xviii, 9, 17, 18, 51, 53, 63, 91, 96, 109, 130, 131, 132, 133, 134, 141, 145, 146, 147, 199, 200, 201, 215, 216, 217, 218, 223, 240

Tajikistan 141, 157, 227

Tanzania 47, 57, 123, 124, 125

TAZARA Line 57

Telegram 114

THAAD xviii

Thailand xiii, 166, 173, 193, 199

The Little Match Girl 43

Thousand Talents Program 28

Three Poles Environment Project (TPE) 181

Tiananmen Square massacre 17

Tibetan 181, 183, 185

TikTok 227

Total factor productivity (TFP) 25, 29

Treaty of Nanjing xiii

Donald J. Trump 115

Tsai Ing-wen 53, 134, 147

Tsinghua University 39, 50, 237

Turkestan xv, xix

Turkey 66, 106, 109

Turkmenistan 93

Twitter xix, 53, 94, 101, 113, 114, 115, 116, 126, 139, 169, 212, 240

Twitter fingers 139

U

Uhuru Railway 124

Uighur 44, 45

UNCLOS vii, xiv, xvii, xix, 7, 52, 189, 190, 192, 199, 202

UNESCO xix, 176

United Kingdom xv, 51, 109, 116, 192, 207, 209

United Nations vii, xiv, xix, 7, 52, 128, 145, 173, 175, 176, 178, 181, 184, 189, 192, 193, 194, 199, 202, 205, 239

United Nations Development Program xix

United States xv, xix, 1, 17, 19, 23, 27, 28, 29, 34, 49, 51, 71, 75, 93, 94, 96, 99, 100, 101, 102, 109, 121, 139, 140, 143, 146, 152, 168, 190, 193, 194, 195, 196, 197, 204, 207, 208, 209, 210, 215, 222, 223, 230, 238

U.S. Customs and Border Protection xiii

U.S. Immigration and Customs Enforcement xvi

Uyghur vi, vii, xix, 43, 44, 115, 121, 141, 221

Uzbekistan 93, 228

V

Vaccine Diplomacy ix, 98, 99, 101, 102, 239

Vanka 43

Vietnam xiii, xvi, xvii, xviii, 50, 73, 141, 170, 173, 190, 196, 199, 201, 202, 205, 227

Virtual Private Network xix

W

Wang Yi 52, 93, 140, 237

Dr. David Waugh vii

Webex 105

WeChat 114

Weibo 114, 115

Wei Fenghe 131

Widow's villages 177

WikiLeaks 80

Win-Win Diplomacy ix, 92, 93, 239

Wolf Warrior ix, xix, 91, 102, 112, 113, 114, 115, 116, 117, 119, 121, 139, 216, 235, 239

Wolf Warrior 2 113

World Bank xix, 23, 57, 63, 69, 71, 77, 123, 157, 158, 161, 162, 168

World Economic Forum 51, 119, 137, 183, 187

World Wide Fund for Nature xix

World Wildlife Fund xix

Wuhan, China xiv, 89, 99, 114, 142

X

Xenophobia 128

Xiaodong Zhu 25, 33

Xi Jinping viii, ix, x, 11, 15, 20, 38, 39, 40, 41, 42, 43, 45, 47, 49, 50, 51, 53, 57, 58, 59, 60, 69, 70, 72, 75, 85, 89, 90, 91, 93, 94, 96, 97, 99, 105, 113, 114, 117, 119, 137, 141, 142, 151, 165, 166, 183, 187, 202, 203, 211, 217, 221, 224, 235, 236, 237, 238, 239

Xinhua 40, 60, 69, 85, 110, 140, 183, 217, 224

Xinjiang Province vi, 7, 187, 221, 223, 224, 225

Xinjiang Uyghur Autonomous Region vii, xix

XUAR xix

Y

Yang Hengjun 120

Yang Jiechi 91, 224

YouTube 114, 116, 117, 227

Yuan xviii, 32, 151, 152, 153, 154, 158, 239

Z

Zambia xvi, 57, 123, 124, 125, 157, 160, 161

Zhao Lijian 114, 115, 216

Zimbabwe 142

Zoom 105

ZTE xix, 67

Jacob Zuma 64

www.ingramcontent.com/pod-product-compliance
Lightning Source LLC
Chambersburg PA
CBHW041323110526
44592CB00021B/2803